DECODING
CHINA

A Handbook for
Traveling, Studying,
and Working in
Today's China

Matthew B. Christensen
Content Adviser: Michael A. Paul

TUTTLE Publishing

Tokyo | Rutland, Vermont | Singapore

The Tuttle Story: "Books to Span the East and West"

Most people are surprised to learn that the world's largest publisher of books on Asia had its humble beginnings in the tiny American state of Vermont. The company's founder, Charles E. Tuttle, belonged to a New England family steeped in publishing. And his first love was naturally books—especially old and rare editions.

Immediately after WW II, serving in Tokyo under General Douglas MacArthur, Tuttle was tasked with reviving the Japanese publishing industry. He later founded the Charles E. Tuttle Publishing Company, which thrives today as one of the world's leading independent publishers.

Though a westerner, Tuttle was hugely instrumental in bringing a knowledge of Japan and Asia to a world hungry for information about the East. By the time of his death in 1993, Tuttle had published over 6,000 books on Asian culture, history and art—a legacy honored

by the Japanese emperor with the "Order of the Sacred Treasure," the highest tribute Japan can bestow upon a non-Japanese.

With a backlist of 1,500 titles, Tuttle Publishing is more active today than at any time in its past—inspired by Charles Tuttle's core mission to publish fine books to span the East and West and provide a greater understanding of each.

Published by Tuttle Publishing, an imprint of Periplus Editions (HK) Ltd.

www.tuttlepublishing.com

Copyright © 2013 Matthew B. Christensen
All photos © Matthew B. Christensen.

All rights reserved. No part of this publication may be reproduced or utilized in any form or by any means, electronic or mechanical, including photocopying, recording, or by any information storage and retrieval system, without prior written permission from the publisher.

Library of Congress Cataloging-in-Publication Data is available for this title.

ISBN 978-0-8048-4267-9

First edition
15 14 13   5 4 3 2 1   1301RP

Printed in China

Distributed by

North America, Latin America & Europe
Tuttle Publishing
364 Innovation Drive
North Clarendon, VT 05759-9436 U.S.A.
Tel: 1 (802) 773-8930
Fax: 1 (802) 773-6993
info@tuttlepublishing.com
www.tuttlepublishing.com

Asia Pacific
Berkeley Books Pte. Ltd.
61 Tai Seng Avenue #02-12
Singapore 534167
Tel: (65) 6280-1330
Fax: (65) 6280-6290
inquiries@periplus.com.sg
www.periplus.com

TUTTLE PUBLISHING® is a registered trademark of Tuttle Publishing, a division of Periplus Editions (HK) Ltd.

To my wife Sharon, for always being there for me
and to my kids for keeping me grounded

Acknowledgments

The idea for this book came over a decade ago. I want to thank my many students who have participated in various assignments related to the contents of this book while studying in China and in the U.S. Their insights helped shape my thinking on many of the topics.

My content adviser, Michael Paul, did some of the background research, proofread and provided valuable insights for the many drafts, and contributed many of the personal anecdotes. He was always ready to bounce ideas around and discuss every topic addressed in the book. His practical and no-nonsense ideas were greatly appreciated.

My research assistant, Hongyi Jia, was invaluable in making sure that all the information in the book was current and accurate. Her network of family, relatives, and friends in China was essential to the research. She also assisted with the Chinese that appears throughout the book.

Finally, I thank my wonderful wife and kids for the support and stability they have constantly provided me for many years, especially during my absences while traveling in China.

Contents

Introduction

CHINA'S CULTURAL CODES

Going to China for the first time can be an intimidating experience, even for those who have studied the language. In fact, going to China for the second, third, or fourth time can also be a challenging experience, especially if you intend to be fully immersed in daily life, get off the beaten path, and experience the real China.

This book is about how to get things done in China. It describes how to act and what to expect in common everyday situations, such as eating at a restaurant or renting an apartment. It deals specifically with Chinese behavioral culture, that is, the codes that people live by and use in their day-to-day behavior.

It is helpful to understand the rules of behavior in terms of scripts or codes. This notion of scripts has been described as:

> ...a set of expectations about what will happen next in a well-understood situation. In a sense, many situations in life have the people who participate in them seemingly reading their roles in a kind of play. The waitress reads from the waitress part in the script, and the customer reads the lines of the customer. Life experience means quite often knowing how to act and how others will act in given stereotypical situations. That knowledge is called a script.
>
> Scripts are useful for a variety of reasons. They make clear what is supposed to happen and what various acts on the part of others are supposed to indicate. They make mental processing easier by allowing us to think less, in

essence. You don't have to figure out every time you en-
ter a restaurant how to convince someone to feed you.
All you have to know is the restaurant script and your
part in that script.... One just has to play one's part, and
*events usually transpire the way they are supposed to.**

Scripts can also be thought of as cultural codes. The code tells you what to expect and how to get things done. The notion of a cultural code implies that there are those who understand how to do things (i.e., native speakers), and those who don't know the code (i.e., non-natives). Decoding cultural practices enables you to understand and act like a native. This then puts natives at ease, which leads to the opportunity to develop and maintain relationships with them.

I tell my students of Chinese that the reason we study Chinese, or any foreign language for that matter, is to develop and maintain relationships with people. Even if you do not study the Chinese language in any depth, living and working in China will necessitate that you develop and maintain relationships with people. In order to do this effectively, you need to behave the way the Chinese expect people to behave. We call this cultural coherence. If the Chinese have to adapt their behavior in order to interact with you, you are not as likely to be able to develop lasting relationships with them. This is similar to the idiom "When in Rome, do as the Romans." The Chinese have an idiom for this as well, **rù xiāng suí sú** 入乡随俗. This means, when you enter the countryside, follow the customs. When you adapt to the way people think, act, and get things done, the Chinese will be comfortable with you. If the Chinese are uncomfortable with your behavior, they are less likely to want to spend time with you. Whether you are living, studying, working, or just traveling to China,

---

* Schank, Roger. *Tell Me a Story: A New Look at Real and Artificial Memory* (New York: Scribner, 1990), pp. 7–8.

understanding these cultural codes gets you into the game, and allows you to participate in the daily lives of Chinese.

A sports analogy may help to highlight how important this idea can be. Let's say that Western culture's codes are like the game of baseball, and Chinese codes are like tennis. In both games there are players, balls, instruments to hit the balls, a playing field, boundaries, and so on. There are specific rules to each game to ensure that play is smooth. The players expect their competitors to understand and obey the rules. If someone disregards the rules, there are penalties.

If you as a Western person only understand the rules (codes) of the Western game, and all your experience has been with playing baseball, you will have difficulty adapting to the rules of the Chinese game. If you've never before been on a tennis court and don't know how to play that game, you will have no choice but to resort to playing by the rules that you are familiar with. When the ball is served to you, your first inclination may be to hit the ball as hard as possible, preferably over the fence. From your perspective this would be a good thing (home run!). However, the Chinese would find this strange. If you insisted on hitting the ball as hard as you could each time it was served, and disregarded the rules of tennis, the Chinese would soon get frustrated and eventually would give up, take their ball and racquet and go home. It is doubtful if they would be eager to invite you to play tennis again.

If you show up in China not knowing the rules, so to speak—the cultural codes—you are likely in for trouble, frustration, misunderstanding, and perhaps even hostility.

Several years ago I was in China leading a group of study-abroad students. We had been in the country for only two days. I was in a small restaurant, in a back corner, when several of my students entered. They were pretty good students and had two to three years of Chinese language study under their belts. They did not see me and I observed the following:

They entered the restaurant and stood just inside the door, waiting to be greeted and shown to a seat. After several minutes, the students were visibly disturbed as they perceived that they were being ignored by the waitresses. At the same time, the waitresses seemed perplexed. I overheard one say to the other, "What are they doing?" "I don't know, maybe waiting for someone." What these students did not understand is that in China you generally find your own table and seats without waiting for anyone to help you. (This is just the beginning of a relatively complex Chinese restaurant script or set of codes.) They assumed that the "rules" of eating in a restaurant were the same as eating at a restaurant in the United States. Even though they had pretty good language skills and knew what to say when ordering, how to ask for the check and so on, they did not know what to do or what to expect in a Chinese restaurant. This was an eye-opening experience for me and was the impetus for this book.

When we go to another country and find out that the restaurant script or code is different there than where we came from, a problem arises. Indeed, we find ourselves trying to figure out how to convince someone to feed us. If you know nothing about the restaurant code in China, you have no choice but to work from your American script. This often leads to frustration and anxiety. Even if you don't know any Chinese, if you do know what to expect in a given situation, then you are more likely to be able to get things done.

For example, if you know about the different kinds of bank accounts that are available, and that you will need your passport to open an account, you will likely be able to open that account even with minimal language skills.

Or, if you are familiar with the different classes of trains, and the different seating and sleeping options on trains, you will be prepared when buying train tickets. Every communicative situation (i.e., buying a train ticket, ordering a meal, etc.) has a set of expectations that if followed will ensure a successful experience. These expectations can be viewed as a cultural code. If you know the code, you will know what to expect, and be able to get things done smoothly.

Culture is a tricky concept to describe, let alone to fully understand its many connotations. Culture can be conveniently divided into three main categories: achievement culture, informational culture, and behavioral culture.

Achievement culture refers to the great achievements of a civilization. For China, this would include things like Beijing opera, the Great Wall, Tang Dynasty poetry, Confucianism, and so on.

Informational culture is the information that defines a people, or the information that is important to a civilization. This would include things like geography, political systems, philosophical traditions, and so on.

Behavioral culture refers to the daily practices and beliefs of individuals within a society. This would include such seemingly mundane things as eating habits, how to greet people, protocols of transportation, how to buy things, etiquette, how to conduct a transaction at a bank, how emotions are displayed, how to develop and maintain relationships, and other related everyday things.*

Though knowing some achievement and informational culture is certainly valuable, it is behavioral culture that is tied directly to cultural codes and is of the most immediate concern for those traveling to China. And unfortunately, many important cultural behaviors are not dealt with in any systematic way in Chinese language classes. Even Chinese culture classes deal almost exclusively with achievement and informational culture. In order to get things done in China

---

* For a more detailed discussion about culture, see pages 12–16 in Christensen, Matthew B. and J. Paul Warnick, *Performed Culture: An Approach to East Asian Language Pedagogy* (Columbus, OH: Foreign Language Publications, National East Asian Languages Resource Center, The Ohio State University, 2006).

smoothly, it is imperative that you understand Chinese behavioral culture and the codes that will form the context of the situations in which you'll need to communicate.

This book describes in detail a number of typical situations that anyone spending time in China will encounter. It explains what to expect in these situations and how to get things done. If you understand how things are done in China, you will be able to actually use your hard-learned language skills in useful and practical ways with a minimum of frustration and confusion. And even if you don't have any Chinese language skills, you will at least know what to expect and how to get things done. This will significantly lower your anxiety levels and give you the confidence needed to navigate Chinese society.

The vast majority of books on living and working in China addresses the needs of expatriates relocating to China to work. In the past these individuals had most things provided for them, including drivers, interpreters, housing, and so on. That kind of situation is becoming increasingly less common. Things are changing as more and more individuals are going to China with language and cultural skills. Companies in China are often providing less for the people they hire, and are expecting individuals to provide their own housing and other needs. Sometimes they'll hire a foreigner for a position originally intended for a native Chinese person; these positions are sometimes called "foreign national hire" and you may even be paid in yuan.

This is a hands-on guide for anyone planning to spend time in China, whether you speak some Chinese (even a little) or not. It is for those who want to live and work independently among the Chinese, and *not* live in some secluded expatriate housing compound with Western standards while relying on Chinese colleagues or friends to get things done for them.

Though this is not a language textbook, it does provide valuable vocabulary and common phrases (in both characters and pinyin) applicable to each of the situations described. This will give those of you who are studying Chinese the language context that applies. For those with no Chinese language skills, the vocabulary will expose you to key phrases that will enrich your understanding of how the language is used in Chinese society.

It is not possible to cover every imaginable situation that you may encounter in China, but this book covers those situations that are most immediate and practical. By studying each chapter, you should know enough about interacting with the Chinese that you'll be able to improvise in other similar situations you may encounter in your travels.

USING THIS BOOK

You will get the most out of this book by following a few strategies. First, read through each chapter based on your particular interest or need. Pay attention to the "Behind the Scenes" sections as these are essential in decoding these cultural practices. If you know some Chinese, take note of the vocabulary items and useful phrases. Practice them until you are confident you can use them in a real communicative situation. Then, go out and accomplish the task. Take notes during and after. What worked well? What did not go so well? Add to the book's lists any other vocabulary and phrases that came up during your experience. Talk to your tutor or a Chinese friend or colleague and have them give you some feedback and advice.

Perhaps more important than the linguistic aspects are the cultural codes you will understand by studying and applying the principles in this book. Several years ago I knew a student who had truly exceptional linguistic skills. He had near-native pronunciation, a wide vocabulary, and a solid grasp of grammar. He had never been to China before, having learned his Chinese in a Chinese-speaking community in Los Angeles. He didn't seem to understand the importance of cultural skills. He was placed in an internship in Beijing with a Chinese organization where he was the only foreigner. Within a short time, the majority of his coworkers did not like him. Because his Chinese language skills were so good, when he offended his Chinese colleagues they naturally assumed it was intentional. He was just acting like an American, using American humor, mannerisms, and so on. But the Chinese will naturally assume that if you have good Chinese language skills you will know how to play the game: that you'll know the cultural codes.

A year or two later, I encountered another student preparing to go to China to do an internship. His Chinese was decent, but not great. But he had an open mind, was very eager to learn, and was a very keen observer of the many cultural things that were going on around him. He was very receptive to the cultural training he received before he left. He thrived in his internship. As a result of his attitude his Chinese language skills took off. He was given significant responsibilities in his work and when it came time to finish the internship he was offered a full-time job.

The difference between these two students, of course, is that the latter student paid attention to Chinese culture codes. When he didn't know something, he asked about it or watched, learned, and tried things out. The former student didn't see the importance of cultural codes and simply behaved as an American would in an American company. In fact, the most dangerous person in China is the person with excellent language skills, but little to no cultural skills. These kinds of people routinely offend, irritate, and annoy their Chinese hosts.

As you use this book to prepare for interacting with the Chinese, you will be able to decode those cultural practices and become more and more fluent in the culture of China.

Chinese language learners will benefit by being able to apply this learning immediately in necessary communicative situations. I am confident that studying this book and applying its principles will allow you to get deeper into Chinese culture and society than most foreigners are able. As a result of this, your Chinese language skills will improve faster than they ever could in a class or by traditional book study. You will learn by doing. With understanding of the cultural codes this book unveils, you will be able to move around in Chinese society smoothly and confidently.

When I first started traveling to China, there was little information available about contemporary Chinese society. The information in *Decoding China* is precisely what I wish I had. With this book you will be able to approach your tasks with the confidence that comes with knowing the code.

Living, working, and studying in China is a great and challenging adventure. After spending some time in China, you will likely see the world in a slightly different way than you did before. Don't be surprised if your whole outlook on life changes.

Throughout the book I provide anecdotes, stories, or experiences that highlight the cultural differences foreigners experience in China. These anecdotes appear in sidebars. They are all true stories, experienced by me, my content adviser, or our students or colleagues.

1

Traveling & Transportation

交通 jiāotōng

Getting around in China may not be as difficult as you might imagine. Unlike some parts of the United States where it is challenging to get around without a car, there are a variety of convenient and efficient ways to get around in China. Transportation within a city is similar to most large international cities. You have a number of options, from walking or riding a bike to public buses, taxis, and subway systems. Personal cars are becoming increasingly popular, but only among the more well-off Chinese. It is still rather expensive to buy a car and drive in China, even though it is still probably cheaper than in the U.S. The cheapest Chinese cars are in the 30,000–40,000 yuan range. The majority of cars are found in the larger metropolitan areas, primarily Beijing, Shanghai, Tianjin, and Guangzhou. Because of the traffic problems in Beijing, private cars can only be driven four out of five days. For example, on Thursdays of a given week, license plates that end in 4 and 9 cannot be driven. Every thirteen weeks, they change the numbers. To further help reduce traffic, one person can only have one license plate. So if you want to buy (and drive!) a new car, you must first sell your old car.

Intercity travel includes long distance buses, trains, and air travel. One may also hire a private car or minivan, called **miànbāochē** 面包车, literally "bread cars," because they are shaped like a loaf of bread. Prices are negotiable depending on the distance and the condition of the roads. This is usually a viable option in rural areas where regular buses do not travel.

> One may also hire a private car or minivan, called **miànbāochē** 面包车, literally "bread car," because they are shaped like a loaf of bread.

Train and bus stations in most cities will have city maps available for purchase. These are usually sold by vendors outside the station. Throughout cities, newspaper and magazine kiosks also sell city maps. GPS units are becoming increasingly popular in China. Radio programs offer traffic reports.

The majority of Chinese get around by using public transportation. It is inexpensive, convenient, and quite easy to navigate most systems. For example, in Beijing it costs only 0.4 RMB to ride a public bus. In some cities it is free for those over 65 years old.

Successful travel in China involves knowing what to expect in a given situation—so that you can crack the codes. For example, buying a train ticket involves knowing where to buy the ticket, which ticket to buy, and so on. Below I describe the various travel codes you need to understand to get to, and travel around in, China.

GETTING TO AND FROM CHINA
往返于中国 wángfǎn yú zhōngguó

Getting to China from the United States will most certainly involve traveling by plane. If you are traveling from Hong Kong, Taiwan, Japan, or Korea, other options are available, such as ferries or trains. The vast majority of international flights to China end up in either Beijing, Shanghai, or Hong Kong. These large modern airports are well equipped for international travelers. Their staff are used to dealing with foreigners, and it is generally easy to get around in these airports. Some connections to cities other than Beijing and Shanghai may go through Seoul or Tokyo.

Security in Chinese airports seems less rigorous than in the United States. It also seems a bit random. I have had water bottles confiscated, but other times I have completely forgotten to take my liquids out of my luggage and I passed through with no questions. Once while I was going through the Guangzhou airport, they made me take a drink out of my own water bottle! I guess they wanted to make sure it was really water.

A few years ago while going through the Gansu Lanzhou airport, my dad who was in his late sixties at the time got a complete search of his bag and all his stuff, while my brother and I walked through with no problem. They ended up taking away my dad's metal fork he had brought.

All international flights into Shanghai arrive at the newer Pudong Airport, which is about an hour's drive by taxi into the city proper. If you have a domestic connection in Shanghai, be aware that some connections may be at the old Hongqiao Airport. This is not very convenient, as the Hongqiao Airport is about an hour away from the Pudong International Airport. Flights within China from Shanghai are usually from Hongqiao Airport as this is the domestic airport, but if you have a connecting flight you usually will take this from Pudong.

Since the bird flu and SARS epidemics, you may also have to pass through a health check station.

There are a few ways to get from the Pudong Airport to the Hongqiao Airport. There are regular shuttle buses that are cheap and convenient, but if the traffic is bad (which it often is), it could take a long time, up to three hours. A taxi is also an option, but is more expensive and can also take a long time due to traffic. Perhaps the best way is to take the Shanghai Metro Line 2. This can be taken directly from Pudong Airport. You will need to change trains at the Guanglan Road Station (**guǎng lán lù** 广兰路). At the Guanglan Road Station you will transfer to the Main Line 2 toward East Xujing which will take you all the way to Hongqiao Airport. Because there are various transfers, taking the subway can still take up to two hours, so plan accordingly.

Most airports in China, and certainly in Beijing and Shanghai, have signage in both Chinese and English. Getting around is pretty straightforward. After picking up your luggage, you'll need to go through customs. In most cases this is a very quick process. There are usually separate lines for locals and foreigners, so make sure you check the signs and get in the correct line. Since the bird flu and SARS epidemics, you may also have to pass through a health check station. This consists of having your temperature taken via infared sensors as you walk by. If you do have a fever you may be stopped and required to fill out some medical forms. Sometimes, a health official will board international flights before passengers are allowed to disembark and will take everyone's temperature via infared sensor. This involves pointing the sensor at you and does not involve touching you in any way. Those with a fever may be quarantined.

DOMESTIC TRANSFERS
国内转机 guónèi zhuǎnjī

If you are connecting to another city within China, you will need to go from the international terminal to the domestic terminal. This should be a pretty straightforward process of following the signs. Unfortunately, it may not be that easy. Finding the domestic terminal and the specific gate that you need in the Beijing airport can be a bit frustrating. It's not always well marked, and you will probably have to ask at least once where to go. You will also have to go through security again.

Sometimes it's also not terribly obvious how far it is to the domestic terminal. We had to walk for at least 30 minutes at the Guangzhou Airport to get from the international terminal (**guójì tōngdào** 国际通道) to the domestic terminal (**guónèi tōngdào** 国内通道), all indoors. Luckily it was not a tight connection. Again, you may have to ask how to get to the domestic terminal. There may be airport shuttle carts that are willing to transport passengers, but take care: they may be asking for an unreasonable price to do so.

AIR TRAVEL WITHIN CHINA
在中国坐飞机 zài zhōngguó zuò fēijī

■ **At the airport** 在机场 zài jīchǎng
In the U.S., airline tickets usually need to be purchased in advance, and usually the earlier they are purchased the cheaper the tickets. In China, it is common to buy a ticket the day before or even the day of travel with no penalty and often at the same price you'd pay if you booked it two or more weeks

in advance. However, buying your tickets in advance can save money, as discounts are sometimes given. I have arrived in Shanghai's Pudong Airport, bought a domestic ticket to another city, and flown out the next morning from Hongqiao Airport with no surcharge on the ticket. It is also possible to change your ticket, such as the time or even the day of departure, without a penalty as long as there is room on the other flight that you want. Go to the counter of an airline and ask about flights to the city where you want to go. The big three airlines in China are all government owned. They are: Air China, CA **zhōngguó guójì hángkōng gōngsī** 中国国际航空公司, China Southern Airlines, CZ **zhōngguó nánfāng hángkōng** 中国南方航空, and China Eastern Airlines, MU **zhōngguó dōngfāng hángkōng** 中国东方航空.

> In the U.S., domestic airline tickets usually need to be purchased in advance—but in China, it's common to buy a domestic ticket the day before or even the day of travel.

The fourth big airline is Hainan Airlines, HU **hǎinán hángkōng** 海南航空, which is a private joint-stock airline. Other smaller airlines include Dragonair **gǎnglóng hángkōng** 港龙航空 and Shanghai Airlines **shànghǎi hángkōng** 上海航空. Numerous other smaller Chinese airlines also operate domestic flights.

If you are flying internationally on a U.S.-based airline and need to change your ticket, do it after you have arrived in China, not while you are in the U.S. The fees associated with changing your international tickets are very low in China, unlike in the U.S.

■ **Using a travel agent** 联系旅行社 **liánxì lǚxíngshè**

Travel agents can be found through referrals from business associates, classmates, or teachers. Most universities also have a travel office. Many big hotels also have travel agents who can book flights for you. Some travel agents may not be reliable, so it's best to get a referral from a friend or colleague. Even small hotels and large apartment buildings can usually arrange a car or buy train tickets. The fees are surprisingly low.

■ **Booking flights online** 网上订票 **wǎngshàng dìng piào**
China has quite a few online travel agencies. One of the bigger, more popular sites is www.elong.net **yìlóng lǚxíng wǎng** 艺龙旅行网. On it you can book international and domestic flights and hotels. This site is similar to and functions the same way as sites like Orbitz and Travelocity.

Chinese universities often have a travel office to help arrange your travel needs.

Another online travel service similar to www.elong.net is www.ctrip.com. It is quite popular, and I have had good luck using this service as well. Flychina.com is a good place to look for international flights from the U.S. to China.

■ **Getting into town from the airport**
从机场进城 **cóng jīchǎng jìnchéng**
Larger cities, such as Beijing and Shanghai, will have more options for getting from the airport into town. When arriving in a new city, I like to buy a map and familiarize myself with the city. This is helpful whether you will be traveling by bus, taxi, bicycle, or walking. Nearly every airport, train station, and bus station will have city maps for sale. As soon as you leave the station buildings, there are usually hawkers waiting for you to sell you a map of the city. The prices are generally quite low, 2 to 6 yuan. City maps can also be purchased at bookstores or newspaper kiosks found throughout the city.

■ **Shanghai** 上海 **shànghǎi**

Shanghai Pudong Airport (**pǔdōng jīchǎng** 浦东机场) has a high-speed train called the Maglev train, or **shànghǎi cífú lièchē** 上海磁浮列车. Unfortunately, this train does not take you all the way into the city center. It ends at the Longyang Road (**lóngyáng lù zhàn** 龙阳路站) subway station (Metro Line No. 2). From there you will have to take the subway into the city center or take a taxi. The Maglev Train runs from 6:45 AM to 8:40 PM. If your flight arrives later than that, you will have to try another option. The Maglev Train is quite expensive, but you do get to travel at speeds up to 430 km/h. The subway, Metro Line No. 2, now extends all the way to Pudong Airport as well. It runs from 6:30 AM until 11:40 PM from Pudong. This is a quick, convenient option and much cheaper than the Maglev Train. Public buses are also an option, albeit slower. There are also airport buses that go to the city center, the train station, and Hongqiao Airport (**hóngqiáo jīchǎng** 虹桥机场).

Taking a taxi into the city center or other parts of Shanghai is straightforward. It usually takes about an hour by car to get into the city center but during rush hour it can take considerably longer. Another option is to take an airport shuttle bus into the city center, then hop into a taxi to reach your specific destination. This can be a good method if you are not in a hurry.

If you need to get to a city in the general region around Shanghai, you usually have two options: train or bus. If you are going to a city like Nanjing, Suzhou, or Hangzhou, taking a bus may be the most convenient and can be faster than taking the train. Oftentimes buses leave directly from the airport to major cities in the region. For smaller cities you may have to go to the long distance bus station **chángtú qìchēzhàn** 长途汽车站. Inside the airport there will be information about bus routes that leave from the airport to cities in the region.

■ **Beijing** 北京 **běijīng**

In Beijing, the comprehensive subway system extends to the airport, so the subway may be the cheapest and most convenient way to get into the city. At the Beijing Airport there are also buses that go to different areas in Beijing and other cities in Hebei Province. If you are going to the areas in Beijing, it generally costs 25 yuan. There are also a number of hotel buses as well. If you have booked a room at a hotel in the city, many will offer a shuttle service. Make sure to check with your hotel to see if this is an option. A taxi into the city center will take about an hour or much longer depending on the traffic. Beijing has experienced an astonishing increase in the number of cars which has made traffic terrible—thus another reason to take the subway, though it can be very crowded during rush hour.

The subway line from Beijing Airport is actually a light rail line. It is called **běijīng jīchǎng guǐdào jiāotōng xiàn** 北京机场轨道交通线, or ABC (Airport Beijing City). There are currently only four stops on this line, Terminal 2 and 3 at the airport and **dōngzhímén** 东直门 and **sānyuánqiáo** 三元桥 in the city. Train service to and from the airport starts early in the morning and runs late into the evening.

TAXIS
出租车 chūzūchē; 的士 dìshì

Taking a taxi is usually a quick and easy way to get around a city. The price varies from city to city. Generally, large cities are more expensive than small cities. The flag-down rate may range from 5 to 10 yuan depending on the city. About 2 yuan will be added for each kilometer. A fee may also be charged for waiting. Taxis tend to congregate at train and bus stations and major markets and other places of commerce.

Make sure you go to the area where there is an official taxi stand or place where taxis can stop. Be aware that taxis are generally not allowed to stop at or near major intersections. Because many Chinese streets have fencing separating bike lanes from traffic lanes, you will need to get to an area where there is a significant break in the fencing.

Finding an empty taxi during rush hour or when it is raining can be very difficult. An empty taxi will have a flag inside the car displaying the character **kōng** 空, meaning "empty."

Be very cautious about taking unmarked cars. There will most likely be many people who will offer you a ride to wherever you want to go. These cars are illegal and do not have meters. All fares have to be negotiated. It can be a tempting option during busy times when the wait for a taxi is long, but I don't recommend it.

In some smaller cities, taxis may not use their meters, or they may not even have meters. In these kinds of taxis, all fares have to be negotiated. If you know the going rate, then it is pretty straightforward, but if you are new to the city, you may be taken advantage of. One strategy is to ask a local what

the going rate is to get to the general area where you are going.

Although the color of a taxi may vary by region, taxis are easy to identify. Make sure the taxi has a meter and that the driver uses it. If it is evident that you are new to the city a taxi driver may take you for a ride, using a circuitous route to your location. This is known as **ràolù** 绕路.

Some big cities, like Beijing, have a lot of one-way streets. Sometimes a taxi will seem to be going the long way when in reality, the driver is taking the best way possible. Tourist places like Beijing sometimes have really unhelpful taxi drivers. Often the ones with nice cars won't take you to an address close by, or will pretend not to know where it is, or they may pretend they can't understand your Chinese. In reality, they are waiting for a longer run and bigger fare. I recommend you pick a taxi that's a little bit run-down and the driver usually won't complain. Getting a taxi in Beijing is becoming increasingly difficult. Drivers seem to be only interested in long, more expensive routes, such as to and from the airport.

It is also possible to hire a taxi for routine transportation. I had a colleague who lived in Tianjin with his wife. They found a taxi driver whom

The first time I went to Changsha, I jumped in a taxi from the airport and told the driver where I wanted to go, which was a hotel recommended in the Lonely Planet guide. As we entered the center of town and neared the address, the taxi driver asked if I had been to Changsha lately. I lied and said it had been several years. He said that he'd guessed that, since the hotel had been demolished two years before. He recommended a neighboring hotel that ended up being super swanky and really cheap.

they really liked and contracted him to take him to and from work every day. He also took his wife to work and back. Sometimes they would hire him for a whole evening. They would go out to eat, then to shop, then to the park or just drive around. He would wait outside for them or come back at a specific time.

If you are staying at a hotel, the staff can call a taxi for you. This is especially important if you have an early flight or an unusual destination.

TRAIN TRAVEL IN CHINA
在中国坐火车 **zài zhōngguó zuò huǒchē**

Traveling by train is by far the most popular way to get around in China. Take a look at any train station in any major city and the crowds will attest to this. Trains can be quick, clean, and convenient, or they can be slow, uncomfortable, and really crowded. There are numerous classes of trains in China that vary considerably in terms of speed, cleanliness, and comfort.

■ **At the train station** 在火车站 **zài huǒchēzhàn**
Train stations can be pretty chaotic places. With the crowds and confusion at most of them, it is important to keep a very close eye on your belongings. Train stations are notorious for pickpockets and petty thieves.

The stations usually have small stores where you can buy food items to eat on the train. They also sell basic items like hand towels, plasticware, and other travel needs.

There are separate waiting rooms for different classes of tickets. Waiting rooms are called **hòuchēshì** 候车室. Once you have purchased your ticket, you will need to check the departure boards **xiǎnshìpái** 显示牌 to see which platform **zhàntái** 站台 your train departs from. These boards list the

train numbers, locations, and platform numbers. Your train ticket will list the train number and your location. Each platform area will have a waiting room. Sometimes these waiting rooms are crowded with people not only occupying the seats but also sprawled out all over the floor. Sometimes mountains of luggage are scattered all over as well.

Airports, train stations, and bus stations are all equipped with water stations that dispense boiling water. This is provided for the Chinese to make tea, and to reconstitute dried ramen-type noodle bowls, a very popular meal when traveling because it is cheap and easy to prepare.

■ Buying train tickets 买火车票 mǎi huǒchēpiào

There are a few ways of obtaining train tickets. One is to book train tickets through a travel agency. Some agencies only sell train tickets and are called **huǒchēpiào dàishòu chù** 火车票代售处. Travel agencies can be found in large hotels, college campuses, or large corporations. They can also be found around the city. This is a convenient way to purchase tickets without having to actually go to the train station, where there are usually long lines and crowds of people. Fees are generally

• BEHIND THE SCENES •

THE TRAIN CLASS NUMBERING SYSTEM

Here are the classes of trains in China, in order of speed. (For more info on seat types, see p. 36.)

 High Speed Train 350km/h
高速铁路动车 **gāosū tiělù dòngchē** or 高铁 **gāo tiě**

These are the fastest, bullet-type trains. Technically, they are called high speed electric multiple units (EMU) trains. They are fairly limited and only run on very popular routes, such as Beijing to Shanghai, Shanghai to Nanjing (and points in between), Guangzhou to Wuhan, and so on. The trip from Shanghai to Nanjing is only 73 minutes, and the Guangzhou to Wuhan train (1,049 km) is only 3 hours 16 minutes. Seating in G class trains is limited to:

- **First class** 一等 **yī děng** These are comfortable seats, similar to airline seats; there are two seats in each side of an aisle.
- **Second class** 二等 **èr děng** These are similar to first class seats but do not have as much padding; There are five seats per row in these carriages.

 High Speed Train 350km/h
城际动车组列车 **chéngjì dòngchē zǔlièchē** or 城际列车 **chéngjì lièchē**

These are the same as the trains described above, but they are for shorter intercity routes, like the Beijing to Tianjin line.

 High Speed Train 250km/h
动车组列车 **dòngchē zǔlièchē** or 动车 **dòngchē**

These are high-speed express trains that usually travel shorter distances during the day, but longer distances do exist, such as Beijing to Xi'an and Beijing to Harbin. These trains generally have only soft seats and soft sleepers and are air-conditioned.

 Non-stop Direct Express Train
直达特快旅客列车 **zhídá tèkuài lǚkè lièchē** or 直特 **zhítè**

Though **zhídá** means non-stop, these trains generally have one stop along the way, and some may have several stops. Regardless they are very fast, modern, and efficient trains. Some of them may have only soft seats and soft sleepers. They are air-conditioned.

Extra Fast Train 140km/h
特快旅客列车 **tèkuài lǚkè lièchē** 特快 or **tèkuài**

These trains run on most railways and stop at major stations. There may be numerous stops which may make them a bit slower than Z trains. These trains have a wider variety of seating options—hard seats, soft seats, hard sleepers, and soft sleepers.

 Fast Train 120km/h
快速旅客列车 **kuàisù lǚkè lièchē** or 快速 **kuàisù**

These are the most popular trains for the average Chinese traveler. So they tend to be the most crowded as well. There are more K trains than any other passenger kind in China. These trains have all types of seats—hard seats, hard sleepers, soft seats, soft sleepers, and standing room in the hard-seat area. The hard-seat area can be crowded, chaotic, and dirty. Many of these trains do not have air conditioning. The seriously hard core traveler on a budget could get a standing-only ticket in the hard-seat carriage, but it is not recommended for long distance travel, as it could be truly miserable. For short distances, say up to about four hours, hard seats are fine.

Numbered Trains 数字编号的列车 **shùzì biānhào de lièchē**

- **1001–5998** 普通旅客快车 **pǔtōng lǚkè kuàichē** Stops at most big towns. About 40 percent of these trains have AC.
- **6001–7598** 普通旅客慢车 **pǔtōng lǚkè mànchē** Stops at every station. There is no AC on these trains.
- **7601–8998** 通勤列车 **tōngqín lièchē** For train personnel only; these stop at every station. There is no AC on these trains.

These are the slowest trains in China, and consequently the cheapest. If you are traveling to a small city or town, you will need to take these trains, as faster trains do not stop at smaller towns. They are only hard seat. Some may have air conditioning, but most will not. These trains are for intrepid travelers only. If you get on a slow, miserable train, one option is to upgrade by getting off at a major stop and waiting for a better train to come along. You'll have to buy another ticket, but that may be better than suffering for hours.

 Temporary Trains (during holiday periods)
临时旅客快车 **línshí lǚkè kuàichē**

These trains stop at most county level stations and run during Chinese New Year, summer holidays, and the National Day holiday. No air conditioning.

pretty cheap, and the service is fast. Buying tickets a day or two ahead of time guarantees you'll get a seat. The other option is to buy your ticket at the train station. Be aware that it is increasingly difficult to get tickets for sleeper cars, both hard and soft, on short notice. Plan on buying these kinds of tickets about a week in advance; otherwise you may be stuck sitting in seats for an overnight trip.

The train system in China is now computerized. This means that you can buy train tickets for anywhere in the system. For example, if you are in Shanghai, you can buy train tickets from Beijing to Xi'an. (In the past you could only buy train tickets in the city of your departure.) Keep in mind that large cities may have more than one train station. Different train stations will have trains departing for different locations. Make sure you show up at the right train station that serves the city where you want to travel. You will have to show your ID or passport to buy a ticket in your name.

At the train station, you will find a ticket office or offices, **shòupiàochù** 售票处. At large train stations there may be dozens of ticket booths. There are usually long lines of people waiting to buy tickets, especially leading up to and during holidays. There may be different booths for different classes of train tickets, so make sure you are in the correct place. Large cities like Beijing and Shanghai may also have specific ticket booths with English speaking staff. I highly recommend this if you don't want to fight the crowds. I have used this service before in Shanghai, and it was pleasant; they were happy to speak English or Chinese with me and bent over backwards to help me secure AM tickets from Shanghai to Suzhou and then PM tickets from Suzhou to Nanjing.

■ **Luggage on trains** 火车上的行李 **huǒchē shàng de xínglǐ**
Most of the time you will carry your luggage onto the train with you. There are racks above the aisles where you can

store your large luggage. Smaller bags can be stored under the seat or bed. Make sure to keep personal items, and especially valuables close to your person. Because the hard sleepers are open to the aisles, it is especially important to keep valuables close to your head (not at your feet) when sleeping.

There are luggage cars on many trains. If you have large, especially heavy, or oversized luggage, you may ask to have it be checked onto a luggage car. Theoretically the baggage is limited to 20 kg for adults and 10 kg for children and should not exceed 160 cm, but staff seldom will weigh or check your luggage, unless it is obviously excessively large or heavy. On some high-speed trains, this luggage requirement may be even less.

If you want to bring a bicycle on a train, make sure to tell the clerk when you are booking your train ticket. Bicycles can be checked to a luggage car for an extra fee. And if the train you are taking does not have a luggage car, your bicycle may be booked on the next available train to your destination. Some travelers have reported that re-moving the pedals of your bike will discourage joy rides. When checking your bike, staff will usually make note of the condition of the bike and if anything is

Removing the pedals of your bike will discourage joy rides.

missing, so they are not responsible if something is amiss at the final destination. For example, if you were to remove the pedals, they would take note of that so they are not responsible for the pedals.

You will be given a luggage ticket. When you arrive at your destination, find the luggage office (which may be around the back of the station), present your ticket, and they will retrieve your bicycle or large luggage.

■ **Eating on trains** 在火车上吃饭 **zài huǒchē shàng chīfàn**
The options for eating depend on the train and length of the trip. On longer, especially overnight trains, there is often

• BEHIND THE SCENES •

TYPES OF SEATING/SLEEPING ON CHINESE TRAINS
座位的种类及在中国的火车上睡觉
zuòwèi de zhǒnglèi jí zài zhōngguó de huǒchē shàng shuìjiào

No Seat 无坐 **wú zuò**
These are standing-room only tickets. I recommend these only for very short trips. The hard-seat carriages where these are available are usually loud, crowded, and chaotic. Sometimes you might get lucky and score a seat, but usually not. Keep in mind that you can usually buy a **wú zuò** ticket if a train is otherwise full, or if the local ticket office doesn't sell sleeper berths on that particular train. Once on the train you can make your way to the dining car, where usually the conductor will come by and you can buy your sleeper berth ticket there. For some high-speed trains, such as the train between Beijing and Tianjin, you can also buy **wú zuò** tickets.

Hard Seat 硬座 **yìng zuò**
Other than no-seat tickets, this is the cheapest way to get around China. These carriages are usually crowded and can be dirty and loud. Though the seats do have some padding, they do not recline and the backs are almost straight up. However, millions of Chinese who cannot afford sleeper cars take hard seats all the time, even for very long cross-country trips. I once took the hard seats for an overnight trip and it was pretty challenging. Needless to say, I did not sleep much. But it could have been worse. I had a friend who was riding in the hard seats, and a peasant's bare breast rhythmically slapped his arm while she was nursing her baby, as the train clickity-clacked up the track. Then another baby peed on his leg.

Soft Seat 软座 **ruǎnzuò**
Soft seats are similar to what you would find on a bus. The seats are individual and nicely padded. They are a great option for longer trips but not necessarily overnight. Soft seats are more limited than hard seats and are not available on all trains. Sometimes soft-seat carriages have two seats facing each other with a small table between them.

Hard Sleeper 硬卧 **yìng wò**
Hard sleeper carriages consist of cabins with six berths each: upper 上 **shàng**, middle 中 **zhōng**, and lower 下 **xià** on each side. The cabin has no door and opens onto a narrow aisle, so there is no privacy and it can be noisy. Between the beds, under a window, is a small table for eating, playing cards, and so on. At the end of the cabin facing the aisle is a small metal ladder for accessing the middle and upper bunks. The beds have a thin mattress and clean linens. I find the beds pretty comfortable, though if you are used to a very soft mattress, you may find them too firm. It's debatable which bunk is the best. The lower bunk is nice because you always have a place to sit, but that also means the other people in your cabin will want to sit there too, even if they are strangers. The top bunk can get hot in the summer. Sometimes these carriages are air-conditioned, but it may not be as cool as you would like. When there is no air conditioning, there are usually small fans at the head of each bed.

On the other side of the aisle there are small fold-down seats. This is how most middle-class Chinese travel long distances. Many foreigners also choose hard sleepers for long trips. Traveling by hard sleeper is a great way to mingle and meet ordinary Chinese people and I have found them quite comfortable.

A word of caution: make sure you keep your valuables close to your body at all times, even when you are sleeping. Unfortunately it is not uncommon for thieves to work these carriages at night, when most people are sleeping. A student of mine had his belongings stolen out of a backpack that was on his bed when he was sleeping. Too bad the backpack was at his feet instead of up near his head. I recommend you get a small cable lock to lock your bag to the luggage rack. Zip ties also work well to lock zippers together on your luggage. I have also seen a thief jump up from the outside of the train and snatch a bag from the small table next to the window, so keep that in mind too.

Soft Sleeper 软卧 **ruǎnwò**
Soft sleepers are very comfortable. They consist of private four-berth cabins with two beds on each side of the cabin, one below and one above, bunk-style. They have regular single size mattresses that are soft and comfortable, with clean linens. The cabin has a door that can be closed for privacy. There is also a small table against the window between the lower beds. This is the most comfortable way to travel long distances in China. However, because the cabins are private, there is less chance to mingle with other passengers. Soft sleepers can be expensive, sometimes as much as you would pay for an airline ticket to the same destination.

> *A few years ago I was traveling with my family by train. Our four-year-old son was insistent on going into the bathroom by himself to do his business. I stood outside the door waiting for him to finish. After several minutes I began to get a little impatient. After I knocked on the door several times, he finally opened the door a crack. There was this little boy standing spread-legged with a bundle of clothes held high above his head and a look of severe stress on his face. He had missed the hole, was afraid of getting his clothes wet, and did not know what to do. After a good laugh, I rescued him.*

a dining car. These cars function like a restaurant: you go to the car, find a seat, and order a meal. The meals are generally pretty basic. In other words, don't expect fine dining. Also, don't expect to show up anytime and be fed; service may be limited to typical meal hours.

Most long-distance trains also have snacks and other small items of food, like instant noodles and fresh fruit, for sale. These are sold by a train employee pushing a cart down the aisles of the various cars.

Probably the most popular and reliable way to eat on long train rides is to bring your own food. Instant noodles are popular among Chinese travelers since train attendants will supply boiling water to cook your noodles. Some train cars have water boilers at the end of the cars where you can get your own boiled water. In extremely rural areas, these boilers are coal fired. On more expensive high-speed trains between cities, bottled water is provided for passengers.

■ **Using the bathroom on trains**
使用火车上的厕所
shǐyòng huǒchē shàng de cèsuǒ
Some trains, particularly older trains, T and K class, as well as numbered

trains, may have fairly primitive bathroom facilities. Squatter type toilets can be challenging for the Westerner. Add the swaying and lurching of a train and squatters can be downright treacherous. Fortunately, there are usually grab bars to steady yourself. It is not uncommon for the floors in these bathrooms to be completely wet with…water or urine. They can smell pretty bad as well.

There will be sinks outside the bathrooms for washing up. Keep in mind that they probably will not offer soap or towels to dry off, so plan on providing your own. It is always a good idea to carry hand sanitizer while traveling in China. (Most bathrooms, except in higher-end hotels, will not have soap or towels to dry your hands.)

BUS TRAVEL IN CHINA 在中国坐公共汽车; 公车; 汽车; 巴士 **zài zhōngguó zuò gōnggòng qìchē; gōngchē; qìchē; bāshì**

Many Chinese rely on buses for most of their travel, whether around town or long-distance.

■ **Getting around town** 在城市中 **zài chéngshì zhōng**
In most large metropolitan areas, there are usually two kinds of buses, those with air conditioning and those without. City buses will cover most areas of the city and many Chinese rely on the bus systems for commuting and general travel around town. Traveling by bus is cheap and convenient. Local buses usually cost 1 or 1.20 yuan and more comfortable air-conditioned buses cost 2 or 2.5 yuan depending on where you are. Fares are listed on the outside of bus doors and no change is provided, so either have exact fare or be willing to pay more than the fare.

More modern buses have a coin box inside the front door where passengers get on the bus. These boxes also scan transit

cards (IC cards); the amount of the fare is deducted from your card's account. IC cards can be purchased at certain banks where there may be a specific booth or area for this purpose. Cards can be recharged at these banks as well as at other locations like grocery stores. On buses the card can be swiped multiple times if you are paying for friends. Besides being convenient, IC cards also offer significant discounts on bus fares, as much as 40 percent off. Older buses may still have a conductor on board. If this is the case, one simply boards the bus and pays the conductor the appropriate fare. The conductor will usually have a small booth located near the center of the bus. In some areas of China, particularly on smaller mini buses, you pay your fare when you get off the bus.

Bus stops around town are quite visible. At larger bus stops, where several buses pass, there may be boards listing all the buses with route information. This can be a bit intimidating as these signs tend to be only in Chinese and can be pretty complicated. Websites like www.trav elchinaguide.com, www.wikitravel.org, www.synotrip.com, and www.chinatour360.com often have bus schedule and route information in English.

City buses can be extremely crowded, especially during rush hour. Expect to be pressed up against other passengers on all sides. A student once told me that one time while she was riding a bus in Beijing during rush hour she counted 13 individual people touching her. Forget about any modesty or private space. Traffic during rush hour on main thoroughfares in town can be very heavy and slow. Getting on and off buses during rush hour can also be challenging.

Because buses can be so crowded, you need to be fairly aggressive when boarding a bus or you will get left behind. Oftentimes there are no neat lines, and when the bus arrives it becomes a bit chaotic with people clamoring to get aboard. If you maintain an American attitude of restraint and courtesy, you will have a hard time boarding a bus because teams of Chinese will push their way ahead of you. It is necessary to do a little pushing to get aboard. Likewise, when it is time to disembark from the bus, you have to do some gentle pushing to make your way to the door. Air-conditioned buses are most definitely worth the extra money, especially in the steamy summer months. They are also usually less crowded and have more comfortable seating. Fellow passengers will usually be willing to help you figure out where you need to get off the bus. Though many Chinese speak some English, particularly student-age people, don't count on being able to use English on a regular basis.

■ **Long distance bus travel**
长途汽车旅行 **chángtú qìchē lǚxíng**

Long-distance travel by bus is by far the cheapest way to go. It can be quite comfortable in large air-conditioned Greyhound-like coach buses on modern highways...but can be quite epic on crowded, uncomfortable, unreliable buses over steep, winding, mountainous roads that are often washed out.

Most cities will have a long distance bus station, **chángtú**

qìchēzhàn 长途汽车站, oftentimes located near the train station. Larger cities may have more than one long distance station. It is important when you buy bus tickets that you pay close attention to which station your bus departs from.

Buying long distance bus tickets is similar to buying train tickets. You may use a travel agent, buy tickets at the bus station, or some hotels may provide this service for a modest fee. Tickets can usually only be purchased ten days to two weeks prior to a trip. However, during Chinese New Year and other holidays, you may be able to buy tickets only five days in advance. Bus tickets must be purchased in the city of departure. In other words, you cannot buy a bus ticket from Shanghai to Xi'an while in Beijing.

Altitude can be an issue on some routes. Be sure to bring warm clothing.

The main routes between large cities generally have coach buses similar to Greyhound buses in the U.S. An added advantage is that long bus routes may also have sleeping berths similar to the hard sleepers on trains. The beds are fairly basic, and can be quite narrow. Sometimes you actually have to share a berth with someone else. When sleeping on the bus, keep valuables close on hand, as buses and trains attract thieves. Most buses do not have bathrooms on board and will stop occasionally for this purpose, but be aware that drivers can be impatient and will not wait for passengers if they're not back when the bus is ready to leave. When disembarking make sure that you take all your belongings with you as they are not secure on the bus.

Long distance bus routes in rural and mountainous areas, such as Yunnan, Sichuan, or Gansu, can be scary. These buses tend to be older and you may experience rough roads that can cause severe "turbulence." Some travelers will even take a motion sickness medication like Dramamine before taking buses in mountainous areas. This can really help. If you are in a sleeping berth you may be rudely awakened by the bus hitting potholes or swerving wildly. In some cases travelers have reported being thrown from their sleeping berths. If you are on an upper berth, be especially careful. Likewise if you have valuables, like cell phones, iPods, laptop computers, and such, make sure they are secure. If they were to fly off your berth in the middle of the night, you might not ever see them again.

In these mountainous areas it is not uncommon for roads to wash out which can delay travel for up to several days. Altitude can also be an issue on some routes. If you are planning a bus ride into mountainous areas, be sure to bring warm clothing, even in summer, as many buses will not have any heat. You should also plan to bring some food along. Buses may stop at meal times, but it is best to at least bring some snacks and some water along just in case the bus does not stop at convenient times for you.

It is strongly advised that when traveling long distances in China, you travel light. Not only is it inconvenient to lug around heavy suitcases, but on many buses there is not much room to store luggage. Also, you will probably want to keep your things with you at all times. For these reasons a backpack or duffle bag works best.

Rural buses frequently break down, so travelers should be prepared with food, water, toilet paper, and warm clothes. Roadside bathrooms in rural areas are often so bad, it is advisable to run up or down the road a ways to do your business. While trains and buses in city areas are mostly very punctual, rural buses may wait until the bus is full before leaving. They may also wait if a ticketholder doesn't show up on time. One evening in Yunnan, there were a 7:00 PM and a 9:00 PM sleeper bus scheduled for departure, and the 9:00 PM bus actually left before the 7:00 PM bus.

Rural buses may wait until the bus is full before leaving.

TRAVELING BY SUBWAY
坐地铁 zuò dìtiě

Subways in China are much like subway systems around the world. About a dozen large Chinese cities currently have subway systems. However, these rapid transit systems—including subway, monorail, light rail and tramway systems—are rapidly growing with another 20 cities either building them or in the planning stages. Cities with some kind of rapid transit system include Anshan, Beijing, Changchun, Chongqing, Dalian, Guangzhou, Hong Kong, Nanjing, Shanghai, Shenyang, Shenzhen, Tianjin, and Wuhan. Most stations tend to be clean, orderly, and safe.

Traveling by subway is the way to go in large, congested cities. While the traffic snarls above ground, subways offer a quick and convenient means of traveling around the city. Some cities, like Beijing, have many lines that can get you just about anywhere in the city, including the airport. However, subways, like buses, can be very crowded during rush hour.

Most subway systems use tokens or plastic fare cards. When you first enter the subway station, there will be token or card machines that look like ATM machines. Most of these self-serve machines have either Chinese or English options. Some cities have a flat rate for anywhere in the system and some will charge according to your final destination. One usually pushes a touch screen for your destination station, then the fare is displayed. Machines take coins or small bills and provide change. As with city buses, an IC card is also available for purchase. Once you have your token or card, go to the turnstile entry point and either insert it or wave it in front of a small screen. You will retain your token or fare card until you exit the subway. There is usually an attendant around if you have questions or trouble but they may not speak much English.

Subway stations have maps showing the various exits. At large stations there will be numerous exits. Some stations will exit directly into a building, such as a shopping mall, or other large business.

TRAVELING BY BICYCLE
骑自行车 qí zixíngchē

The streets of nearly all Chinese cities used to be swarming with bicycles. In fact, in many cities the bicycle lanes were wider than the automobile lanes. As private cars have become more popular, the bicycle lanes have shrunk, as has the number of bicycles on the street. But bicycling is still very popular and a very convenient way to get around town.

There are more bicycles and bicyclists in China than any other country in the world. It is said that there are more than 10 million bicycles in Beijing alone. But bicycles are not seen as fitness machines as they are in many parts of the world. In China they are viewed and used as simple transportation.

Though there are designated bike lanes in Chinese cities, this is not to say that bicycling in China is completely safe. In fact, bicyclists and pedestrians must yield to motorized vehicles, which will not stop for you even if you are in a crosswalk or bike lane. Be cautious and keep your eye on the traffic.

Bicycling through a Chinese city feels quite liberating. While the traffic in most Chinese cities gets slower and slower, the bicycle is your ticket to nearly unimpeded progress. Rush hour does exist for the cyclist, but it is still often faster and more convenient than buses or cars. Of course, this depends on how far you have to travel. Rush hour on a bike may find you literally shoulder-to-shoulder and wheel-to-wheel with thousands of other cyclists and traffic seems to flow like a river. Riding a bicycle in China is like being in a big school of fish, slowly merging and navigating around obstacles without quick movements that would disrupt the flow. Chinese cyclists seldom yell out, but they use their bells. Even if you're about to crash, ring your bell. Never shout out.

> **Even if you're about to crash, never shout out. Ring your bell.**

■ Buying a bicycle 买自行车 **mǎi zìxíngchē**

There are several options for buying a bicycle. The easiest might be buying a bicycle at a large department store or large discount-type store similar to Walmart. Most of these kinds of stores have a sporting goods department where bicycles are available. It may not be possible to test-ride bikes from these kinds of stores because the sporting goods department may be on an upper floor. Another option is a dedicated bicycle shop. These can be found scattered around most cities. You may need to ask a friend, colleague, or hotel concierge where such shops can be found. The advantages of a bike shop are that there will usually be a better selection, the staff will be more knowledgeable about bikes, and you will probably be able to test-ride bikes before you buy. A third option is to find a used bicycle market. These can be a bit more challenging to find, but they do exist. The downside to these markets is that it is easy for a foreigner to get ripped off. I have had students who bought bikes at these kinds of markets and

were quite proud to show off their inexpensive new wheels, only to have them start falling apart in a couple of days. Some of these students then spent almost as much on repairs as they'd paid for the bike. The other disadvantage to buying from a used market is that not all the bikes will be properly licensed. According to law all bicycles in China must have a license (more about this below). A final option is to buy a used bicycle from someone. If you would like to do this, ask around your network of friends and associates and they may have a bike for sale, or know someone who does.

When buying a bicycle, make sure you also buy a good lock and a bell. A bell is essential on China's crowded streets. Use it as you would the horn in a car, to warn others—cyclists and pedestrians—of your presence. It used to be that locks were permanently attached to the frame of the bike and consisted of a curved bar that went through the spokes of the back wheel of the bike, thus preventing the bike from being rolled. These kinds of locks are not as secure as cable-type locks.

When you buy a new bike, you also need to buy a license and register it. This can be done at the store where you buy your bicycle, and the sales clerk can help you with filling out the form to do this. You will need your identification, such as your passport. Once the bike is licensed and registered, a metal tag license will be installed on the bike, behind the seat, and you will get a paper license as well. Keep this in a safe place because you'll need it if you ever want to sell the bike in the future. If you are buying a used bike, the previous owner should have the license, and it can be transferred into your name. At used bike markets, many of the bikes may be stolen property and will not have a license. In reality you may never be asked to show the license on your bike, and you will probably never be stopped for riding a bike that does not have a license, but if you are ever in an accident, or want to sell your bike, you will need to have that license.

■ **Electric bicycles** 电力自行车 **diànlì zìxíngchē**
Another increasingly popular option is to buy an electric bike. More and more of these are showing up on the roads of China. They are silent, quick, and efficient but they do need to be plugged in at night to recharge their batteries. They are more expensive than traditional bicycles but if you anticipate traveling longer distances, such as for your commute, this might be a good option. Just make sure that the battery will hold a charge for as long as you need it to.

There are two kinds of electric bikes. One uses a normal lead-acid battery, which is quite heavy. These bikes cost about 1600 yuan. A 36-volt battery can run approximately 25 kilometers and a 48-volt battery can go about 30 to 40 kilometers on a charge. These kinds of batteries need to be replaced once a year or so, and cost around 240 to 320 yuan. The other kind of electric bike uses a lithium battery, **lǐ** 锂, which is very lightweight. These bikes are quite a bit more expensive, from around 2000 to over 4000 yuan. A 36-volt lithium battery can go about 30 kilometers and a 48-volt lithium battery can go about 40 to 50 kilometers. Lithium batteries need to be replaced approximately every three years, and a new one costs about 1800 yuan. New batteries need to be charged for around 12 hours. Each subsequent charge takes six to seven hours.

■ **Parking your bike** 存放自行车 **cúnfàng zìxíngchē**

At large commercial centers you can usually find bike parking lots. These lots can be very large. They are staffed by an attendant and are fenced or at least partitioned off. To use these lots, simply find a place to park your bike—it may be squeezed in among thousands of other bikes—then pay the attendant. It usually only costs about 0.5 yuan for regular bikes and 1 yuan for electric

bikes. The attendant will then give you a small ticket and a corresponding ticket will be placed on your bike. When you return to pick up your bike, you must show the ticket to the attendant before retrieving your bike. There are no time limits with these kinds of lots and they are secure.

The other common place to park your bike is on the street. Many streets have areas between the sidewalk and the street for bicycle parking. It is a good idea to park your bike in a designated area, or at least where other bikes are parked. If there is a rack, make sure you secure your frame to it. Often there will be no rack, so just thread the lock through the frame of the bike and the front tire.

There usually will be a designated place to park your bike at your

> If you park in a no parking zone, your bike may be impounded.

apartment building. However, if no such place exists, try to find a rail or other secure object to lock your bike onto. Despite your best efforts of locking or otherwise securing your bike, bikes do get stolen in China. The newer and shinier the bike, the more attractive it will be to potential thieves. Also, if you park in a no parking zone, your bike may be impounded. In other words, you will probably never see it again.

■ Renting a bicycle 租自行车 zū zìxíngchē

Most areas that cater to tourists will have places where you can rent a bike. Prices will vary by region and the type of bike you rent. Hotels may have information about where bikes can be rented. Travel agents and outfitters will also have this kind of information. Bikes are usually rented by the hour, half day, or full day. You will need proper identification to rent a bike, and will probably have to leave a cash security deposit that will be returned when you return the bike. Places that rent bikes will be pretty obvious as there will usually be dozen of used bikes lined up outside the shop.

■ Getting your bicycle repaired 修理自行车 xiūlǐ zìxíngchē

Sooner or later you will need to get your bicycle repaired. All over Chinese cities, bicycle repair people have set up shop on

sidewalks, street corners, and small repair booths along the street. Some are as simple as a guy with a pump, a small basin of water, and a few tools; others are large booths with numerous bicycles, tools, and multiple repairpeople. Repair stations are usually located in areas with

lots of traffic: near schools and college campuses, near large shopping areas, and scattered throughout blue-collar neighborhoods. Most of them are located on smaller side streets. You won't find many on major thoroughfares.

Getting your bicycle repaired is as simple as finding one of these repair stands, telling them about or pointing out your problem, and either waiting for it to be repaired, or leaving and coming back later to pick it up at an arranged time. Most repairs are quick and inexpensive. I have found most repairpeople to be very fair and competent. The more complete operations can fix everything, from a flat tire to rebuilding a rim. The more simple operations usually can only fix a flat tire, adjust your brakes, or make other very simple fixes.

DRIVING IN CHINA
在中国开车 **zài zhōngguó kāichē**

A final option for travel in China is driving a car. It is debatable whether China accepts international driver's licenses. If

> *Several years ago I had a badly bent rear rim, with several broken spokes, from a minor accident. I was concerned that it would be a difficult and costly repair, if it was even possible to fix the damaged rim. I took it to a local bicycle repair booth, expecting the worst. The repairman took a look, grimaced a bit, and told me that he could fix it but it would take several hours. When I returned, the rim was as true as the original and looked great. The bill was 31 yuan (at that time, about US$3.85). Pretty good deal.*

you plan to drive in China you may need to take a written test and a driving test to get a Chinese driver's license.

Those who have foreign driver's licenses can go to the Vehicle Management Office **chēliàng guǎnlǐsuǒ** 车辆管理所 in the police station. There you can take a test of Chinese traffic laws, and then get a Chinese driver's license. You'll probably need to study Chinese traffic laws as there are many that are different from laws in other nations.

Buying a car in China is increasingly inexpensive, but still usually only the upper class can and do drive cars. The tax on new cars is quite high. The traffic in nearly every major city in China is getting progressively worse. This results not only in frequent traffic jams and long waits, but also in chaotic driving conditions. Driving in China is most likely not like the driving you're used to. Though vehicular traffic usually does obey traffic lights for the most part, the flow of traffic tends to be more fluid. In other words, lane changes can be erratic, and you must constantly be on the lookout for pedestrians, bicycles, and scooters weaving in and out of traffic. The rule of the road seems to be to yield to the larger vehicle. This means that buses or trucks may simply pull out in front of you and expect you to yield, sometimes quite abruptly.

The other major problem with driving in Chinese cities is that most cities were not designed with so many cars in mind. As a result parking is a serious problem. Yes, you may be able to get to your favorite restaurant—but finding a parking place may be the real challenge.

> The rule on the road: yield to the larger vehicle.

The bottom line is this: expensive taxes on cars, major traffic, challenging driving conditions, and a serious lack of parking space should lead one to seriously consider whether driving in China is worth the effort. Perhaps a better option, if you can afford it, is to hire a car and driver. Some expats working for large non-China-based companies may be provided with a car and driver. This will not alleviate the traffic and parking problems, but it will give you the freedom of driving when and where you want to go, without actually having to drive yourself.

WALKING
走路 zǒulù

Walking can be a great way to get around, especially if you don't have far to go. During rush hour or other busy times, by the time you wait for an available taxi, or navigate the crowds on a bus or subway, often you could have walked to your destination without the hassle. It is also a wonderful way to see a city and observe the daily lives of ordinary people.

Walking does have its challenges. Though there are usually sidewalks in Chinese cities, sometimes they are not the smooth, wide walkways you might expect. Be cautious about uneven surfaces, potholes, drop offs, and so on. Those with disabilities will find most Chinese cities very difficult to navigate. There are very few handicap-accessible services for those who need them. The other thing to keep in mind when walking is that cars, buses, motorcyles, and bikes will not yield for pedestrians. Be very careful when crossing streets. Always cross with a green light, and even then, watch for cars, bikes, and so on. They will sometimes be turning into your path, or going through a red light. Just follow the rest of the people crossing the street and it is not too scary.

■ ■ ■

USEFUL PHRASES

ABC (Airport Beijing City): light rail line from the Beijing Airport **Běijīng jīchǎng guǐdào jiāotōng xiàn** 北京机场轨道交通线

book flights online **wǎngshàng dìng piào** 网上订票

domestic terminal **guónèi tōngdào** 国内通道

domestic transfers **guónèi zhuǎnjī** 国内转机

getting into town from the airport **cóng jīchǎng jìnchéng** 从机场进城

Hongqiao Airport **hóngqiáo jīchǎng** 虹桥机场

international terminal **guójì tōngdào** 国际通道

Maglev train **shànghǎi cífú lièchē** 上海磁浮列车

Pudong Airport **pǔdōng jīchǎng** 浦东机场

buy train tickets **mǎi huǒchēpiào** 买火车票

ticket offices **shòupiàochù** 售票处

C class **chéngjì dòngchēzǔ lièchē** 城际动车组列车/**chéngjì lièchē** 城际列车

D class **dòngchēzǔ lièchē** 动车组列车/**dòngchē** 动车

G class **gāosù tiělù dòngchē** 高速铁路动车/**gāo tiě** 高铁

L class **línshí lǚkè kuàichē** 临时旅客快车

K class **kuàisù lǚkè lièchē** 快速旅客列车/**kuàisù** 快速

T class **tèkuài lǚkè lièchē** 特快旅客列车/**tèkuài** 特快

Z class **zhídá tèkuài lǚkè lièchē** 直达特快旅客列车/**zhítè** 直特

long distance bus travel **chángtú qìchē lǚxíng** 长途汽车旅行

long distance bus station **chángtú qìchēzhàn** 长途汽车站

buy a bicycle **mǎi zìxíngchē** 买自行车

get a bicycle repaired **xiūlǐ zìxíngchē** 修理自行车

park your bike **cúnfàng zìxíngchē** 存放自行车

rent a bicycle **zū zìxíngchē** 租自行车

Vehicle Management office **chēliàng guǎnlǐsuǒ** 车辆管理所

NAMES OF AIRLINES

Air China, CA **zhōngguó guójì hángkōng gōngsī** 中国国际航空公司

Cathay Pacific Airlines **guótài hángkōng gōngsī** 国泰航空公司

China Airlines (Taiwan) **zhōnghuá hángkōng gōngsī** 中华航空公司

China Southern Airlines, CZ **zhōngguó nánfāng hángkōng** 中国南方航空

China Eastern Airlines, MU **zhōngguó dōngfāng hángkōng** 中国东方航空

Delta Airlines **dáměi hángkōng gōngsī** 达美航空公司

Dragonair **gǎnglóng hángkōng** 港龙航空

Hainan Airlines, HU **hǎinán hángkōng** 海南航空

Korean Airlines **dàhán hángkōng gōngsī** 大韩航空公司

Shanghai Airlines **shànghǎi hángkōng** 上海航空

Singapore Airlines **xīnjiāpō hángkōng gōngsī** 新家坡航空公司

United Airlines **měilián hángkōng gōngsī** 美联航空公司; in Taiwan, **liánhé hángkōng** 联合航空

USEFUL WORDS

airport **jīchǎng** 机场

bicycle **zìxíngchē** 自行车

bus **gōnggòng qìchē** 公共汽车; **gōngchē** 公车; **qìchē** 汽车; **bāshì** 巴士

driving **kāi chē** 开车

empty **kōng** 空

electric bicycle **diànlì zìxíngchē** 电力自行车

hard seat **yìng zuò** 硬座

hard sleeper **yìng wò** 硬卧

long distance bus station **chángtú qìchēzhàn** 长途汽车站

minivan **miànbāochē** 面包车

no seat **wú zuò** 无坐

soft seat **ruǎnzuò** 软座

soft sleeper **ruǎnwò** 软卧

subway **dìtiě** 地铁

taxi **chūzūchē** 出租车 / **dìshì** 的士

traveling/touring **lǚxíng** 旅行

walking **zǒulù** 走路

2

Living

居住 jūzhù

Living in the People's Republic of China has changed significantly in the past twenty years. Previously, foreign students were required to live in approved and designated student dormitories on university campuses and businesspeople and the diplomatic corps were required to live in foreign compounds designated specifically for foreigners and where local Chinese were usually not allowed. This created isolated islands or enclaves of foreigners in the major cities in China. Under these conditions it was wholly possible to interact primarily with other foreigners for the majority of the time. Being isolated from Chinese communities prevented foreigners from living in and experiencing real Chinese neighborhoods. Thus it was difficult to get a feel for how the Chinese live on a day-to-day basis.

With the continuous opening up to the West, the housing situation has changed considerably. In the past, private ownership was prohibited and locals lived in housing compounds provided by their work unit. Now in China, private housing is allowed and the construction rate of new apartment buildings and complexes is staggering. Whereas in the past housing was very tightly controlled creating a housing shortage, now in many cities finding an apartment is not that difficult, though prices continue to rise.

The hotel situation in the past was also different. Foreigners were only allowed to stay in hotels that were approved by the state to house foreigners. Often only the most luxurious and expensive hotels were open to foreigners. There has long been the assumption that foreigners, especially Westerners, have an abundance of money to throw around. Traveling on a budget was challenging, though not impossible. Now, most hotels are open to foreigners. Those that may not be open to foreigners are typically very modest guesthouses or hostel-like accommodations that cater to migrant workers, construction crews, and other working-class groups. These are advertised with signs saying **zhùsù** 住宿 and are sometimes rented by the hour as well as nightly. Most Chinese businesspeople would

Several years ago some friends of mine pulled into the tourist town of Lijiang in Yunnan province in the middle of the night after a grueling 10-hour drive from Sichuan. They stopped at the first lodging they saw, only to discover that the hotel could not house foreigners.

For a couple of yuan, the taxi driver was persuaded to check into the hotel with his ID card. My friends had an uneasy night's sleep in less-than-desirable conditions, but it only cost the equivalent of one U.S. dollar and saved them from having to search for an approved hotel.

not stay at these kinds of guesthouses. As a foreigner you will most likely be turned away from these kinds of places.

In this chapter I discuss three kinds of accommodations: staying in a hotel, living in a student dormitory, and renting an apartment.

STAYING IN A HOTEL
住宾馆 zhù bīnguǎn

If you are in China for only a short time, staying in hotel-type lodging is probably your best choice. This option ranges from the most elegant five star hotels to university guesthouses and youth hostels.

There are a number of different terms used for hotels in Chinese. The larger, more expensive hotels usually use the term **fàndiàn** 饭店 or **jiǔdiàn** 酒店 sometimes with the character **dà** 大 added indicating a very large hotel. Generally, a **jiǔdiàn** 酒店 is bigger and more modern than a **fàndiàn** 饭店. Both are typically four- and five-star level hotels.

A **bīnguǎn** 宾馆 is a simple hotel or guesthouse that is typically less expensive and smaller than the bigger hotels described above, and is similar to a three-star hotel.

A **zhāodàisuǒ** 招待所 is a guesthouse or hostel that in the past was owned and operated by work units (**dānwèi** 单位) or universities.

Today they are similar to a **bīnguǎn** 宾馆 though usually cheaper and not as nice and anyone can stay at them. Finally, there are **lǚguǎn** 旅馆 which are very simple, small, one- or two-star hotels that do not have restaurants. Youth hostels, **qīngnián lǚshè** 青年旅社, can be found in larger cities like Beijing. They are

• BEHIND THE SCENES •

Characteristics of Hotels in China 中国旅店的特点 **zhōngguó lǚdiàn de tèdiǎn**

- When checking into a hotel you'll need your passport. The staff will probably scan or make a copy of it. At the very least they will fill out some paperwork.

- Bigger hotels usually provide the following: toothbrush, toothpaste, comb, soap and either bodywash or shampoo.

- In many government hotels you have to ask to have the Internet turned on and often it is not wireless. You may need to pay a deposit as well.

- Just inside the door, there is usually a small card slot where you insert your key card to activate the power in the room. This is designed to save energy since when you leave the room and take your key, the power to the room is disconnected. There are ways to get around this; for example, if you want to keep the room cool in the summer, or you are drying clothes that you have hand washed, you can simply use a business card or other similarly sized card.

- Some hotels have wood floors. Disposable slippers are provided for you to wear in the room. (If you don't, sometimes hotel staff may get irritated.)

- Some old-style government hotels still will not give you a room key. A hotel employee will open your door for you. In these kinds of hotels, there is usually a staff member on each floor of the hotel.

- At smaller, older hotels, it is a good idea to ask to see a room before checking in. Hotels often have various levels of rooms and for a little more money, you may be able to get a newly updated one.

- If it isn't peak season, ask for a discount **dǎzhé** 打折. Hotels will often give you one.

- Many hotels still have Ethernet cables in the rooms and wireless only in the lobby. Keep this in mind if you are an iPad or tablet user.

even more inexpensive and usually have shared rooms and bathing facilities. Some universities, such as Nanjing University, have foreign student dormitories, **xuéshēng sùshè** 学生宿舍, that are also available to travelers. They are similar to youth hostels with shared bathrooms and private or shared rooms. They are usually quite inexpensive and are located on or adjacent to university campuses (see below for more information).

Staying in a hotel in China is not that different from staying at a hotel elsewhere in the world. Booking a room at a hotel in advance (**yùdìng fángjiān** 预定房间) can be done online at the largest hotels, or by calling on the phone and making a reservation with a credit card. At larger (i.e., expensive) hotels, typically foreign-owned chains, most personnel speak some English. But otherwise, calling and making a reservation at smaller hotels will require that you speak some Chinese. Or, you can use an online travel company like www.elong.com or www.ctrip.com. These are Chinese companies that work similarly to online travel companies in the West such as Orbitz or Travelocity. One can use a credit card to make reservations at a wide variety of hotels, from expensive to very modest, and these websites have both English and Chinese options. Travel guidebooks also have detailed information (including phone numbers, addresses, rates, etc.) regarding accommodations in a large number of Chinese cities. It is advised that during peak travel season, such as around Chinese New Year, you book your rooms several days, or even weeks, in advance. Those mentioned in popular guidebooks may fill up fast.

When staying at small Chinese-owned hotels do not expect the same level of service that you might at larger, more expensive hotels. Do not assume that everyone will speak and understand English. In fact, the traveler who speaks Chinese will probably have a much smoother experience and receive better service.

Be warned that the system of assigning stars to hotels can be quite different for Chinese hotels. I recently stayed at a three-star hotel in Yangzhou and it was not even as nice as a Super 8 motel in the U.S. But by Chinese standards it was okay.

Many universities have hotels, guesthouses, or dormitories (宾馆 **bīnguǎn**, 招待所 **zhāodàisuǒ**, 宿舍 **sùshè**) for foreign students that also will rent rooms to the general public. These accommodations range from typical hotel-like rooms to basic dorm rooms with shared bathroom facilities. Many of these guesthouses or dormitories are listed in travel guidebooks.

> Universities offer lodging to the general public, too—not just students.

Many hotels may have a "service charge" which is similar to room taxes that are paid for hotels in the U.S. This charge can be as high as 15 to 20 percent. When booking a room be sure to ask if there is a service charge (服务费 **fúwùfèi**) or any other additional charges.

Remember to not drink the water in hotels or guesthouses. I also recommend using boiled or filtered water to brush your teeth. Thermoses, filled daily with boiled water, may be provided in lower level hotel rooms. Even more common now are electric kettles. With these you can boil your own water as needed. Larger hotels may provide a couple of bottles of spring water for your use.

STAYING IN A UNIVERSITY STUDENT DORMITORY (宿舍 sùshè) or FOREIGN STUDENT HOUSING
住在大学生宿舍或外国留学生公寓
zhù zài dàxuéshēng sùshè huò wàiguó liúxuéshēng gōngyù

There are two kinds of foreign students studying in China: those that are on study abroad programs specifically to study Chinese language and culture, and those who are matriculated

> *On my first trip to China, in 1985, we were housed in a Chinese student dormitory at a large university. We thought it was pretty nice, even spacious, with two single beds, two desks, and two wardrobes for clothes. It was about the size of a typical dorm room in the U.S. There were clean bathrooms down the hall. We later learned that usually this same room would house eight Chinese students.*

students earning a degree from a Chinese university. (For more details see Chapter 7 on studying in China.) Many universities have a department for foreign studies, that is, for foreigners studying Chinese. For example, Nanjing University has a department called **hǎiwài jiàoyù xuéyuàn** 海外教育学院, or the "College of Overseas Education." Many of these kinds of colleges have housing designated for foreigners. In the past, foreigners were generally required to stay in these foreign student dormitories. As such they sometimes turned into foreigner ghettos with a host of restaurants and bars in the vicinity that catered specifically to Westerners. This does not exactly encourage a real immersion experience into the language and culture. These foreign student dormitories may be freestanding buildings or a wing or two of an existing building. Accommodations are usually adequate with two people per room and with communal bathrooms at the end of the hall.

The nice thing about foreign student dormitories is that you don't have to deal with a landlord, negotiate rent, pay utility bills, and so on. They will usually require a security deposit and rent may either be paid in full, or monthly depending on the arrangements. If you are studying through a U.S.-based university, housing will probably be part of your fees, so you do not have to worry about monthly rent.

Most universities and work units (**dānwèi** 单位) have older, more basic guesthouses **zhāodàisuǒ** 招待所, but many now also have pleasant newer guesthouses (**bīnguǎn** 宾馆) as well. These guesthouses are not only for foreign students but for anyone who would like to stay there. They are usually very reasonably priced compared to other hotels. In these university guesthouses, there are often dormitory-style accommodations, as well as private rooms with private bathrooms for a higher price. The more nicely appointed single rooms are usually rented by travelers or visiting faculty members.

It may be possible to stay in a regular student dormitory. Dorms that Chinese students live in are quite a bit more basic than what you see in the U.S. Dorm rooms typically house up to eight students and are very crowded. Furniture typically consists of bunk beds, some small wardrobes, and maybe a small desk. Private space is very limited. In fact, it is not uncommon for a student's bed to be all the private space they have. I have seen dorm rooms where half of the bed was piled with books, clothes, and other personal items because there simply is no other place to store things. Bathrooms are communal and are usually at the end of the building. Sometimes bathrooms do not have bathing facilities, so taking a shower may require going to a different building altogether. Many dorms lack air conditioning and south of the Yangtze River, most buildings do not have central heat. Beds in student dormitories can be rather hard with very thin mattresses. Living in a Chinese student dormitory would certainly give you an authentic experience, but know what you are committing to.

RENTING AN APARTMENT
租公寓 / 租房子 **zū gōngyù/ zū fángzi**

Renting an apartment in China can be an intimidating experience. Unfamiliar vocabulary and contracts with legal terminology can be challenging for even the linguistically sophisticated. However, it is not an impossible task if you have sufficient information. Below, I outline the various steps in finding housing in a moderately sized Chinese city. This information may not apply to small towns or villages where housing may not be as readily available as it is in larger metropolitan areas.

■ **Finding an apartment** 找房子 **zhǎo fángzi**

There are three general strategies to finding an apartment. One is to get a recommendation or referral from a friend or colleague, the second is to find your own, and the third is to use a real estate company. If you are working for a company in China your employer may provide housing or have suggestions about where to live. Your colleagues may also have suggestions or know someone that is renting an apartment. In China having connections is very important and can allow one to get things done much more easily and less painfully than if one has no connections. Chinese colleagues or friends will have a network of friends and associates whom they may call on for favors. If you are lucky they may know someone (who may know someone) who has an apartment for rent. Oftentimes, landlords own multiple properties, and your friend's or colleague's landlord may have other apartments they can show you. If you are a student, you might ask other students in the area for recommendations.

> As always, connections help: Chinese colleagues or friends may know someone (who may know someone) who has an apartment for rent.

If you are not in a hurry and have some time to look around, you may be able to find something on your own. The best strategy is to go to apartment buildings and ask if there are any apartments for rent. In larger, more refined buildings there will be a **guǎnlǐyuán** 管理员, or person who manages the door, similar to a security guard, and many will know if there are landlords renting apartments in their buildings. Some communities have bulletin boards where the daily paper is displayed. Sometimes apartments for rent are advertised there. The advantage to using this approach is that you do not have to pay a finder's fee; but of course it will also require more work on your part.

If you do not have any connections in the city in which you're planning to live, using a real estate company is a good way to go. Again, ask around for a recommendation for a good company to use. These kinds of companies are typically called **fángchǎn** 房产, **dìchǎn** 地产, or **fángdìchǎn gōngsī** 房地产公司. They may also be referred to as **zhōngjiè** 中介, meaning a go-between or broker.

The first thing that you will be asked at these companies is what kind of apartment you are looking for. Apartments in China are typically categorized in one of two ways: by square meters (**píngmǐ** 平米), or by the number of rooms. Try to familiarize yourself with how square meters convert into square footage. Also, keep in mind that Chinese apartments are typically smaller than apartments in the U.S. One square foot is equal to .09 square meters (and one square meter is equal to 10.76 square feet).

The other method used is number of rooms. This is usually expressed in terms of the number of bedrooms and living or sitting rooms. For example, a three-bedroom apartment with a living

Square meters	Square foot equivalent
60	646
65	700
70	753
75	807
80	861
85	915
90	969
95	1023
100	1076
105	1130
110	1184
120	1292

or sitting room, and one bathroom, would be expressed as **sānshì yìtīng yíwèi** 三室一厅一卫 which is the equivalent of "3 bedrooms, 1 room, 1 bath" **sānjiān wòshì yìjiān kètīng yìjiān wèishēngjiān** 三间卧室一间客厅一间卫生间. The term **dānyuán** 单元 is used to refer to a residential unit or apartment. For example, you might say **wǒ jiā zhù zài sān dānyuán** 我家住在三单元, "My house is in Unit 3."

If you are in China for a short term (a semester to a year) you will probably want a furnished (**dài jiājù** 带家具) or at least partially furnished apartment. This is something you should bring up with the **zhōngjiè** 中介 before you go out looking. Furnished apartments are common and come equipped with appliances, furniture, and sometimes some kitchen pots and pans. You usually will need to buy your own sheets, blankets, and pillows, and most of your cooking supplies, like a wok, rice cooker, electric teapot, and so on.

Once you have agreed on what you are looking for, the **zhōngjiè** 中介 will then offer to show you some apartments. They usually charge a fee to do this, which will often be dropped (or deducted from other fees) if you actually rent the apartment. Real estate companies usually will also charge an additional finder's fee for finding you an apartment. This fee will often be the equivalent of half a month's rent for the apartment that you decide on. Some companies may also charge a flat finder's fee. This finder's fee is in addition to the **zhōngjiè**'s fee. Make sure you know what the company policy is before you go out looking.

Another good strategy to get a feel for what apartment rents currently are in the area where you're looking is to use an online real estate company like **wǒ ài wǒjiā** 我爱我家, www.5i5j.com. On this site you can search for rentals by city and district, as well as by size, price, and so on. Some people go to this site to see what typical apartment rents are, then go to a local real estate company and have a **zhōngjiè** 中介 show

them some places. Doing this may help you more successfully negotiate a rental contract without getting ripped off. This site is only in Chinese and covers the following cities: Beijing, Tianjin, Shanghai, Hangzhou, Suzhou, Nanjing, Ningbo, and Taiyuan.

Once you have found an apartment that you like you will usually need to negotiate to determine a monthly rental price and what appliances and other things will be covered in the rent. With some apartments you will deal directly with the landlord, and with some you will deal with the real estate company that will also act as the property manager. Sometimes the **zhōngjiè** 中介 may help with the negotiations, but most often you will be on your own to negotiate with the landlord. Most landlords are only willing to rent their apartments for a full year. If you want to rent an apartment for a shorter period of time, like a four-month semester, it will take some dealing; be prepared to pay more to get a shorter contract.

It is important when looking at an apartment that you carefully inspect the furnishings and appliances to make sure everything is in working order. Flush the toilets, run the hot water, turn on the stove, check the lights, the air conditioner, televisions, telephone, etc. Most apartment buildings that rent apartments will have Western style sit toilets. However, sometimes the plumbing systems in certain areas are not designed to handle toilet paper in the toilets. In these situations there is usually a small waste basket next to the toilet for used toilet paper. This may sound a bit gross, but it is a fairly common thing in many parts of China. Ask about this when looking at an apartment.

■ **Signing a contract** 签合同 **qiān hétong**
Usually landlords will require that you pay three months' rent up front when you sign a contract. Sometimes the term **jìdù** 季度 is used, meaning quarterly. This three months' rent then serves as your security deposit, which you will get back when you move out. Sometimes, such as in Beijing, if the rent of the apartment is more than 3000 yuan, the landlord is expected to pay the finder's fee.

When renting to foreigners, some landlords may want the entire amount of rent due at the time of occupancy. This may seem a bit daunting, but if you have a housing budget, paying it all up front means that much less to worry about later. A security deposit is also usually required at signing time as well. The amount of the deposit (**yājīn** 押金) may vary but is often the equivalent of one month's rent. When you move out, if there are no problems or damage to the apartment, the deposit will be refunded to you.

The contract should outline the furniture (**jiājù** 家具) and appliances (**qìjù** 器具) that the apartment includes. It should also list which services are and are not included in the monthly rent. This may include things such as cable television fees (**yǒuxiàn diànshì fèi** 有限电视费), Internet access fees (**shàngwǎng fèi** 上网费), telephone fees (**diànhuà fèi** 电话费), and so on. Also make sure that you understand how to pay utility bills, which are usually not included in the rent. Make sure that you retain a copy of the contract.

■ Paying utility bills 付水电费 fù shuǐdiànfèi

Most apartments do not include utilities (typically water, electricity, and gas). Monthly or bimonthly you will receive the bills. Your landlord should have information on how to pay these bills. Most of the time bills are paid at local banks or maybe at the post office. It should say on the bill which banks will accept payment. You must have an account number (which you should get from your landlord) when paying your bill. Take the actual bill, which will have a measurement of the water, gas, or electricity used during the time period, but will not show a payment amount, to the bank along with the account number. You will then find out how much the bill is, and can pay on the spot with cash. Though credit and debit cards are becoming more common in China, most commerce is still based on cash, including paying utility bills.

■ Bathrooms and sanitation
卫生间和卫生 wèishēngjiān hé wèishēng

Sanitation is continually improving in China, especially in the larger cities. However, the countryside is still another matter. Though there are increasing numbers of Western style sit toilets (**mǎtǒng** 马桶/**zuòbiànqì** 坐便器), especially in hotels and shopping malls, the squatter type toilet (**dūnshì mǎtǒng** 蹲式马桶/**dūnkēng** 蹲坑) is still the most common throughout China. These types of toilets can be intimidating at first, but with practice and an open mind one can adapt without much trouble. Getting acclimated to squatters is not just a matter of training the leg muscles to squat without any support, but it also requires one to get used to the stench that is often ubiquitous at Chinese public restrooms. Part of the problem is how bathrooms are cleaned (usually just sprayed down with water), and Chinese squatter toilets and urinals seldom have a U-bend in the pipes to prevent fumes from coming back up into the bathroom, as is customary in the West. The smell in some public bathrooms can be overpowering, especially in smaller cities or in rural areas. The best advice is to breathe through your mouth and be as quick as possible. Another potential hazard in public restrooms is that the floors are frequently wet, sometimes with standing water. This makes it challenging to do your business without getting your pants wet. It can be done, you just have to be more careful. A small fee may be charged at public restrooms. Finally, always carry toilet paper or small packets of tissues with you whenever you leave your hotel or apartment since most public restrooms do not provide toilet paper. Because of the possible primitive conditions, it is wise when you are out to find a hotel or maybe a restaurant and use its bathroom, which will undoubtedly be cleaner than public restrooms.

> **The squatter type toilet can be intimidating at first, but with practice one can adapt.**

Most apartments that rent to foreigners will have Western style toilets. However, in some older apartments the toilets were not designed to handle toilet paper and will easily clog if it is flushed down. With these kinds of toilets a special waste basket (**zhǐlǒu** 纸篓) is provided to dispose of used toilet paper (**shǒuzhǐ** 手纸). This can contribute to a smelly bathroom.

Unlike in the West where the trash goes out once a week, in China, you typically take the trash out every day or whenever your wastebaskets are full. Different apartment buildings will have different policies, but there is usually a designated place, sometimes just an area outside the building, where trash is deposited. There may be garbage cans, but often it is just a pile where you throw your trash bags. In densely populated areas, the trash collector will have a wheeled cart to pick up the trash. It will then be transported to a larger facility. Most apartments do not have recycling bins, but rest assured that your trash will be checked and sorted for recyclable items. In fact, you may notice three-wheeled bicycles or other carts full of cardboard, plastic, metal, and so on, on their way to a recycling center.

■ **Problems in the apartment**
公寓的问题 **gōngyù de wèntí**
In North America if something breaks or stops working, such as a washing machine, refrigerator, or air conditioning unit, and it is not due to your abuse, it is usually the landlord's responsibility to fix (**xiūlǐ** 修理) it. In China, on the other hand, the landlord (**fángdōng** 房东) will expect you to get it fixed at your expense.

If something breaks and you can't fix it yourself, you have a few options to try. You can contact the landlord or property manager and ask them to arrange to send someone over to fix it. You can ask your neighbors for a recommendation of a handyman. Or, using your network of friends and associates,

*Several years ago we were living in China in a typical working class apartment complex. We noticed that the main drain in the bathroom was getting progressively slower. Finally, after every shower there was standing water in the bathroom (the drain was located in the middle of the floor). I was hesitant to call a plumber (**shuǐnuǎngōng** 水暖 工) because they are so expensive in the U.S. Also, there was no phone book or other obvious resource available. I finally called the **zhōng jiè** 中介 who'd helped us find the apartment. I explained the situation and he called a plumber for me. The plumber arrived promptly, cleared the drain, and charged us 35 yuan, which at that time was equivalent to about US$4.35. A real bargain.*

you can find someone yourself to fix it. Some places in China, primarily large cities, may have something like the yellow pages where you can look up information and services. However, these sorts of reference books are usually only available at large hotels or post offices.

China does have a directory assistance service for getting information and phone numbers. The China Telecom number is 118114, and the China Unicom number is 116114. Theoretically, you can call these numbers to get phone numbers of businesses and services. However, they are generally limited to large cities like Beijing and Shanghai. There is also a companion website, www.wo116114.com, but we found it had few listings outside of Beijing. A better site is 58.com. This site is very easy to use and has a great deal of useful information for cities all over China, including smaller cities. You simply select a city (they're listed alphabetically by pinyin) then select a category for the services you need. One thing to keep in mind is that these listings may not be very comprehensive—there are countless small businesses all over every city in China that will not be part of these kinds of networks.

■　■　■

USEFUL PHRASES

book a room at a hotel in advance **yùdìng fángjiān** 预定房间

guesthouse (belongs to a university or a large company) **zhāodàisuǒ** 招待所

high-level hotel that also offers dining for guests only **bīnguǎn** 宾馆

low-level hotel (generally does not have food services) **lǚshè/lǚguǎn** 旅社/旅馆

restaurant, hotel **fàndiàn** 饭店

restaurant, hotel **jiǔdiàn** 酒店 Both 酒店 and 饭店 can refer to restaurants, but they also can mean hotels. Sometimes 酒店 is more modern than 饭店, and offers more amenities.

student dormitory **xuéshēng sùshè** 学生宿舍

youth hostel **qīngnián lǚshè** 青年旅社

look for or find an apartment **zhǎo fángzi** 找房子

furnished rental unit **dài jiājù** 带家具

sign a contract **qiān hétong** 签合同

real estate **fángchǎn** 房产; **dìchǎn** 地产

real estate agency; property company **fángdìchǎn gōngsī** 房地产公司

rent an apartment **zū gōngyù; zū fángzi** 租公寓; 租房子

3 bedrooms, 1 living room, and 1 bathroom **sānshì yìtīng yíwèi** 三室一厅一卫

to pay utility bills **fù shuǐdiànfèi** 付水电费

cable TV fees **yǒuxiàn diànshì fèi** 有限电视费

Internet access fees **shàngwǎng fèi** 上网费

telephone fees **diànhuà fèi** 电话费

USEFUL WORDS

accommodation **zhùsù** 住宿

air conditioning **kōngtiáo** 空调

apartment **gōngyù** 公寓

bathroom **wèishēngjiān** 卫生间/ **cèsuǒ** 厕所

bedroom **wòshì** 卧室

bill **zhàngdān** 账单

book (a room at hotel) **yùdìng** 预定

contract **hétong** 合同

deposit **yājīn** 押金

discount **dǎzhé** 打折

dormitory **sùshè** 宿舍

electricity **diàn** 电

electric light/lamp **diàndēng** 电灯

fee; expense **fèi** 费

fix, repair **xiūlǐ** 修理

furniture **jiājù** 家具

gas **ránqì** 燃气

heating system; central heating **nuǎnqì** 暖气

landlord **fángdōng** 房东

living room **tīng** 厅; **kètīng** 客厅

manager **guǎnlǐyuán** 管理员

neighbor **línjū** 邻居

pay **fù** 付

plumber **shuǐnuǎngōng** 水暖工

RMB dollar **yuán** 元

refrigerator **(diàn)bīngxiāng** (电)冰箱

rent (v) **zū** 租

rent (n) **fángzū** 房租

restroom; bathroom **xǐshǒujiān** 洗手间

room **fángzi** 房子; **fángjiān** 房间

service charge **fúwùfèi** 服务费

sign (your name) **qiān** 签

sit toilet **mǎtǒng** 马桶/**zuòbiànqì** 坐便器

special waste baskets for used toilet paper 纸篓 **zhǐlǒu**

square meter 平米 **píngmǐ**

squatter type toilet **dūnkēng** 蹲坑; **dūnshì mǎtǒng** 蹲式马桶 (Taiwan & Southern China)

stove **lúzi** 炉子

telephone **diànhuà** 电话

television **diànshì** 电视

toilet paper **shǒuzhǐ** 手纸

real estate broker **fángchǎn zhōngjiè** 房产中介

utility fee **shuǐdiànfèi** 水电费

washing machine **xǐyījī** 洗衣机

water **shuǐ** 水

3

Eating

吃饭 chīfàn

Eating in China can be a wonderful experience. Good food can be had at all price ranges, from very inexpensive sidewalk stalls to elaborate multicourse feasts. However, eating out in China can also be a frustrating experience if you don't know how to go about doing it. Even with good Chinese language skills it can be challenging trying to make sense of a restaurant menu that could be seven or eight pages long, and protocols and etiquette in most restaurants in China are quite different than in North America. Knowing what to expect when you go out to eat will make for a considerably smoother and more comfortable experience.

Eating out in China is a viable option because it's so inexpensive, relatively speaking. For those on a truly tight budget, cooking in your apartment is also a good option as buying foodstuffs is often even cheaper. This chapter focuses on eating out (at restaurants, and at street stalls) and the basics of buying food and cooking.

EATING AT RESTAURANTS
下饭馆(儿) **xià fànguǎn (er)** / 下馆子 **xià guǎnzi**

It would be nearly impossible to describe the precise conditions one can encounter in the myriad of Chinese restaurants throughout China. Very expensive formal restaurants resemble Western restaurants more than do the inexpensive streetside restaurants. In this section we'll consider typical casual sit-down restaurants that are found all over China.

If you have been invited out by a Chinese friend or associate, it is important that you wear nice clothes. To the Chinese, appearances are very important. Dressing up for your friend or associate tells them that you value the relationship and are honored to be their guest. Otherwise, dressing up is not a requirement at casual restaurants.

> **If you've been invited out to eat by a Chinese friend or associate, dress up.**

Chinese restaurants can be called by a variety of terms. A

typical term used for Chinese restaurants is **fànguǎn (er)** 饭馆 (儿) or **jiǔjiā** 酒家 or even **fàndiàn** 饭店. Other terms include **càiguǎn (er)** 菜馆(儿) (commonly used for vegetarian restaurants, but not exclusively), **jiǔlóu** 酒楼 (more common in the south), **cāntīng** 餐厅, often used for Western or other foreign food restaurants, or for inexpensive Chinese food, **xiǎo chī** 小吃 (used for small, inexpensive restaurants, as well as street food or snacks). For example, you might see a restaurant called **mǎshì càiguǎn (er)** 马氏菜馆(儿), **sìchuān fàndiàn** 四川饭店, **huímín cāntīng** 回民餐厅, **guǎngzhōu jiǔjiā** 广州酒家 or **wángsì xiǎo chī** 王四小吃.

■ **Entering the restaurant and getting a table**
进餐馆(儿)找位子 **jìn cānguǎn(er) zhǎo wèizi**
In China, restaurants may or may not have a reception area to wait for a table. At larger higher-end restaurants there will usually be a hostess who will greet you and show you to a seat, similar to restaurants in the United States. The situation is a little different for small restaurants and noodle shops, where, often, upon entering the restaurant one will be in the midst of the dining floor. There typically is not a host/hostess to greet diners when they come in, or to seat them. In these kinds of small, informal restaurants, it is appropriate for diners to enter and find their own place to sit down. If a small, informal restaurant is especially busy, it is not uncommon to join a table already occupied by other diners.

Americans often make the mistake of entering a small restaurant and standing politely until someone comes to greet them and seat them. If the restaurant is particularly busy, no one in the restaurant may pay any attention to the party, simply thinking that they are looking for someone or trying to decide whether they want to eat there or not. This behavior is usually met with a sometimes impatient server who will approach the foreign diners and ask if they need something. The

Americans will usually say something like "We need a table for six," whereupon the Chinese server will probably wonder why they are standing there and not going to an empty table and sitting down. At this point they will probably motion the party to the empty tables.

■ Tables 餐桌 cānzhūo

In typical larger Chinese restaurants, tables are large and round and seat anywhere from eight to ten diners. At smaller restaurants tables are smaller and may only seat two to four people. Chinese restaurants tend to be quite busy thus the space between tables may only be wide enough for a single person to walk through. Round tables almost always have a lazy Susan (**zhuànpán** 转盘) in the middle of the table. This facilitates the Chinese style of family dining. They may also have a few large round tables with lazy Susans for larger parties. There are usually a few condiments on the table, such as small bottles of soy sauce and/or hot sauce. One will find small ceramic teacups and chopsticks at each place (or they

are brought shortly after one is seated). There may also be a box of tissues or a roll of toilet paper at the table. It's a good idea to bring your own tissue packets to use for napkins, since they are not always provided.

After the diners are seated, tea is often served while they are deciding what to order. Just as water is automatically served in American restaurants, there is usually no charge for tea in a Chinese restaurant. Unless specified, the house tea, usually a green tea, will be brought (see p. 92 for more on tea). If appetizers are available, they are ordered separately from the main dishes so they can be eaten while diners are waiting for the main meal to come. It is more common for Chinese to drink alcoholic beverages during a meal rather than before and after as is common in the U.S.

> It's a good idea to bring your own tissue packets to use for napkins.

■ The server 服务员 fúwùyuán

The server's role in a Chinese restaurant is simply to bring the food to the diners. Some time after diners have seated themselves the server will arrive with a menu. The time will depend on the restaurant and how busy it is. It is not customary to give each person a menu; for most parties, usually only one will be brought out. This reflects the group orientation in Chinese dining: that is, all Chinese meals are shared, family style. Usually one person, or perhaps two, are designated to order the meal (**diǎn cài** 点菜), which is considered somewhat of an honor. Often a person of honor, perhaps the guest, is selected by the host to order the dishes. The honoree may not be totally comfortable with this and there may be a bit of friendly bantering about who should order. In the end, the host may order. After it is agreed upon what will be ordered, the server will take the order, collect the menu, and leave. Normally the server does not check on the table on a regular basis as in a Western restaurant, except in very high-end restaurants. If a diner has questions for the server or if they need anything, they must call out to the server or motion to them for him or her to come help out.

> It is considered an honor to be the one to place the table's order.

At larger higher-end restaurants, it is common to reserve a private dining room. These rooms typically have air conditioning, and sometimes a television and karaoke. These kings of restaurants may also have large, colorful menus with photographs of nearly all the dishes. Each private dining room will often have a server or even two assigned.

■ Making sense of Chinese menus
了解中国菜单 **liáojiě zhōngguó càidān**

Making sense of a Chinese menu is more difficult than one might expect. One of the reasons for this is that Chinese dishes often have special names using characters that are in no way descriptive of the dish. For example, the popular dish **máyǐ shàng shù** 蚂蚁上树 or "ants climbing a log/tree," does not give one much idea about what to expect. Could it really be a dish with ants? This particular dish is actually thin glass noodles stir-fried with a small amount of ground pork and chili peppers. The tiny bits of meat in this dish resemble ants and the strands of noodles represent trees or logs. The term **yúxiāng** 鱼香, "fish fragrance," is also used in a number of popular dishes, such as **yúxiāng ròusī** 鱼香肉丝. It would be natural to think that this dish contained fish, but it merely means that the dish (shredded pork in this case) is made with Chinese spices that are generally used when preparing fish. With no training or insight into Chinese menus, even an individual with relatively advanced Chinese language skills may find menus very difficult to navigate. However, if you understand a little about how Chinese menus are typically arranged and you have a basic knowledge of food vocabulary, you can successfully order a Chinese meal without too many surprises.

Generally, there are three clues to look for when ordering from a Chinese menu. These are all based on how the dish is prepared. The name of Chinese dish will often be an indication of 1) the central ingredient in the dish, 2) how the dish is prepared, and 3) how the ingredient is cut or sliced.

1) A typical Chinese menu is arranged by category, using the character **lèi** 类, based on the main ingredient. A typical menu may have the following categories:

tèsècài 特色菜	special dishes
lěngpán 冷盘 or **lěngcài** 冷菜	cold dishes
hǎixiān lèi 海鲜类	seafood
jī yā lèi 鸡鸭类	poultry
zhūròu lèi 猪肉类	pork
niúròu lèi 牛肉类	beef
ròulèi 肉类 or **hūn cài lèi** 荤菜类	meat dishes
sù cài 素菜	vegetable and vegetarian dishes
dòufu lèi 豆腐类	tofu dishes
fànmiàn lèi 饭面类	rice and noodle dishes
zhǔ shí lèi 主食类, or **miànshi** 面食	noodles (sometimes separated into soft noodles in broth and fried noodles)
tāng gēng lèi 汤羹类	soups and stews
yǐnliào 饮料	beverages

There can be some variation to these basic categories. For example, you might also see:

红烧类 **hóngshāo lèi**	red braised dishes (stewed in a dark soy sauce blend)

家常小炒 **jiācháng xiǎochǎo**   family style fried dishes

铁板类 **tiěbǎn lèi**   dishes cooked on an iron platter

羊肉类 **yángròu lèi**   lamb dishes (particularly at Muslim restaurants)

2) Knowing how a dish is prepared can also be helpful when reading a Chinese menu. Though many kinds of Chinese food are stir-fried (**chǎo** 炒), the Chinese use a variety of other ways to cook food. These include **qīngchǎo** 清炒 (usually refers to fresh stir-fried vegetables, often with garlic, but no sauce; as in **qīngchǎo bōcài** 清炒菠菜, fresh stir-fried spinach), **hóngshāo** 红烧 (red-braised: stewed in a dark soy sauce blend, as in **hóngshāo páigǔ** 红烧排骨 red-braised ribs), **kǎo** 烤 (roast, as in **běijīng kǎoyā** 北京烤鸭 Peking Roast Duck; roast dishes are almost always meat), **zhēng** 蒸 or **qīng zhēng** 清蒸 (steamed/fresh steamed, as in **qīng zhēng guìyú** 清蒸鳜鱼 fresh steamed Mandarin fish), **zhǔ** 煮 (boiled, as in **dàzhǔ gānsī** 大煮干丝 boiled shredded tofu; dishes that use this character are usually served in a large bowl with a broth, like soup), **yóu jiān** 油煎 (fried in oil). **Zhá** 炸 means to deep fry, so **zhá jī** 炸鸡 would be fried chicken.

3) Sometimes the characters used in a dish's name also describe the way in which the food was cut or prepared. For example, the character **dīng** 丁 indicates that the meat in the dish is diced or cubed, as in **gōngbào jīdīng** 宫爆鸡丁, known in the West as "Kung Pao chicken." In this dish the chicken and other ingredients are cubed in small bite-size pieces. Pork is also commonly used in this dish and is called **gōngbào ròudīng** 宫爆肉丁. The character **piàn** 片 indicates that the food is sliced thinly as in the dish **yángròu tǔdòu piàn** 羊肉土豆片 "lamb with sliced potatoes." **Sī** 丝 literally means "silk" or "a threadlike thing," and with regard to food it means "shredded" as in the dish **jiǔcài**

chǎo ròusī 韭菜炒肉丝 "chives with shredded pork." If you see the character **kuài** 块 in a dish, it indicates that the meat is cut into pieces, usually with the bone. Ribs are eaten all over China, usually pork or lamb (mostly at Muslim restaurants) and are indicated by the character **pái** 排 literally meaning a "row" or "line." Pork ribs are usually rendered as **páigǔ** 排骨 and lamb is often seen as **yángpái** 羊排. The characters **táng** 糖 and **cù** 醋 mean "sugar" and "vinegar" respectively. Together on a menu they indicate "sweet and sour." **Táng cù páigǔ** 糖醋排骨 would be "sweet and sour pork ribs" and **táng cù lǐji** 糖醋里脊 is what we know as "sweet and sour pork," the **lǐji** 里脊 meaning "tenderloin."

Even though the strategies described above will be very useful, there will still be many names on a menu that will not provide any clues as to what the dish actually is. For example, **quánjiāfú** 全家福, "Happy Family," certainly is open to interpretation. The name is probably a metaphor, meaning many vegetables together. Another is **sānxiān guōbā** 三鲜锅巴, "three fresh rice crust," basically meaning three ingredients cooked with rice crust. If you are curious and want to try something that you cannot make sense of, and you speak some Chinese, simply ask the server what is in the dish and how it is prepared. Most servers will not mind describing a particular dish to you. As you try new things you will learn that when you see **sānxiān** 三鲜 on a menu it usually refers to fresh vegetables and sometimes a small amount of meat, and that **guōbā** 锅巴 is a delicious crispy rice that is usually served with a broth and vegetables poured over it making it soft and chewy.

It is also a good idea to ask about the house specials (**tèsècài** 特色菜 or **náshǒucài** 拿手菜). Often a particular restaurant will have certain dishes they're known for and that are especially good. And just as in the United States you'd be

• BEHIND THE SCENES •

Eating Like a Native:
Chinese Dining 中国进餐习惯 zhōnggúo jìncān xíguàn

Eating in a Chinese restaurant is a group experience. Unlike in American restaurants, diners order several different dishes and everyone shares them. This is the reason for the lazy Susan—easy access for all to the dishes. Everyone eats directly off the platters in the center of the table.

Sometimes a serving spoon is supplied with each dish. If so, it is appropriate to dish food directly into your rice bowl. Usually one dish at a time is eaten in this way, and usually only a small quantity. Often one will use one's chopsticks to take food from the platter, to his or her rice bowl, whereupon it is consumed bite by bite.

Chinese dishes are delivered to the table as they are prepared. It is not uncommon for some dishes to be completely consumed before others are even brought out. It is common in many parts of China, particularly in the South, to eat plain steamed white rice with a meal. Rice is usually not brought automatically; one must order it when ordering the other dishes. Usually one's rice bowl will be refilled without any extra charge. Each diner will have their own individual rice bowl.

Plates are typically not supplied unless one is at a Chinese fast food establishment, where food is often served heaped on a large plate and eaten by one person with a spoon or sometimes with a spoon in conjunction with chopsticks. This is especially true in Taiwan and Hong Kong.

It is common for the host of a group to serve guests from the dishes in the center of the table. For example, if you were visiting a friend in China, or a friend took you out to eat at a restaurant, the friend might select especially good pieces of meat or vegetables and put them in your bowl with their chopsticks (or they may use a serving spoon, especially on more formal occasions). In situations like this it is polite to thank the person who has done this for you and act grateful.

wiser to order the chicken-fried steak, not the shrimp Creole, at a truck stop in Kansas, the situation is similar in China. If you are at a restaurant that specializes in Cantonese food, do not expect the Mapo Tofu (**mápó dòufu** 麻婆豆腐), which is a Sichuan specialty, to be all that great. When in doubt, look around and see what other people are ordering.

If you do not speak or read Chinese, another strategy for ordering is simply to look around at what other people are eating. If something looks good, indicate to your server that you would like a dish by pointing at it. You may also get a Chinese friend or colleague to write down some good dishes in Chinese that you can show to your server.

■ **Chinese eating etiquette**
中国人吃饭时的礼仪 **zhōngguórén chīfàn shí de lǐyí**
When eating a Chinese meal, whether in a restaurant or at someone's home, there are several rules of etiquette that should be followed.

- The lazy Susan (**zhuànpán** 转盘) in the middle of the table is designed for a group eating experience. Diners should not reach across the table to serve themselves food. It is polite to eat those dishes that are close to oneself. When the food is rotated, *then* one may feel free to select new dishes now within easy reach. Be careful that you don't turn the lazy Susan when someone else is taking food from the dishes. You need to give others time to put food in their bowls. This can take patience, especially when you see your favorite dish quickly disappearing at the other side of the table.

- If you are eating meat that is on the bone, or shellfish, it is appropriate to place the bones, shells, or other non-edible items in a neat pile on the table, just beyond or to the side of your rice bowl. In higher-end restaurants, small plates will be provided for this purpose; when the plate becomes full, the server will replace it with a new plate. It is not appropriate to put bones in your rice bowl as you eat. When at home the Chinese will often spread newspaper on the table before a meal, or provide paper plates or napkins for this purpose. Cleaning up involves simply rolling up the newspaper or napkins (with the bones, shells, and other scraps) and throwing it all away. In rural areas I have even seen bones, shells, and such things spit directly onto the floor.

- Fish is usually served whole, with the head, tail, and fins intact. When one side of the fish has been consumed, turn the complete fish over with your chopsticks to gain access to the other side. (Diners should not dig through the bones to get to the meat on the other side of the fish.)

- It is important to make sure your chopsticks are free of grains of rice or other bits of food before you take food from the dishes in the center of the table, to be considerate regarding hygiene.

- It is considered impolite to place chopsticks in one's rice perpendicular to the table. That action is associated with Buddhist funeral rites.

- It is acceptable to burp, slurp, or make other sounds of satisfaction with one's mouth while at the Chinese dining table. However, in more formal dining, this is subdued.

- The individual rice bowl should be held in your hand and brought close to your mouth when eating rice. Often, the bowl is brought to the lips and the rice is "shoveled" in. This prevents grains of rice from falling on the table and making a mess. Avoid the temptation to lift the rice from the bowl on the table up to your mouth—you will most likely make a mess doing that. In more formal dining occasions, the rice bowl is still held in your hand, but the rice is brought to your mouth with your chopsticks, until the last bit in your bowl, when it's acceptable to bring your bowl to your mouth.

- It's not polite to take the last thing on a plate. It's best to first offer the remaining food to someone else, even picking up the plate or the food item with your chopsticks and physically offering it to another diner. They will almost always refuse and suggest for a different diner to eat it. If someone offers you the last of a dish, politely decline several times, perhaps suggesting someone else to eat it. If the offers are persistent after your several refusals, politely accept.

- When serving soup with a large serving spoon it is polite to dip the spoon into the pot from the back—that is, dip the spoon into the soup from the back edge of the spoon to the front. When drinking soup with one's own individual spoon, it is considered polite to sip from the side of the spoon, and not put the whole spoon in one's mouth.

- Oftentimes no drinks (other than hot tea) are offered at a Chinese meal. The Chinese generally feel that drinking at a meal is not good for digestion. They will drink tea before a meal, and afterward too. It's not a common practice to drink cold beverages during a meal, even in the heat of the summer. Water is typically not served at Chinese restaurants, unless one does not drink tea and specifically requests "boiled water" (**kāishuǐ** 开水). At higher-end restaurants or banquets, it is common to have Sprite and Coke or alchoholic drinks offered, especially if foreigners are present.

- It is polite to accept whatever a Chinese host or friend offers. It does not mean that one has to eat a lot of it, but declining an offer of food or drink may hurt the feelings of the host. It's better to accept something, rather than nothing. For example, if you were offered tea, but did not drink tea for some reason (perhaps religious), it is best to simply indicate that you do not drink tea, but that you would like some "boiled water" (**kāishuǐ** 开水) or other readily available beverage.

- It is appropriate for diners to always be very appreciative and offer thanks to those who have hosted the dinner. Mention that they shouldn't have gone to so much trouble (**máfan nǐ** 麻烦你 or **gěi nǐmen tiān máfan le** 给你们添麻烦 了).

- When a meal is complete, toothpicks are often available. It is typical to clean one's teeth at the table before leaving the restaurant. Be careful to cover your mouth. It is considered rude to clean teeth without obstructing the view with a hand.

- A meal will usually conclude with fresh fruit, such as watermelon or oranges. (It is not common for dessert to be served in Chinese restaurants or even after a meal at a Chinese home.) The serving of fresh fruit is your cue that the meal is over.

■ Concluding the meal and paying the check
吃饭结束及买单 **chīfàn jiéshù jí mǎidān**

At the conclusion of a meal, you must ask the server to bring a bill. Don't assume that the bill will automatically be brought to the table after a meal—it most likely will not be. To the Chinese, eating is a very social affair sometimes lasting for hours. Therefore, when the party is ready to leave, they will be expected to request the bill.

Requesting the bill can be done by saying to the server, **mǎidān** 买单, **jiézhàng** 结帐, or **suàn zhàng** 算帐. Paying the bill at a Chinese restaurant is a memorable experience. Because of the Chinese group orientation, it is considered an honor to be able to pay the bill for a group of friends. At the conclusion of a meal, it is very common for an argument to erupt over who will pay the bill. Typically, several in the party will offer and banter with each other for this privilege. Paying the bill brings some prestige and honor to a person. Sometimes the arguing can get fairly vigorous, with money pushed into another's hands, then thrown back and so forth. In the end one person will pay the bill. It's not customary, even among a group of friends, for everyone to pitch in and split the bill into equal payments.

It's very common for an argument to erupt over who will pay the bill.

There is an informal order that says if one person pays the bill this time, they will not be expected to the next time. Everyone usually takes even turns paying the bill. Nevertheless, it is still important to offer to pay the bill after a meal, and banter with the others who will also be offering to pay it as well. After the bill has been paid, sincere thanks is offered to the person who eventually paid the bill. When you are visiting a friend in China, they will almost certainly pay for the meals, even if it is a financial burden to them. The Chinese view this as their responsibility to take care of their guest while they are visiting. Among younger people it is becoming more common for each person to pay for their own food (i.e., "going Dutch"). In Chinese this is called AA制 and in Chinese is pronounced **ai ai zhi**.

Tipping is not required nor expected at Chinese restaurants. Insistence on leaving a tip will usually be met with uncomfortableness from the Chinese. (In other service industries such as hotels, service charges are usually automatically added to the price.)

THE CHINESE BANQUET
中国式宴会 zhōngguóshì yànhùi

Banquets can be defined as any hosted dinner. The banquet is an important part of Chinese hospitality. It is a way to show respect, gratitude, or friendship to a guest. Incidentally, all foreigners in China are usually regarded as guests, even if you are a long-term resident. For example, if you are visiting China in a business capacity, your host organization will invite you to a banquet; students going to China for study will often be hosted by the unit in the University to a banquet meal; your visit to friends in China will very often result in eating out at a fancy restaurant.

Banquet dinners often take place in private dining rooms in higher-end, large restaurants, or many companies or universities and other organizations have on-site restaurants for this purpose. However, if friends are taking you out to eat, it may be in a regular restaurant.

In the Chinese business world, drinking alcohol can be an important part of building relationships, and toasting (**gānbēi** 干杯) is an integral part of this ritual. See Chapter 9 for more detailed information about banquets.

EATING CHINESE HOTPOT
吃火锅 chī huǒguō

Eating Chinese hotpot (**huǒguō** 火锅) is a wonderful and delicious experience. It is the kind of meal, like most Chinese meals, that needs to be enjoyed as a group. Hotpot meals vary depending on where you are in China. It is generally acknowledged that Chinese hotpot has its origins in Mongolia. Legend has it

Legend has it that Mongol warriors originated hotpot.

that Mongol warriors, ever on the move on horseback, would stop out on the steppes to make camp. They would build a fire, fill a metal helmet or shield with water and place it over a small fire. Because it is so cold on the northern steppes meat would freeze quickly after slaughter. The meat would then be carved off the frozen carcass in paper thin shavings. These thin shavings would then be tossed into the hot "pot" on the fire and would cook very quickly—these warriors did not have a lot of time to dilly-dally around camp. Modern hotpot dinners resemble these early origins. Some Chinese will contest the Mongolian origins of hotpot; the Sichuanese maintain that hotpot originated in Chongqing.

The actual hot pot varies by region. In the north, including Beijing, the hot pot has a central conical chimney in the center of a circular pot, shaped like a doughnut. Hot coals are placed in this chimney which heats the water in the circular ring. Herbs like ginger, garlic, and scallions as well as dried shrimp are thrown into the boiling water to season it. Several plates of thinly sliced meat, fish, and vegetables like cabbage and mushroom are ordered and each diner places food into the hotpot to cook. Each diner also receives a bowl of a mixture of sesame paste and other spices that is used to dip the meat and vegetables. As all the food is brought raw, the diners themselves do all the cooking in the hotpot that is placed in the center of the table.

In other parts of China the hotpot looks more like a traditional wok. In some hotpot restaurants the woks are built into the tables and can be divided into two halves. In one half will be a mellow broth and in the other side a very spicy broth. Raw meats and vegetables are ordered and cooked by the diners as described above. Sichuanese hotpot is also very popular, as is Chongqing style hotpot: rather than being in a tame broth, meat and vegetables are cooked in a very spicy oil. At some newer hotpot restaurants, diners can make their own dipping sauces from a buffet-like bar with all kinds of dips and condiments.

GOING OUT FOR DIMSUM
去吃广式早茶 qù chī guǎngshì zǎochá

In the south of China, particularly with the Cantonese in Guangdong Province, going to a tea house for **diǎnxīn** 点心, dimsum, is widely popular, even a way of life. This kind of meal differs considerably from the typical Chinese meal. It is usually eaten at breakfast or brunch and Chinese will often spend a great deal of time over the meal socializing. This is not the kind of meal to rush over. A **chálóu** 茶楼, tea house, in Guangdong and Hong Kong can be a very large restaurant that serves thousands of diners every day. They are usually  very loud and lively places. These tea houses serve a vast array of **diǎnxīn** 点心 which can be described as small bite-sized appetizer-type food, though they are not eaten as appetizers. The food is freshly prepared and delicious. Some typical dimsum dishes include **xiājiǎo** 虾饺, shrimp filled ravioli-like dumplings, **chāshāobāo** 叉烧包, steamed buns filled with barbecued pork, **shāomài** 烧卖, open-ended dumplings with minced meat, **niúròu qiú** 牛肉球 or **niúwán** 牛丸, beef meat balls, **dòushābāo** 豆沙包, sweet bean paste buns, **chūnjuǎn** 春卷, spring rolls, **nuòmǐjī** 糯米鸡, chicken and sticky rice wrapped in lotus leaves.

Tea houses do not have a menu, or if they do they're not often used. What you will encounter instead is servers walking

Chinese Tea 中国茶 **zhōngguó chá**

Tea is also an important part of a dimsum meal. There is a great variety of teas available, though all come from the same plant. The differences are in how the tea leaves are processed. Teas can be generally classified by the amount of fermentation used in the processing. Green teas, like **lóngjǐngchá** 龙井茶 *dragon well tea and* **xiāng piàn** 香片 *or* **mòlìhuāchá** 茉莉花茶*, jasmine tea, are not fermented but are allowed to oxidize. As a result they have a fresh aroma and flavor and are green or light green in appearance. Green teas are the most commonly drunk in China. Semi-fermented teas, such as* **wūlóngchá** 乌龙茶 *oolong tea and* **tiěguānyīnchá** 铁观音茶 *Steel Guanyin tea, are a bit stronger and are yellow to brown in appearance. Fully fermented teas are referred to in the West as "black" teas, though in Chinese they are referred to as* **hóngchá** 红茶, *red tea. These have a dark red appearance, are sweeter and may have a roasted taste. Post fermented teas, like* **pǔerchá** 普洱茶 *Pu'er tea, is allowed to ferment, then is fermented again at a later time. This tea is popular in south and southwest China and has a strong, full, earthy taste. Herbal teas, though traditionally not consumed in China, are becoming more widely available there. The more popular flower teas include* **júhuāchá** 菊花茶 *chrysanthemum tea,* **shuǐxiānchá** 水仙茶 *daffodil tea, and* **lìzhīchá** 荔枝茶 *lychee tea. Often these flower teas are blended with tea leaves, usually green. If you want a purely herbal tea, you can ask if the tea has tea leaves in it, 茶叶* **cháyè***. Herbal teas may be called 草药茶* **cǎoyàochá***. Larger tea houses and regular restaurants will have a wide variety of teas available, but small restaurants will often only have one typical green tea.*

around the restaurant pushing carts, or carrying large trays, calling out what they have in Cantonese. As they come by your table you are welcome to inspect what they have and select what you want. At  the end of the meal, the server will tabulate the bill based on the plates on your table; sometimes there are larger and smaller plates indicating cheaper and more expensive dishes. Or at some tea houses a menu of sorts will be provided listing the various dimsum offered, and diners will mark how many of each dish they want on the form and return it to a server. Or, when a cart comes by and you select a dish, the server will stamp on the dimsum list which dish you had. At the end of the meal the bill is easily tabulated from this list.

EATING ON THE STREET
路边小吃 **lùbiān xiǎochī**

The term **xiǎo chī** 小吃 refers to either snacks or informal dining, often from street vendors or in small, casual restaurants. Street food is readily available in cities all over China. Vendors peddling a vast array of food, from snacks to entire meals, can be found near college campuses, shopping districts, bus terminals and train stations, and just about anywhere else people congregate. In some big cities, there are designated areas where street vendors set up. Foreigners should use some caution when eating on the street as this type of food has the potential of not being as sanitary as at larger restaurants. You may want to ease into street food when you first arrive in China to allow your stomach some time to adapt to the new food and bacteria.

Ordering food from a street vendor can be a little tricky. This is because there often is no menu because everyone knows what the vendor is selling. Crowds of people around a particular vendor is also common, thus getting to the front of the line only to stammer questions about what's being sold does not go over too well. If you are unfamiliar with what is being sold or how to order, simply eavesdrop for a few minutes. Observe what the Chinese are saying, how they are ordering and so on. At times when it's not crowded, vendors are usually happy to chat with you about what they are selling. When ordering have your money ready and use small bills as most vendors cannot or are unwilling to make large amounts of change.

Early in the morning there will be a number of breakfast vendors which will be replaced by another set of vendors for the lunch and dinner hours. The kinds of food available on the street will vary depending on where in China you are, but some foods are fairly common all over China. Common food sold on the streets may include **yóutiáo** 油条, a fried bread; **cōngyóubǐng** 葱油饼, a kind of scallion bread fried in a pan; **bāozi** 包子, steamed buns of all kinds, such as **xiǎolóngbāo** 小笼包, **càibāo** 菜包, **ròubāo** 肉包, **guōtiē** 锅贴, pot stickers, and so on. Roasted sweet potatoes are common in the north during autumn, as is fresh fruit in season all over China.

Roasted meat on skewers **kǎoròuchuàn** 烤肉串, grilled meats, and seafood with dipping sauces are readily available as well. Soups with dumplings are also quite common.

Some kinds of food items, such as **jiǎozi** 饺子 (dumplings), are sold by weight, in measures of Chinese **liǎng** (两). A **liǎng** is equivalent to 50 grams or 1.76 ounces. **Jiǎozi** is the generic term for "dumpling" in Chinese; they are the typical and traditional Chinese fast food. **Shuǐjiǎo** 水饺 are **jiǎozi** that are boiled and served in a bowl of broth or on their own. **Guōtiē**, 锅贴 "potstickers," are **jiǎozi** that are fried, then steamed, and have a delicious brown crust on the bottom. Many small restaurants specialize in and serve only **jiǎozi**, with a number of different fillings. (Some chain restaurants such as the popular **dàniáng shuǐjiǎo** 大娘水饺 are found all over China in the big cities.)

SHOPPING AND COOKING
买菜做饭 **mǎi cài zuò fàn**

If you'll be living in China for longer than a couple of months, and you have access to a kitchen, it may be worth your while to learn to cook some basic Chinese dishes. Most furnished apartments have some basic cooking implements such as a wok, spatula, a knife or two, maybe some rice bowls and other dishes. Even if your apartment does not have these things they are relatively inexpensive to purchase.

■ Shopping for cooking supplies 买厨具 **mǎi chújù**

If you decide to do some cooking at home, there are a number of places you can shop for supplies and food. For supplies you can shop at department stores (expensive) or small shops (inexpensive). Many department stores have housewares departments where you can buy just about anything you might need in the kitchen. Increasingly common in China are large discount-type department stores similar to Walmart in the United States. (In fact, Walmart stores themselves are cropping up in China.) These kinds of large stores sell kitchen goods as well as a wide variety of other goods, including groceries. Throughout China there are also markets, usually indoor, that are a large collection of individual stalls or shops within the larger building. They are often located near larger housing complexes and cater to the average Chinese citizen. These kinds of "malls" have an astonishing array of goods for very reasonable prices, and there are dozens of stalls that deal exclusively with kitchen and household goods and are very inexpensive compared to department stores and even discount stores. Outdoor night markets also may sell household goods, but the selection will not be as extensive.

■ **Shopping for food** 买菜 **mǎi cài**

You have a couple of options when it comes to buying foodstuffs and produce in China. The first? The increasingly popular grocery store. These can be small, resembling the size of a convenience store, or very large like a Western style grocery store. Some of the large discount department stores mentioned above have large quantities of food items, including canned and bottled goods, produce, meat, refrigerated foods, and frozen foods.

The other option is to shop at outdoor markets or meat and produce markets, which offer an excellent variety of meat and produce with good prices. Keep in mind that when shopping at outdoor markets, prices are usually not marked and may be negotiable. Shopping here will give you more of an authentic experience, though it may not be as convenient as shopping at a grocery store. Outdoor markets are lively and crowded places, and can be found on the street in specific locations as well as in partially indoor areas. Street

• BEHIND THE SCENES •

Where Are All the Buffets? 哪里有自助餐 nǎlǐ yǒu zìzhùcān?

Chinese buffets have become very popular in the United States. Many travelers to China wonder where all the buffets are. Actually most large, higher-end restaurants do have buffets, catering to foreign expectations. Often big hotels will include a buffet breakfast for their guests. But outside large hotels you will not find buffets serving Chinese food. Most Chinese food is prepared fresh to order. The exception to this is in food courts or outdoor night markets where large quantities of food are prepared and served as customers arrive and order.

The reason the Chinese are not too fond of buffets is that the very essence of Chinese food is that it is cooked to order and served right out of the wok. The Chinese insist on eating fresh food. They will often buy meat and produce every day rather than storing things in a refrigerator. When eating at a restaurant the dishes arrive as they are prepared, and not all at the same time like in U.S. restaurants. To cook food, then let it sit around, is a strange concept to the Chinese. Their insistence on freshly prepared and served food is not compatible with buffets. Taiwan is an exception to this where you can find buffets. They are called **zìzhùcān** 自助餐.

markets are usually only open from early to late morning; where these markets are located in a building, they'll usually be open only during the day. Ask your neighbors or associates where to find street markets.

■ Basic cooking equipment
基本的烹饪设备 jīběn de pēngrèn shèbèi; 炊具 chuījù

If you decide to do some Chinese cooking in your home or apartment there are some basic things that you will need to invest in. The first thing you will need is an electric teapot (**diàn shuǐhú** 电水壶) as it is not advised that you drink tap water in China. It is essential to boil all water that is consumed. Electric teapots are inexpensive and efficient. Next you will need a wok (**guō** 锅, **chǎoguō** 炒锅), a cleaver or other kitchen knife (**dāo** 刀), a cutting board (**ànbǎn** 案板, **zhēnbǎn** 砧板, or **qiēcàibǎn** 切菜板), a spatula for cooking with the wok (**guōchǎn** 锅铲 or **chǎnzi** 铲子), a rice cooker (**diànfànbǎo** 电饭煲 or **diànfànguō** 电饭锅), some rice bowls (**wǎn** 碗), a plate or two to serve the food on (**pánzi** 盘子), some chopsticks (**kuàizi** 筷子), and maybe a couple of spoons (**sháozi** 勺子 or **sháor** 勺儿) for serving. With these basic things you can cook a good variety of food.

■ **Basic pantry supplies**
　基本的食品储备 **jīběn de shípǐn chǔbèi**
Likewise, with a few basic food items on hand, you can cook a wide range of dishes. You will first need rice (**dàmǐ** 大米). It is inexpensive and available just about everywhere. Keep in mind, however, that rice is more commonly eaten in the south than in the north, though northerners do eat rice as well. You can buy rice in bulk (and get as little as you want), in grocery stores or special rice shops, or you can buy bags that range from a few kilos to fifty or more kilos. It's best to begin with a small bag until you find a brand and variety that you like. There is a wide variety, and where you are will dictate what kinds of rice are available. Many people will not be able to taste much difference, but those with a discriminating palate will be happy to find rice ranging from short to medium to long grain and fragrant jasmine rice (**xiāngmǐ** 香米). Generally speaking, cheaper rice will be a bit coarser and less soft. That is not to say that inexpensive rice is not good, and it's what you will be accustomed to eating at small, casual restaurants. The one thing you will probably not be able to find in China is brown rice. The Chinese simply do not eat brown rice.

　You will also need cooking oil, like peanut oil (**huāshēngyóu** 花生油). Other staples are soy sauce (**jiàngyóu** 酱油), vinegar (**cù** 醋), cooking wine (**liàojiǔ** 料酒), garlic (**dàsuàn** 大蒜), ginger (**jiāng** 姜), salt (**yán** 盐) and if you like spicy food you

will want a bottle of hot pepper paste (**làjiāojiàng** 辣椒酱).
You can add other ingredients as you get more adventurous
with your cooking.

■ ■ ■

USEFUL PHRASES

eat at a restaurant **xià guǎnzi** 下馆子
  or **xià fànguǎn (er)** 下饭馆(儿)

eat Chinese hotpot 吃火锅 **chī
  huǒguō**

eat on the street **lùbiān xiǎochī** 路
  边小吃

go out for dimsum **qù chī guǎngshì
  zǎo chá** 去吃广式早茶

menu **càidān** 菜单

paying the check **mǎidān** 买单;
  jiézhàng 结帐

restaurant **fànguǎn (er)** 饭馆(儿)

restaurant; dining room; dining hall
  cāntīng 餐厅

shop for cooking supplies **mǎi chújù**
  买厨具

shop for food **mǎicài** 买菜

snacks; small restaurant **xiǎo chī** 小
  吃

teahouse; a place that has drinks,
  pastries and dimsum dishes similar
  to a coffee shop or coffee bar in
  the West **chálóu** 茶楼

to box; take-out box **dǎ bāo** 打包

toasting **gānbēi** 干杯

waiter; server **fúwùyuán** 服务员

What can I do for you?/What do
  you want to order? **yào diǎn (er)
  shén me** 要点儿什么?

What do you want to order? **nǐ yào
  diǎn shénme?** 你要点什么?

Are you ready to order? **xiànzài jiù
  diǎn ma?** 现在就点吗?

(We want to) order (now) **diǎn cài**
  点菜

(Let us) have a look the menu **kàn
  yí xià càidān** 看一下菜单

What drinks (do you have)? **yǒu
  shénme yǐnliào?** 有什么饮料?

What main food (do you have)?
  yǒu shénme zhǔshí? 有什么主
  食?

What do you not want to eat or
  what can you not eat? **nín chīfàn
  yǒu shénme jì huì de?** 您吃饭有什
  么忌讳的?

(I) want this one **yào ge zhèi ge ba**
  要个这个吧。

We want some water **gěi wǒmēn lǎi
  diǎn (er) shuǐ ba** 给我们来点儿水
  吧。

(Please) change the plate **huàn yí xià
  pánzi** 换一下盘子

USEFUL WORDS

ants climbing a log/tree (a popular
  dish) **máyǐ shàng shù** 蚂蚁上树

banquet **yànhùi** 宴会

beef dishes **niúròu lèi** 牛肉类

beverages **yǐnliào** 饮料

boiled shredded tofu **dà zhǔ gānsī**
  大煮干丝

boiled water **kāishuǐ** 开水

braised in soy sauce dishes
  hóngshāo lèi 红烧类

buffet **zìzhùcān** 自助餐

chives with shredded pork **jiǔcài
  chǎo ròusī** 韭菜炒肉丝

cold dish, hors d'oeuvres **lěngpán**
  冷盘; **liángcài** 凉菜

crispy rice **guōbā** 锅巴

dumplings **jiǎozi** 饺子; **shuǐjiǎo** 水饺

fish dishes **yú lèi** 鱼类

fish-flavored **yú xiāng** 鱼香

fish-flavored pork (a popular dish) **yúxiāng ròusī** 鱼香肉丝

fresh stir-fried vegetables **qīngchǎo** 清炒

fresh stir-fried spinach **qīngchǎo bōcài** 清炒菠菜

fresh steamed Mandarin fish **qīngzhēng guìyú** 清蒸鳜鱼

fresh steamed **qīngzhēng** 清蒸

fresh vegetables and sometimes a small amount of meat **sānxiān** 三鲜

fried chicken **zhá jī** 炸鸡

fried dough sticks 油条 **yóutiáo**; 果子 **guǒzi** in Tianjin

fried in oil **yóu jiān** 油煎

green onion pancake 葱油饼 **cōngyóubǐng**

"Happy Family" (a popular dish) **quánjiāfú** 全家福

homemade fried dishes **jiā cháng xiǎo chǎo** 家常小炒

hotpot **huǒguō** 火锅

house specialty **tèsècài** 特色菜/ **náshǒucài** 拿手菜

Kung Pao Chicken **gōngbǎo jīdīng** 宫保鸡丁 or **gōngbào jīdīng** 宫爆鸡丁

lamb dishes **yángròu lèi** 羊肉类

lamb with sliced potatoes **yángròu tǔdòu piàn** 羊肉土豆片

lamb ribs **yángpái** 羊排

Mapo Tofu (a popular dish) **mápó dòufu** 麻婆豆腐

meat kebab **kǎoròuchuàn** 烤肉串

meat dishes **ròulèi** 肉类; **hūn cài lèi** 荤菜类

Peking roast duck **běijīng kǎoyā** 北京烤鸭

potstickers; fried dumpling **guōtiē** 锅贴

pork dishes **zhūròu lèi** 猪肉类

pork ribs **páigǔ** 排骨

poultry dishes **jī yā lèi** 鸡鸭类

principal food such as noodle **miàn-shi** 面食

red-braised; stewed in a dark soy sauce blend **hóngshāo** 红烧

red-braised ribs **hóngshāo páigǔ** 红烧排骨

rice and noodles dishes **fànmiàn lèi** 饭面类

rice crust with three ingredients **sānxiān guōbā** 三鲜锅巴

seafood dishes **hǎixiān lèi** 海鲜类

sizzling or served on an iron plate **tiěbǎn lèi** 铁板类

soup, stew **tāng gēng lèi** 汤羹类

staples or main food (such as noodle, rice, or pancake) **zhǔ shí lèi** 主食类

steamed stuffed bun **bāozi** 包子

steamed stuffed meat bun **xiǎolóngbāo** 小笼包

steamed vegetable bun **càibāo** 菜包

steamed meat bun **ròubāo** 肉包

sweet and sour pork **tángcù lǐji** 糖醋里脊

sweet and sour pork ribs **tángcù páigǔ** 糖醋排骨

tofu dishes **dòufu lèi** 豆腐类

tenderloin **lǐji** 里脊

vegetable dishes **sù cài** 素菜

Cooking methods

to boil **zhǔ** 煮

to cook **zuò fàn** 做饭

to deep fry **zhá** 炸

to roast **kǎo** 烤

to steam/steamed **zhēng** 蒸

to stir-fry **chǎo** 炒

Kitchen vocabulary

bowl **wǎn** 碗

chopsticks **kuàizi** 筷子

cooking supplies; cooking equipment **chújù** 厨具

cutting board **ànbǎn** 案板 or **zhēnbǎn** 砧板 or **qiēcàibǎn** 切菜板

electric teapot **diàn shuǐhú** 电水壶

knife **dāo** 刀

lazy Susan **zhuànpán** 转盘

plate **pánzi** 盘子

pot **guō** 锅

rice cooker **diànfànbǎo** 电饭煲 or **diànfànguō** 电饭锅

spatula **guōchǎn** 锅铲 or **chǎnzi** 铲子

spoon **sháozi** 勺子 or **sháor** 勺儿

wok **chǎoguō** 炒锅

4

Communicating

通讯 tōngxùn

Communicating in China has changed dramatically in the past two decades. The digital age has arrived in China in a big way. Cell phone use in China is growing faster than any other market. Internet use likewise is on the rise and it has been estimated that the Chinese language will be the most common language on the Internet in the near future. But these are all rather recent developments.

As recent as the mid 1980s personal telephones were not a common possession in people's homes. Public telephones were scattered all over the streets in China's larger metropolitan areas. It was not uncommon to find long lines of people waiting to use these phones. You will still see these public phones around, usually at newspaper stands, but they are used far less frequently than in the recent past.

In this chapter I discuss the main modes of communication for urban Chinese: telephone (including cell phones), computer (including

Internet and email), and the old-fashioned post office. We'll look not only at how to use these modes of communication, but how to go about buying and using a cell phone, how to get Internet service, and what to expect at a Chinese post office.

TELEPHONES
电话 diànhuà

There are a variety of ways to communicate with a telephone in China: private telephones in an apartment or hotel, public telephones, and cell phones. In China's cities, the majority of urban dwellers have telephones in their apartments. Many in rural areas also have telephones in their apartments. And almost everywhere in China people use cell phones **shǒujī** 手机, even in remote areas where you would not think cell service was possible.

Local calls, **shìnèi diànhuà** 市内电话, do not require a city or region code. However, if calling another city in China, you must first dial the city code (**qūhào** 区号), followed by the number.

With most telephones, landlines as well as cell phones, you cannot make international calls without a special service or with a phone card. Making international calls from a hotel can be very expensive or pretty reasonable depending on the hotel and where it is located, so check with your hotel. Most larger hotels have international direct dialing available, sometimes at very reasonable rates. If you are in China for a short time, and you are just making an occasional international call, it may be worth the convenience to use the phone in a hotel room. However, if you are making regular calls, it is best to use a more cost-effective way.

There are three large national companies that offer tele-

phone services. China Telecom **zhōngguó diànxìn jítuán gōngsī** 中国电信集团公司 (**zhōngguó diànxìn** 中国电信／**diànxìn** 电信) and China Unicom **zhōngguó liántōng gōngsī** 中国联通公司 (**liántōng** 联通) offer landline service, cell phone service, and Internet services. China Mobil **zhōngguó yídòng tōngxìn jítuán gōngsī** 中国移动通信集团公司 (**zhōngguó yídòng** 中国移动／**yídòng** 移动) only offers cell phone service. It is debatable as to which company is the best for which services, and opinions vary.

■ **Landline phones** 座机 **zuòjī**

Landline telephones are called **zuòjī** 座机 or the more formal term **gùdìng diànhuà** 固定电话. To get long distance service on a landline or cellular telephone, either for in-country or international, you will need to go the phone company and open an account. The desk you need at the phone company is either **kāitōng guónèi chángtú yèwù** 开通国内长途业务 or **kāitōng guójì chángtú yèwù** 开通国际长途业务. (**Kāitōng** 开

通 is to open or set up). At these desks you can set up long distance service. To set up this service you will need your passport or identification card, and some cash for a deposit. The deposit may be as much as 2500 yuan. Phone bills are paid monthly and can be paid at the telephone company office, post offices, some banks, and sometimes online. Check with your telephone company to find out where you can pay your monthly bill.

■ **Cell phones** 手机 **shǒujī**

China is the fastest growing region in the world for cell phone use. It seems that just about everyone on the streets of large Chinese cities, large and small, has a cell phone glued to his or her ear. Even small children sometimes have cell phones. Recently a friend and I were trekking in a remote valley in Yunnan Province near the border of Tibet, and met some Tibetan teenagers along a dirt road. We were surprised to see them carrying and using their cell phones.

Cell phone service in China is available through all three of the large national companies, China Unicom **zhōngguó liántōng** 中国联通, China Mobil **zhōngguó yídòng** 中国移动, and China Telecom **zhōngguó diànxìn** 中国电信. There are two kinds of cell phones that are available in China.

The first type of cell phone works only in China, on a different frequency than is used by cell phones in North America. The second type of cell phone has dual frequencies that will work in China or North America. In China GSM network phones use 900MHz and 1800MHz, and CDMA phones use 800MHz. In the U.S. GSM phones use 1900MHz. In China some cell phones can support 1900MHz. Both of these kinds of cell phones can make local as well as long distance calls. For people who want the flexibility of being able to use the phone anywhere in China, these kinds of phones are the best choice. However, using a cell phone from the U.S. in China without getting a new SIM card, will undoubtedly incur huge roaming charges. It is best to get your U.S.-based phone switched over to a Chinese cell phone service. However, if you are only using your smartphone to check email, an international data plan can be reasonable way to go for a short period of time.

■ Buying a cell phone 买手机 **mǎi shǒujī**

Cell phones vary considerably in terms of features and price, and they can be purchased at a variety of places. Many large department stores will have an electronics department with extensive cell phone offerings. Cell phones are usually arranged by brand, with different counters offering different brands of cell phones. It can be intimidating to walk into one of these stores because the selection can be truly huge, and it's often very crowded and somewhat chaotic. There are also specialty electronic stores in China that have extensive selections of cell phones. The three major cell phone companies also have stand-alone stores.

Buying a cell phone in China is not too different than buying one elsewhere. After you've decided what kind of phone you want, then decide on what features you need. Many brands sold in the West, such as Sony-Ericsson, Motorola, Nokia, Samsung, and Apple's iPhone, are also available, but Chinese brands are usually less expensive than foreign brands. You may want to ask some friends or colleagues for a recommendation if you want to try a Chinese brand, since some are quite good and others are not. Popular Chinese brands include Lenovo (**liánxiǎng** 联想), Huawei (**huáwéi** 华为), and Zhongxing (**zhōngxīng** 中兴). Another type of product that is widely sold and used in China is called **shānzhài** 山寨. A **shānzhài** 山寨 product is not a brand, but is a copy of a name brand product. In other words, you might have a Chinese made Nokia cell phone that is not a genuine Nokia

• BEHIND THE SCENES •

Making Sense of Cell Phone Plans

Once a phone has been selected, you need to select a calling plan. Of the three large telephone companies in China, China Mobil **zhōngguó yídòng gōngsī** 中国移动公司 may have the most customers, but it depends on the region of China. In some regions different companies have more customers, as each of the companies may have coverage for different parts of the country.

Cell phone plans initially require that you purchase a startup SIM card **shǒujīkǎ** 手机卡 for your phone, that will also give you some initial start-up minutes. When your minutes are running low, you will receive a text message indicating this. The normal procedure is to then buy a new phone card **chōngzhíkǎ** 充值卡 (available in various denominations, usually 50 or 100 yuan). These cards are available at electronics stores or more conveniently at the many newspaper kiosks scattered around large cities in China. With these cards, you call a number and enter a PIN, which in turn adds the amount of time (in money) to your phone.

phone, but will look like one and have the Nokia name on it. Everyone knows these are not genuine products. **Shānzhài** 山寨 cell phones are quite popular in China and sometimes even have more features than the originals. (The term **shānzhài** 山寨 can also refer to someone who looks like a movie star, or a television program that copies the name and format of an original program. There are also **shānzhài** 山寨 electronics, snack foods, and so on.)

If you already know what brand you want, find that counter in the electronics store. Salespeople selling cell phones are generally pretty knowledgeable about the products. There may be a fair amount of technical jargon associated with cell phones but if you are familiar with cell phones in your own language you can understand a great deal through context. If you are not familiar with cell phones, you will need to ask lots of questions and get as much help as you can. It may be a good idea to take a Chinese friend or colleague along to help.

■ Texting 发短信 fā duǎnxìn

Texting on cell phones is very popular in China, even more so than talking. This is because texting is often cheaper than talk. It may sound cumbersome to text Chinese characters on a cell phone, but it's fairly straightforward, albeit a bit more complicated than English. Texting is typically done via pinyin or through the strokes method, called **wǔbǐ** 五笔. The pinyin method is the same as if you were typing Chinese on a computer. For example, if you want to type the word **nǐ** 你 (you), simply type "n" and "i" and the characters for **ni** will pop up. You then select which character you want. With practice one can get very fast and efficient.

■ Telephone cards 电话卡 diànhuàkǎ

There are two basic kinds of telephone cards: IP cards, which are used for international long distance, and IC cards which are used for domestic calls with public phones and phone booths.

IP cards work like phone cards in the United States. The user first dials an access number, enters the PIN, then enters the number of the other party. These cards are based on time. Per-minute rates vary, but are very reasonable compared to rates in the U.S. IP cards will work on most telephones, including some cell phones. As mentioned above, some cell phones require a certain calling plan to make international calls. Another option, if you do not have a phone card, is to simply dial an IP phone service, such as 96446, and the number. To make calls to the United States, for example, dial 96446001. You still have to have a long distance service plan with your phone to use this kind of service, but these kinds of numbers have considerably cheaper rates than the phone companies. Using an IP card is an excellent and cheap way to make occasional calls to the U.S. or other areas. Some cards will list on the front (in Chinese) where you can call. For example, you may have an IP card that is good for calling the U.S., Canada, Singapore, Hong Kong, and domestic long distance locations. I recently bought an IP card in a 100-yuan denomination that is only .3 yuan per minute for long distance calls.

The other type of telephone cards used regularly, IC cards, have a small chip like the SIM chips on cell phone cards. These kinds of cards must be used with specific public telephones that accept them. The cards are swiped or inserted into the public phone and minutes are deducted as you speak. You do not have to enter an access number or PIN. The cards are convenient to use, though you must have access to one of these public phones, which are common all over China.

Telephone cards can be bought from street vendors, often from a box on the back of a bicycle; from vendors with handbags near post offices; or at street markets, at newspaper kiosks, at the telephone company, railway stations, airports, small supermarkets, and so on. Prices for telephone cards are often negotiable. In fact, seldom do you pay full price for a phone card. For example, 100-yuan phone cards do not usually cost 100 yuan. The price will usually be lower, sometimes considerably. However, you cannot negotiate the price of phone cards with the telephone company or at the post office.

■ Public telephones 公用电话 gōngyòng diànhuà
There are three kinds of public telephones. One is the kind described above that requires the use of a special phone card. The other is like a typical pay phone where one inserts money. The third kind of public telephone is a regular-looking telephone that can be found at newspaper and magazine kiosks and at small convenience stores. These public-use phones usually charge a flat per-minute rate for local and domestic long distance calls. The person running the kiosk will moni-

tor the time and charge you accordingly, or sometimes these phones have a built-in digital monitor that keeps track of the time and fee. This phone option works well if you are out on the street (and you don't have a cell phone) and need to make a quick call. In one small city I needed to make a call to the U.S., but was staying in a small traveler's hostel that didn't have phones. I found a small convenience store along the street where there was a telephone. I was able to call directly to the States using this phone, and its built-in monitor kept track of the time and the cost. It can be a very convenient and inexpensive way to make international phone calls.

■ Setting up standard landline telephone service
开通座机 **kāitōng zuòjī**

Many rental apartments will have telephone service provided, that is, there will be a landline telephone and service already set up. But maintaining the service is usually the responsibility of the renter. Phone service is usually billed by the month. You may not receive a typical phone bill in the mail, but will be expected to go the phone company and pay the bill, usually within the first five days of the month (it's often possible to pay in advance). If you do not pay your bill on time, you may get a recorded message on your phone when you try to use it. Failing to pay your bill will result in your phone line being cut off, **tíngjī** 停机. To pay the bill, go to the nearest location of the phone company, find the place to pay bills **fù zhàngdān** 付账单, then provide the clerk with your telephone number. You may also pay at kiosks in grocery stores, banks, post offices or online.

COMPUTERS AND THE INTERNET
电脑与网络 **diànnǎo yǔ wǎngluò**

Computers have become widespread throughout China. By 2011 there were 400 million Internet 网络 **wǎngluò** users in

China. To put this in perspective, keep in mind that as few as fifteen years ago, computers were not commonly used, even in business and education. Though home computers are still not as widespread as in the West, computers are available to an increasingly large number of individuals. More and more Chinese are relying on computers and the Internet for news, communication, and gaming.

Some universities may have computer sites available to use, if you're a student. Large hotels usually have a business center where you can use computers, sometimes for a fee. If you are traveling with a laptop or iPod (or other device) with Wi-Fi capability, you may be able find free Wi-Fi hotspots at coffee shops and cafes.

■ **Internet bars** 网吧 **wǎngbā**

Internet bars or cafes are found all over China's cities, and even in small out-of-the-way towns in rural areas. They are usually identified with signs indicating Internet and the character 网 **wǎng**. These bars are not really bars in that they do not serve drinks, but they may resemble bars by the thick cloud of cigarette smoke you must endure if you frequent these places. Technically they are not supposed to allow smoking, but it may not be enforced. Some of the Internet bars may have smoking and non-smoking areas. There are all kinds of Internet bars from little shops with a few aging computers to large establishments with literally hundreds of fast, modern terminals.

The details of using a computer at Internet bars may vary, but here's the typical procedure: Most Internet bars have a reception desk or area. They charge by time, usually in quarter or half-hour increments. Prices are generally quite reasonable, from 2 to 4 yuan per hour. Sometimes you are free to select any open computer, and sometimes you will be assigned a specific computer. You may be given a card that has the computer number on it as well as a log-in name and password. When you arrive at a computer, if there is a log-in screen, enter the required information.

Public computers are generally geared toward Internet use. They are also widely popular for video gaming. You usually cannot use a flash drive or print at public computer sites. Some may offer printing facilities but these will be harder to find.

Most travelers and students will likely use Internet bars to stay in touch with family and friends via email. As long as you have an Internet-based email program, such as Gmail or Yahoo, accessing email is not a problem, though some programs work better than others in China.

■ Setting up Internet access at your apartment
在你的公寓开通网络 **zài nǐ de gōngyù kāitōng wǎngluò**

If you are renting an apartment while in China, and you have a computer, you will probably want to have Internet access. Many apartments, especially those that regularly rent to foreigners, may have Internet access available, but some areas do not have the infrastructure for Internet access. It is wise to ask the landlord about this before signing a contract. If the apartment already has access set up, the Internet fee may be added to your rent, or you may have to pay this on your own independent of your rent.

If access is not provided with your contract, you will need to arrange to have Internet access set up in your apartment. Most areas in China use an ADSL network. Some apartment complexes, universities, big companies or the army may also use a local area network (LAN) as well. The phone companies that set up Internet services can tell you what kind of system is used for your area.

The local office of one of the big three telecommunications offices (China Telecom, China Unicom, China Mobil) is

• BEHIND THE SCENES •

Blogging Like a Native

Blogs **bókè** 博客 and micro-blogs **wēibó** 微博 have become very popular in China. Personal blogs are most often accessed through mainstream websites, such as **xīnlàng** 新浪 (blog.sina.com.cn), **wǎngyì** 网易 (www.163.com), and **sōuhú** 搜狐 (www.sohu.com). On these kinds of sites, there's a vast number of blogs arranged topically, such as sports, emotion, business, current events, and so on. Creating a blog requires you to create an account with a user name and password. As in the West, blogs allow for comments. Micro-blogs are similar to Twitter in that very short messages are used. On **xīnlàng** 新浪 they can be found at www.weibo.com.

Micro-blogs have become a means for many to spread potentially sensitive information via the Internet. By the time China's government censors can block a message it may have already been forwarded to thousands if not millions of people. One way the government has attempted to better control this is by requiring that people register blogs using their real names and personal information.

the place to go to set up Internet access (开通网络 **kāitōng wǎngluò**) for an apartment. The company you use will depend on which companies offer service in your area, and which service you prefer. You may have to have the assistance of your landlord to do this as telecommincations companies will want information about the owner of the apartment and the telephone account information. Internet accounts are typically on a yearly basis or sometimes for half a year. If you are renting your apartment for less than that time, you will need to negotiate with your landlord about the specific terms. For a new account, there may be set-up fees and deposits as well. If you are sharing an apartment with roommates, this can be reasonable, but if you are on your own it can be quite expensive.

■ Navigating the Internet in Chinese

用中文网游 **yòng zhōngwén wǎngyóu**

I will not attempt to identify all popular Chinese websites, as that would be an endless endeavor. Probably the most popular search engine in Chinese, and very similar to Google, is **bǎidù** 百度 www.baidu.com. It functions in the same way as other search engines like Google and Yahoo. You can search for news, pictures, websites, MP3s, maps, videos, etcetera. If you are looking for information in Chinese, such as Chinese news, gossip, or sports, you will get better, more complete results using **bǎidù** than using Google. That is not to say that Google does not work in China or with Chinese, but **bǎidù** was designed specifically for the Chinese-speaking world. A few other popular search engines and information sites are **xīnlàng** 新浪 (www.sina.com.cn), 网易 **wǎngyì** (www.163 .com), and **sōuhú** 搜狐 (www.sohu.com). Again, these sites are all in Chinese and I have not found online translators able to do a very good job translating the sites into English. You may be able to get the gist, but the English translations tend to be pretty rough and literal.

- ■ **Online news and information**
  网上新闻和消息 **wǎngshàng xīnwén hé xiāoxi**

The official newspaper of the Communist Party in China is *People's Daily*, **rénmín rìbào** 人民日报 (www.people.com.cn). At the above website there is a link to the English version (http://english.peopledaily.com.cn). There are numerous national and local newspapers in China, with most having online versions. Most cities, large and small, have their own newspaper. Some of the larger and more popular Chinese language national newspapers include *China Daily* **zhōngguó rìbào** 中国日报 (English: http://usa.chinadaily.com.cn and Chinese: http://www.chinadaily.com.cn/hqzx), CCTV **zhōngguó zhōngyāng diànshìtái** 中国中央电视台, and China Internet Television **zhōngguó wǎngluò diànshìtái** 中国网络电视台 (http://www.cntv.cn).

Other popular English language newspapers are the South China Morning Post **nánhuá zǎobào** 南华早报 (www.scmp.com) in Hong Kong, China Daily **zhōngguó rìbào** 中国日报 (www.chinadaily.com.cn), and Global Times **huánqiú shíbào** 环球时报 (globaltimes.cn). A more complete list of news and other useful websites can be found in the appendix at the end of this book.

- ■ **Social networking Internet sites**
  社交网站 **shèjiāo wǎngzhàn**

Social networking is very popular in China, particularly among teenagers and young adults. Because of government regulations Facebook, YouTube, and Twitter are banned and blocked in China. However, there are many Chinese sites similar to these popular sites that are thriving. There are two websites in China that are very similar to Facebook: **kāixīn wǎng** 开心网 (www.kaixin001.cmo) and **rénrén wǎng** 人人网 (www.renren.com). Both of these sites are very popular and can be used to communicate with friends, classmates, and so on. You can post pictures too. These sites as well as other social networking sites in China are entirely in Chinese, so in order to navigate and use them, your Chinese will need to be pretty good.

■ Online communication 网上交流 **wǎngshàng jiāoliú**

There are a number of online and cell phone services that allow instant messaging such as MSN, gtalk, Skype, and Twitter. The most common service is QQ (qq.com). QQ requires that you download their software in order to use their service. This is a very popular service especially among the younger 1980s and 1990s generations. QQ accounts are a series of numbers. It is not uncommon for someone to ask you what your QQ number is. QQ can be accessed through a computer or your cell phone. Since texting is cheaper than talk on many cell phone plans, text-based communication is very popular, more so than talking. If you have QQ on your computer, you can also talk to others for free. MSN is more popular in business offices where QQ is generally not allowed. MSN does not have a Chinese language equivalent. It's also more popular with the 1970s generation. YY (**yǔyīn liáotiān** 语音聊天, www.yy.com) is a voice service similar to Skype that allows instant message–type service with voice capability. Skype can also be used in China, but is less popular with Chinese.

■ Online video 视频网站 **shìpín wǎngzhàn**

Online video and video sharing have become increasingly popular in China, just as in the West. These sites function very similarly to YouTube: you can watch videos, television programs, and movies, as well as post your own videos. The more popular sites include:

yōukù 优酷 www.youku.com	**kù liù** 酷6 www.ku6.com
jīdòng 激动 www.joy.cn	**tǔdòu** 土豆 www.tudou.com
56 www.56.com	**qíyì** 奇异 www.qiyi.com

USING THE POST OFFICE
用邮局 **yòng yóujú**

A Chinese post office is the place to mail letters or packages. Post offices in China also have a department that functions as a savings bank where you can maintain a savings account. Mailing letters domestically is very inexpensive, whereas mailing letters internationally will cost quite a bit more. It's still an economical way of communication, though. The different kinds of mail service include airmail, surface mail, registered mail, post cards, printed material, book rate, printed material bags, and others.

Envelopes **xìnfēng** 信封, writing pads (notepads) **xìnzhǐ** 信纸, and stationery **wénjù** 文具 can be bought at department stores, discount stores, or at stationery shops. Envelopes in China usually do not have self-stick flaps. In fact Chinese do not lick envelopes or stamps **yóupiào** 邮票—envelopes need to be glued closed, and stamps are either self-stick or need to be glued on. Post offices will have an area with a bottle of paste for this purpose. This can be a pretty messy affair as there is often thick white paste, **jiànghú** 糨糊, on the table, the jar, and the handle of the applicator brush. There may also be less-messy liquid glue, **jiāoshuǐ** 胶水.

■ **Mailing letters and packages** 寄信和包裹 **jìxìn hé bāoguǒ**
To mail a letter, bring it to the post office, give it to the clerk, and indicate how you want it mailed. The clerk will then weigh the letter and tell you how much it costs for the stamp. After you pay, they'll give you the stamp(s). Take the stamp over to the pasting table and glue the envelope closed, and the stamp onto the envelope. Beneath this counter or nearby will be the box where you deposit your mail. There are usually separate slots for intercity (to other cities) and intracity (within the city) mail. These slots will be labeled as **běnbù** 本

埠 for local mail within the city, and **wàibù** 外埠 for mail to other cities in China. These terms mean literally "this local" and "outside local" respectively.

Mailboxes (**yóuzhèng xìntǒng** 邮政信筒) on the street and in front of post offices are usually dark green with yellow writing on them and will have the same two mail slots, as well as the hours when mail is picked up. The latter will be indicated with the words **kāixiāng shíjiān** 开箱时间 meaning "open the box times." These mailboxes are only for domestic mail. For international mail, you will need to go into the post office and give the letter to a worker.

If you have things that you want to mail home, you can find boxes and packing materials at larger, main branch post offices. Inside there will be a station with packing materials for sale. At these stations, they'll even pack up your materials for you. The price for this service is very modest. Once your package is ready, take it to the counter. (Sometimes the package will not be sealed until you take it to the counter and show the contents to the postal worker.)

You have three options for packages, in order of speed and cost: air **hángkōng** 航空, a combination of surface and air **hángkōng jiā lùyùn** 航空加陆运, and surface and boat **hǎiyùn jiā lùyùn** 海运加陆运. Airmailing heavy boxes, like books, is quite expensive, but is quite fast, as short as one to two weeks to the United States. Surface and air usually takes close to a month. If you're on a budget and in no hurry, your best option is surface and boat, which will take anywhere from four weeks to three months. There will be a form to fill out which the clerk can help you with. Most forms of this nature will have Chinese as well as English, though the English may not be as helpful as you might think. If you don't understand something on the form you can always ask the clerk for help.

If you've packed a box of things yourself, do not seal the

box before you go to the post office. The contents will need to be checked by a postal worker first, then it will be sealed.

■ ■ ■

USEFUL PHRASES

to set up in-country long distance service **kāitōng guónèi chángtú yèwù** 开通国内长途业务

to set up international long distance service **kāitōng guójì chángtú yèwù** 开通国际长途业务

to set up standard landline telephone service **kāitōng zuòjī** 开通座机

to buy a cell phone **mǎi shǒujī** 买手机

to pay bills **fù zhàngdān** 付账单

a card to add minutes to your cell phone **chōngzhíkǎ** 充值卡

copycat of branded products or services **shānzhài** 山寨

mail pick-up times **kāixiāng shíjiān** 开箱时间

mailing letters and packages **jìxìn hé bāoguǒ** 寄信和包裹

online communication **wǎngshàng jiāoliú** 网上交流

online news and information **wǎngshàng xīnwén hé xiāoxi** 网上新闻和消息

online video 视频网站 **shìpín wǎngzhàn**

social networking Internet sites **shè jiāo wǎngzhàn** 社交网站

voice chat online **yǔyīn liáotiān** 语音聊天

I would like to set up an Internet account **wǒ xūyào kāi gè shàngwǎng de zhànghù** 我需要开个上网的帐户

Is Internet available for my area? **zhèr néng shàngwǎng ma?** 这儿能上网吗？

How is the account charged? Monthly? **zěnme shōufèi? shì měiyuè fù fèi ma?** 怎么收费？是每月付费吗？

Is there a set-up fee? **hái yòng jiāo kāihù fèi ma?** 还用交开户费吗？

Deposit? **yājīn ne?** 押金呢？

Telephone companies

China Mobil **zhōngguó yídòng tōngxìn jítuán gōngsī** 中国移动通信集团公司

China Mobil abbreviation **zhōngguó yídòng** 中国移动

China Telecom **zhōngguó diànxìn jítuán gōngsī** 中国电信集团公司

China Telecom abbreviation 中国电信 **zhōngguó diànxìn**

China Unicom 中国联通公司 **zhōngguó liántōng gōngsī**

China Unicom abbreviation 中国联通 **zhōngguó liántōng**

Cell phone brands

Apple (iPhone) **píngguǒ** 苹果

Blackberry **hēiméi** 黑莓

HTC **duō pǔ dá** 多普达

Huawei 华为 **huáwéi**

LG **LG**

Lenovo **liánxiǎng** 联想

Motorola **mótuóluólā** 摩托罗拉

Nokia **nuòjīyà** 诺基亚

Samsung **sānxīng** 三星

Sony Ericsson **suǒní** 索尼

Zhongxing **zhōngxīng** 中兴

Chinese search engines
Baidu **bǎidù** 百度 www.baidu.com
Sogou **sōugǒu** 搜狗 www.sogou
 .com

Social networking sites
Kaixin 开心网 **kāixīn wǎng** www
 .kaixin001.cmo
Renren 人人网 **rénrén wǎng** www
 .renren.com

Online video sites
Youku **yōukù** 优酷 www.youku.com
Ku66 **kù liu** 酷 www.ku6.com
Jidong **jīdòng** 激动 www.joy.cn
Tudou **tǔdòu** 土豆 www.tudou.com
56 **56** www.56.com
Qiyi **qíyì** 奇异 www.qiyi.com

USEFUL WORDS

air **hángkōng** 航空
ADSL modem **kuāndài
 tiáozhìjiětiáoqì** 宽带调制解调器
bill **zhàngdān** 账单
blog **bókè** 博客
cell phone **shǒujī** 手机

cell phones whose functions are like
 landline telephones **xiǎo língtōng**
 小灵通
computer **diànnǎo** 电脑
envelope **xìnfēng** 信封
ethernet cable **wǎngxiàn** 网线
Internet **wǎng** 网; **wǎngluò** 网络
Internet bar 网吧 **wǎngbā**
landline telephone 座机 **zuòjī**/固定
 电话 **gùdìng diànhuà**
letter pad **xìnzhǐ** 信纸
local **běnbù** 本埠
mail **xìn** 信
mailbox **yóuzhèng xìntǒng** 邮政信筒
micro-blogs (like Twitter) **wēibó**
 微博 (**wēixíng bókè** 微型博客)
packages **bāoguǒ** 包裹
post office **yóujú** 邮局
prepay **yùfù fèi** 预付费
public telephones **gōngyòng diànhuà** 公用电话
SIM chip **shǒujīkǎ** 手机卡
telephone 电话 **diànhuà**
telephone card 电话卡 **diànhuàkǎ**
to open or set up 开通 **kāitōng**
to send, to mail 寄 **jì**
to text 发短信 **fā duǎnxìn**
stamp 邮票 **yóupiào**

5

Banking
銀行业务 yínháng yèwù

Banking in the United States and banking in China have many similarities. Account types are similar, various kinds of debit and credit cards exist, and both countries have ATM machines. There is a huge variety of banks in China. Among them are many national or regional chains. However, as a foreigner, you may be limited to certain banks for opening your accounts.

Generally, non-Chinese are allowed to open accounts at any of the four large national banks: Bank of China **zhōngguó yínháng** 中国银行, China Construction Bank **zhōngguó jiànshè yínháng** 中国建设银行, Agriculture Bank of China **zhōngguó nóngyè yínháng** 中国农业银行, and Industrial and Commercial Bank of China (ICBC) **zhōngguó gōngshāng yínháng** 中国工商银行. Other Asian and international banks are also options; two examples are Cathay Bank **guótài yínháng** 国泰银行 (originally a Chinese-American bank) and Citibank **huāqí yínháng** 花旗银行. Be aware that large

international banks will not likely have branches in smaller Chinese cities.

There are now eleven nationwide joint-stock commercial banks in China, such as CMB (China Merchants Bank) **zhāoshāng yínháng** 招商银行, which has a branch in New York, and China CITIC Bank **zhōngxìn yínháng** 中信银行, which deals with foreign currencies. Other joint-stock commercial banks are Guangdong Development Bank **guǎngdōng fāzhǎn yínháng** 广东发展银行 (**guǎngfā yínháng** 广发银行), Shanghai Pudong Development Bank **shànghǎi pǔdōng fāzhǎn yínháng** 上海浦东发展银行 (**pǔfā yínháng** 浦发银行), Shenzhen Development Bank **shēnzhèn fāzhǎn yínháng** 深圳发展银行 (**shēnfāzhǎn yínháng** 深发展银行), Industrial Bank Co. Ltd. **xìngyè yínháng** 兴业银行, Hua Xia Bank **huáxià yínháng** 华夏银行, Bank of Communications **jiāotōng yínháng** 交通银行, China Everbright Bank **guāngdà yínháng** 光大银行, China Minsheng Banking Corp. Ltd. **mínshēng yínháng** 民生银行, and Evergrowing Bank **héngfēng yínháng** 恒丰银行.

Some cities also have city commercial banks, such as Bank of Beijing **běijīng yínháng** 北京银行 and Bank of Tianjin **tiānjīn**

yínháng 天津银行. These banks may also allow foreigners to open RMB accounts, but usually not U.S. dollar accounts.

There are also some foreign-invested banks, such as Standard Chartered China **zhādǎ yínháng** 渣打银行, HSBC (The Hong Kong and Shanghai Banking Corporation Limited) **huìfēng yínháng** 汇丰银行, Deutsche Bank China **déyìzhì yínháng** 德意志银行, The Royal Bank of Scotland China **hélán yínháng** 荷兰银行, and so on.

With so many to choose from, you may be wondering which banks are the best for your needs. CMB (China Merchants Bank) has a good reputation, especially for online services. Bank of China is generally reliable. For normal saving and checking business, many people use Bank of Communications and ICBC (Industrial and Commercial Bank of China), as they have many branches all over China. Some people think the service at Bank of Communications is excellent, and some think that the service at the four stated-owned banks, especially Agricultural Bank of China, is generally not that great. Others report that China Construction Bank is very good, especially for housing loans. Information about all these banks can easily be found online with a simple search.

EXCHANGING MONEY
换钱 huànqián

Exchanging money at a Chinese bank is fairly straightforward. However, it can take a while depending on how much experience with exchanging money the person at the counter has. I was at a bank in Kunming once where the clerks were not very experienced with exchanging money, so the process took much longer than usual. In some banks only certain tellers can exchange money, while at larger banks in larger cities you can usually exchange money using any teller. Exchange rates are typically posted on an electronic board in the bank lobby.

In smaller towns and rural areas it is always a good idea to have bills in smaller denominations as many places are unwilling to accept or cannot make change for 50- or 100-yuan bills. One of the reasons for this is the abundance of counterfeit 50- and 100-yuan notes.

To exchange money you will need your passport, a money exchange form, and the cash **xiànjīn** 现金 (and a form for remittance, **xiànhuì** 现汇, if appropriate) or traveler's checks **lǚxíng zhīpiào** 旅行支票 you want to exchange. Sometimes there are different exchange rates for traveler's checks and cash. (Surprisingly, traveler's checks will often get a better exchange rate, but you have to be at a main branch of the bank to exchange them.) Here's the procedure for exchanging money:

1. When you enter the bank, take a number and wait until your number is called. At larger banks the number will be displayed on an electronic board above the tellers. Smaller branches may or may not have this service.

2. When your number is called, go to the appropriate teller and tell her that you would like to exchange (换外币 **huàn wàibì**) foreign currency to Chinese 人民币 **rénmínbì**. You'll give your passport to the teller, who will usually make a copy of your passport for their records.

3. The teller will ask you how much you would like to exchange and what currency you are exchanging. (U.S. dollars are called **měiyuán** 美元.) They will either give you a money exchange form to fill out, or they will fill it out for you. At Industrial and Commercial Bank this form is called "Application Form of Personal Exchange Settlement" **gèrén jiéhuì yèwù shēnqǐng shū** 个人结汇业务申请书. These forms are usually, at least in part, printed with both

Chinese and English, so they are pretty easy to fill out. They usually ask for your name, nationality, phone number, ID type and number (e.g., passport), the amount, and so on. If there is a section of the form that does not have English and you do not understand, the teller can either help you, or fill it out for you.

4. The teller will take the money and count it several times to verify the amount. Don't be surprised if they count the money over and over again. They will also run it through a mechanized counter, which will also check for counterfeit bills. (My brother once had a U.S. bill rejected at several banks and ended up going back to the U.S. with it where his bank accepted it without issue.) Chinese banks tend to be very picky about the condition of bills you are trying to exchange. If you have bills that are torn, excessively crumpled, or have writing on them, they may not accept them. So if you are bringing cash to China, make sure the bills are fairly new.

5. The teller will carefully count the RMB and give you a receipt

> *In smaller Chinese cities or rural areas, don't expect the same banking services that you find in large cities. Recently we were in a small city in Yunnan Province. We assumed we could exchange our U.S. dollars at any of the usual banks. We were surprised to learn that only one bank in town was authorized to exchange foreign currency. Unfortunately it was a Saturday and that bank was closed. We tried a large hotel with a money exchange service, but because we weren't guests at that hotel they wouldn't exchange our money. We finally found a local branch of one of the four national banks, and used the ATM machine there to withdraw Chinese cash.*

showing how much was exchanged, how much RMB you received, the exchange rate, and the service charge.

Keep in mind that exchanging money at the airport will cost you more than using a bank. Airport money exchange booths will often charge a flat fee, usually around 50 yuan, for exchanging money, no matter the amount. It is best to just exchange enough to get you into town, then exchange money as you need at the bank. Larger hotels often also provide money exchange services, and usually offer exchange rates similar to banks.

Don't be surprised if the clerk counts the money over and over again.

Another, and probably the most convenient, option for exchanging money is to use an ATM machine at the bank or at the airport when you land. Most ATM machines have the option of English or Chinese. A service fee is applied to the transaction, and you can only withdraw a certain amount per day, but this is a fast and convenient way to get Chinese currency. Usually the maximum amount that you can withdraw with a foreign ATM card is 2500 yuan per transaction with a total of two transactions per 24-hour time period. Another advantage to this is that you do not need your passport and there's no need to fill out any forms. Make sure your debit card has a Visa logo on it, or that you have a four-digit PIN for your credit card.

HOW TO OPEN A BANK ACCOUNT
开账户 **kāi zhànghù**

Major bank branches typically have service desks with personnel who will help help you get a waiting-line number, explain how to do various transactions, fill out forms, and answer questions.

Opening a bank account at a Chinese bank is quick, easy, and convenient. You will need your passport, local address, a small fee (usually around 1 yuan), and you will need to fill out the appropriate application form, such as the Personal Customer Business Application Form **gèrén kèhù yèwù**
shēnqǐng shū 个人客户业务申请书. Most forms are in English and Chinese, or some banks may have separate English and Chinese forms. The application form will require basic information such as name, local address, passport number, the amount to be deposited, the type of ATM card that you want, and so on. You'll need to decide whether you want to use an ATM card, or use a bankbook. You will also be given various options to manage your account. These include:

1. Online Banking **wǎngshàng yínháng** 网上银行 (sometimes referred to as Internet banking)

2. Telephone Banking **diànhuà yínháng** 电话银行
   This gives you the ability to do basic bank transactions including transferring money with a regular landline telephone. You will need to specify the telephone number you plan to use for this service.

3. Mobile or Cell Phone Banking **shǒujī yínháng** 手机银行 (referred to as WAP, Wireless Application Protocol)
   This allows you to do basic transactions with your cell phone. You will need to provide the cell phone number you will use to access your account.

4. Other Options **qítā** 其他
   • Balance Change Reminder by email or phone **yú'é biàndòng tíxǐng** 余额变动提醒

- Credit Card attached to your account. This requires an additional application.

Once you have filled out the form, you'll take a number and wait until you are called to the counter. You may be given an ATM card at the time you open your account, if that is the kind of account you've chosen. Your account will be immediately activated so you can access your money right away.

It may seem a little scary putting your hard-earned money in a bank in a foreign country. Rest assured that banks in China are safe and secure.

ATM CARDS
银行卡 **yínháng kǎ**; 储蓄卡 **chúxù kǎ**; 借记卡 **jièjì kǎ**

When you open an account you will have the option of using either a bankbook **cúnzhé** 存折 or an ATM card. Whereas bankbooks were the standard in the past, they are usually only used by older people now. To get an ATM card as a foreigner, you have to be at least 18 years old. Typical ATM cards use a magnetic strip like in the U.S., but they may also contain embedded chips as well. Keep in mind that in China, transactions done in a bank usually have a higher fee than online banking.

There are four options available for regular ATM cards:

1. Allows you to bank using RMB only.

2. Allows you to bank using RMB and foreign currencies

3. Allows you to use RMB and foreign currencies, but also allows you to link more than one type of account to the card.

• BEHIND THE SCENES •

Kinds of Bank Accounts 各种银行帐户 **gèzhǒng yínháng zhànghù**
At most banks you'll find the below two kinds of bank accounts.

---

1. 活期存款 **huóqī cúnkuǎn (current deposit)**
This is like a checking account in America. The interest rate is set by the government and is very low (usually less than .35%).

---

2. 定期存款 **dìngqī cúnkuǎn (fixed-term deposit)** or 储蓄帐户 **chúxù zhànghù (savings account)**

This is what we in America would call a savings account. The interest rate is set by the government, but the rate depends on how long you have the money in the account. For example, the table here is based on **dìngqī** 定期 accounts that were posted at ICBC bank.

Your ATM card can be used to access a **huóqī** 活期 account. To withdraw money from a savings account, you usually have to go to the bank.

Months	Interest Rate %
3	1.91
6	2.2
Years	
1	2.5
2	3.25
3	3.85
5+	4.2

---

4. Allows you to use RMB with more than one bank account. (See the box above for the two main types of accounts.)

Using an ATM card in China is very similar to the process used in the U.S., Canada, etc. Most ATM machines have an English option and if they display the Visa or MasterCard symbol you can use an international ATM card (like one from the U.S., provided it also has a Visa or MasterCard symbol on it) to withdraw money. Service fees for international withdrawals vary by bank. There is a cap on the amount you can withdraw from an ATM machine per day. This maximum amount is usually posted on the ATM machine and may vary from 5,000 to 20,000 RMB for domestic bank accounts.

CREDIT CARDS
信用卡 xìnyòngkǎ

Just as in the U.S., there is a variety of credit card options in China. Regular, gold, and platinum cards with corresponding credit limits are available. Credit cards carry the Visa, MasterCard, or Union Pay logo (the Chinese government's credit card system). For more details on Union Pay you can do a simple online search.

Buying things with a credit card in China is not as common as it is in the West. In fact, many Chinese, and especially those who are elderly or in rural areas, use cash for nearly all their transactions. You may be able to use a credit card in bigger, more exclusive department stores, and at large restaurants, but

Nowadays most universities will accept international money transfers to pay tuition and other costs, but up until the early 2000s this was not the case. In 1998, I was directing a study abroad group in China. The university we were dealing with insisted that we pay cash for all the student tuition, housing, and related fees. This left me in the uncomfortable position of hand carrying about US$28,000 in traveler's checks to China. I had large wads of traveler's checks strapped to my waist, around my leg, and around my neck. When I arrived in China, I had several students accompany me to the bank where I spent a long time signing traveler's checks to exchange into Chinese currency. We put all that cash into a bag, then I had four larger male students form a bicycle motorcade, one student in front, one behind, and one on each side of me, as we pedaled our way back to campus to pay the university accountant.

do not plan to use them at small shops, grocery stores, small restaurants, and so on. Debit cards are also not very commonly used in many parts of China. In rural areas and small towns, plan on using cash for everything. Even in big cities, you will find that places like travel agents only accept cash. I haven't had much luck using a U.S.-issued credit card in China except at large hotels. Even places that accept credit and debit cards, like department stores, usually do not accept foreign cards.

> Many Chinese use cash for nearly all transactions; don't plan to rely on your credit card.

Most Chinese have their paycheck directly deposited into an account accessible by their debit card. Some younger people use credit cards because they may be attractively promoted in different ways. Those who do use credit cards pay them off each month. In China there is also a card called a **gòuwùkǎ** 购物卡 "shopping card." It is similar to a gift card, but it can be used anywhere a credit or debit card is accepted. These cards can be bought at the bank in various denominations. You do not earn interest on these kinds of cards.

MONEY TRANSFERS
汇款 **huìkuǎn**

Money can be transferred from your Chinese bank account to another account at the same bank, or to an account at a different bank (domestic or foreign). You can do money transfers in person at the bank, online, or at an ATM machine. Typically the service fee for a transfer is 0.5% to 1% of the amount with the lowest fee being 2 RMB and the highest being 100 RMB. To make a money transfer you will need your account number, the other person's name, bank, and account number, and the proper form. Different forms are required for different kinds of money transfers. For example, the ICBC bank requires the following forms:

1. Personal Banking Voucher **gèrén yèwù píngzhèng** 个人业务凭证
   For money transfers to an account at the same bank.

2. Electronic Transfer Form **diànhuì píngzhèng** 电汇凭证
   For money transfers to a different Chinese bank.

3. Overseas Transfer Form **jìngwài huìkuǎn shēnqǐng shū** 境外汇款申请书
   For money transfers to a foreign bank. You may transfer up to US$50,000 per transfer.

■ **Getting your money from the U.S. to China**
把钱从美国转到中国 **bǎ qián cóng měiguó zhuǎn dào zhōngguó**

If you are going to China for the first time it is not likely that you will already have a Chinese bank account. As such, you will not be able to wire transfer your funds to a Chinese bank. You may have to carry a fairly large amount of money with you, for school fees, rent money, relocation-related things, and so on.

Use common sense when dealing with money in China. Though a foreign currency may seem like "play" money at first, always be careful how you handle and display your money. What may seem like an insignificant amount of money to you may be a fortune to someone else. Foreigners often casually spend and display 100-yuan notes not realizing that some workers in China may only make 500 or 600 yuan in an entire month.

Traveler's checks are a good option as they can be replaced if lost or stolen. You may not be able to use traveler's checks in rural areas, but in large cities they are accepted anywhere that you can exchange money.

Perhaps the best and safest option is to carry some cash, some traveler's checks, and your Visa or MasterCard ATM card linked to funds in your U.S. bank. For your immediate needs, cash will be important, especially if you are initially travelling to less-developed areas. The traveler's checks can then be exchanged for your other pressing needs, such as paying tuition, renting an apartment, and so on. Finally, you can simply use your ATM card to get money as you need to during your stay. Or you may bring the bulk of your money in traveler's checks, take them to the Bank of China and open a checking account, and exchange it into RMB. You can then access your money with a debit card at any ATM machine.

If you are relocating to China for a job, and anticipate staying for an extended period, you will certainly open a bank account and can then have funds transferred from your U.S. bank to your Chinese bank account.

PAYING UTILITY BILLS AT THE BANK 在银行支付（水电费）帐单 zài yínháng zhīfù (shuǐdiànfèi) zhàngdān

As mentioned in Chapter 2, one can sometimes pay various utility bills at the bank. Each situation is different, so you will have to check with your landlord. Some banks accept some kinds of utility bills, and sometimes only certain branches in your neighborhood will accept your bill payments. You may also need to go to different banks to pay different utility bills.

■ ■ ■

USEFUL PHRASES

email or phone reminder of balance change **yú'é biàndòng tíxǐng** 余额变动提醒

exchange foreign currency to Chinese currency 换外币 **huàn wàibì**

kinds of bank accounts **gèzhòng yínháng zhànghù** 各种银行帐户

make money transfers from the U.S. to China **bǎ qián cóng měiguó zhuǎn dào zhōngguó** 把钱从美国转到中国

pay utility bills at the bank **zài yínháng zhīfù (shuǐdiànfèi) zhàngdān** 在银行支付（水电费）帐单

to open a bank account **kāi zhànghù** 开账户

Application Form of Personal Exchange Settlement **gèrén jiéhuì yèwù shēnqǐng shū** 个人结汇业务申请书

Electronic Transfer Form **diànhuì píngzhèng** 电汇凭证

Overseas Transfer Form **jìngwài huìkuǎn shēnqǐng shū** 境外汇款申请书

USEFUL WORDS

ATM/debit card **yínháng kǎ** 银行卡/ **chúxù kǎ** 储蓄卡/**jièjì kǎ** 借记卡

bankbook 存折 **cúnzhé**

banking 银行业务 **yínháng yèwù**

cash 现金 **xiànjīn**

caution 谨慎 **jǐnshèn**

Chinese currency 人民币 **rénmínbì**

credit cards 信用卡 **xìnyòngkǎ**

checking 活期 **huóqī**

checking account 活期存款 **huóqī cúnkuǎn**

deposit 存钱 **cúnqián**

exchange money 换钱 **huànqián**

fixed-term 定期 **dìngqī**

fixed-term deposit 定期存款 **dìngqī cúnkuǎn**

mobile or cell phone banking 手机银行 **shǒujī yínháng**

money transfers 汇款 **huìkuǎn**

online banking 网上银行 **wǎngshàng yínháng**

remittance 现汇 **xiànhuì**

RMB (currency of China) 人民币 **rénmínbì**

savings account 储蓄帐户 **chúxù zhànghù**

shopping card 购物卡 **gòuwùkǎ**

telephone banking 电话银行 **diànhuà yínháng**

traveler's checks 旅行支票 **lǚxíng zhīpiào**

U.S. dollars 美元 **měiyuán**

withdraw 取钱 **qǔqián**

yuan (RMB dollar) **yuán** 元

6

Shopping

买东西 mǎi dōngxi

Many Chinese are passionate about shopping, especially in large urban areas. With the rise of a new middle class in China, the Generation Y youth are especially big shoppers. Even just twenty years ago the options for consumer goods were extremely limited. And what you could find was beyond the budget of nearly all except well-connected and relatively wealthy government cadres.

When I was studying in China in the early 1980s the Chinese wardrobe was very basic, consisting of blue or green baggy trousers, white shirts, and a basic leather belt. It seemed to us that there was only one size as well. On skinny guys the belt would wrap halfway again around their waist and their clothes were especially baggy. We used to joke about going to the big state-run department store to buy clothes, and saying "I'll take a pair of the pants, a shirt, and the belt."

Nowadays it is astonishing what is available in China, from a huge variety of inexpensive

Chinese goods to the most elite European designer boutiques and everything in between. The choices now are practically unlimited.

Whether you like shopping or not, you will have to buy things in China. From buying souvenirs to setting up house, there's always something to purchase. Knowing where to go is the first step in buying things in China. Ideally you will go to the place that has the best prices and selection for what you need. This may be a top department store, or a street market.

There are many bargains to be found in China, but there is also a great deal of money to be made from foreigners. In other words, if you are not careful you can easily get ripped off.

In this chapter I discuss two different categories of shopping in China: shopping for living necessities and shopping for souvenirs or gifts. Of course there is some overlapping of items in these categories, but the principles, and where you shop, are the differences.

WHERE TO SHOP
去哪儿购物 **qù nǎr gòuwù**

Where you shop, of course, depends on what you want to buy. The variety of stores in China can be looked at in three main groups: convenience stores, usually referred to as **biànlì diàn** 便利店, large department stores, and discount stores. Department stores are typically multi-storied and are sometimes called **bǎihuò gōngsī** 百货公司 literally "100 goods" but really meaning general merchandise. However, this term is becoming outdated and now large department stores are just called **shāngdiàn** 商店 or **shāngchǎng** 商场. Discount stores like Walmart and the Chinese equivalents are usually called **gòuwù guǎngchǎng** 购物广场 or **shāngchǎng** 商场. A **gòuwù guǎngchǎng** 购物广场 can also refer to an area, often indoors, where there are many individual booths selling goods. A **gòuwù zhōngxīn** 购物中心 is a shopping mall, and a **shāngyè jiē** 商业街 is a street lined with stores, or a shopping district. A store that sells only one brand of things, usually a designer brand, is called a **zhuānmài diàn** 专卖店, and a **chāoshì** 超市 is a supermarket or other kind of store where you select items off the shelf yourself and take them to a checkout stand.

■ **Convenience stores** 便利店 **biànlì diàn**

Convenience stores are everywhere in China. In larger cities you often find chains similar to 7-11 type stores. 7-11 stores themselves are actually quite common in Taiwan and Hong Kong, and are becoming more common in the mainland. These kinds of stores are often open 24 hours a day (at least in big cities). They sell the same kinds of things you would find at a convenience store in North America: canned and dried food items, dairy and other fresh food items, candy and snacks, drinks, including alcohol, and basic household items

like toilet paper, feminine products, and batteries. You can even buy time for your cell phone, or pay your bills. Chinese convenience stores often also sell fresh food items like steamed buns and boiled eggs. Some also sell some basic fresh produce and fresh eggs.

These stores vary in size, but most are quite small. They are liberally scattered throughout larger cities. They are great for grabbing some snacks between meals, and for buying bottled water when you are out on the streets. They are also a great place to buy tissue packets, which you should always have with you. Besides functioning as toilet paper, they are also handy as napkins when you are out eating, and for mopping your sweaty brow in hot, humid conditions.

Some of the more popular convenience store chains in China include:

C-Store **xǐshìduō** 喜士多
Kedi **kědì** 可的
Alldays **hǎodé** 好德
Dafang Convenience Store **dàfāng biànlì** 大方便利
FamilyMart **quánjiā** 全家

There are numerous other regional chains as well. For example, the largest chain of grocery and convenience stores in Jiangsu Province is Suguo 苏果 **sūguǒ**. In the Beijing area the largest are Wu Mart **wùměi** 物美, Hualian **huálián** 华联, CSF Market **chāoshìfā** 超市发, and Jingkelong **jīngkèlóng** 京客隆. In the Shanghai area it is QUIK **shànghǎi huálián kuàikè biàn-lìdiàn** 上海华联快客便利店 or **kuàikè** for short.

■ **Discount stores** 购物广场 **gòuwù guǎngchǎng;** 商场 **shāngchǎng;** 超市 **chāoshì**
Discount stores are one of the most convenient places to buy household goods and groceries. They are conveniently located throughout large and small cities. Because they are fairly numerous, you can usually find one near your hotel or

apartment. This means you don't have to travel and transport your goods a long distance. You can find just about anything in these large discount stores including groceries, medicine, clothing, appliances, electronics, school supplies, bicycles, books, tools, and so on. Walmart **wòěrmǎ gòuwù guǎngchǎng** 沃尔玛购物广场/**wòěrmǎ** 沃尔玛 and Carrefour **jiālèfú** 家乐福 are probably the biggest chains in China in this category of stores. But there are numerous other regional and national chains throughout China that are just as good, if not better, than their foreign competitors.

These kinds of stores usually have one entry point and one exit. Sometimes you are forced to walk through the store in a circuitous way to get to the exit. The registers are located near the exits. Escalators take you from floor to floor, and many are designed so you can use your shopping cart on them. Paying for your things is done in the same way as in the U.S. Many Chinese still prefer paying cash for just about ev-

> Escalators are designed so you can use your shopping cart on them.

erything. Debit and credit cards are becoming more common, but are only accepted at larger, more established stores—and they usually only accept local cards, not international cards. It's best to have cash on hand when shopping. You may be required to show your receipt to a sales clerk before exiting the store.

■ **Department stores** 商场 **shāngchǎng;** 商店 **shāngdiàn**
Department stores in China can be confusing places to shop. They are typically very large, and multi-storied. They sell the same kinds of products as departments stores anywhere. The

> *China has never been short on manpower and this seems to be particularly evident in department stores. There are sales clerks all over these stores. I remember one time in a department store I asked a clerk a question about a product, and she referred me to another sales clerk one aisle over. When I looked around I realized there were sales clerks stationed about every two to three aisles apart, and each had responsibility for their section.*

Don't expect departments organized by product categories.

goods they sell are typically higher quality and more expensive than at discount stores. Some department stores cater to less expensive goods (think JC Penney or Sears in the U.S.), and others are more up-scale (think Nordstom or Saks Fifth Avenue).

The thing that makes China's department stores different than many in the U.S. is the compartmentalization of various brands. For example, instead of a women's clothing department with numerous brands, each brand has its own section of the store. In this way, if you were shopping for a new coat, you would not just go to the coat department; instead you would have to visit as many as fifteen or twenty individual brand stations within the store to find a coat. Shoes will all be located on the same level and in the same area, but each brand will have their own space within the larger area.

Once you have found something that you would like to buy, you simply tell the sales clerk. She will then fill out a sales slip, usually in triplicate. You will leave the item with the clerk while you take the sales slip to a cashier. The cashier booths are usually located centrally in the store. Different departments may each have their own cashier booth. Look for the signs that say **shōuyín** 收银. After you pay, the cashier will stamp two copies of the sales slip and give them to you. You then give one slip to the clerk, who will give you your item, and you keep one slip as your sales receipt. From an American point of view it seems a rather clumsy process, but it is still very common in department stores. If you are buying several items from different parts of the store, you may need to go through this process multiple times.

■ Markets 市场 shìchǎng or 菜市场 cài shìchǎng

Markets are informal and inexpensive places to shop. Some markets are outdoor with individual stalls lining long walkways, and some are indoors in large buildings, often multiple stories high. As with discount stores, you can find just about anything at these markets. Those that just sell produce are called **cài shìchǎng** 菜市场. These are where many Chinese buy their daily produce and meat. Sometimes these kinds of food markets are called **nóngmào shìchǎng** 农贸市场 and are the equivalent of what we call a farmer's market.

Each stall is operated independently of the others, so when buying things you will pay for each item at each individual stall. Definitely plan on using cash at these kinds of markets. Dealers usually specialize in one kind of item, such as shoes, handbags, scarves, dishes, hardware items, and so on. In large indoor markets, like items will be clustered together in one area. In other words, all stalls selling shoes will be in the same vicinity. In outdoor markets this may not be the case, though some like items may be clustered together in various parts of the market.

Items in markets can be quite inexpensive, even more so than at discount stores. You can usually barter for prices at markets (whereas at discount stores you pay the marked price). You may find Western branded goods in these kinds of

markets, but they most certainly will not be genuine. Most of the products in these markets will be Chinese brands, since they cater to local populations and not to foreigners. Keep in mind that some markets have limited operating times. For example, some may only be open on the weekends.

■ Specialized markets 专项市场 zhuānxiàng shìchǎng

Some markets specialize in specific items. For example, some cities may have an area or district for electronics—a **diànnǎo chéng** 电脑城 or **diànzǐ shāngchéng** 电子商城—where you can buy computers, cameras, and related things. There are usually numerous stores clustered around these markets, too, selling the same. In addition to electronics markets, you may also find markets for books **shūshì** 书市, household goods and hardware **zhuāngshìchéng** 装饰城, flowers **huāhuì shìchǎng** 花卉市场 or **huāshìr** 花市儿, knick-knacks **xiǎo shāngpǐn shìchǎng** 小商品市场, and antiques **gǔwán/wénwù shìchǎng** 古玩 / 文物市场. Don't forget the fish markets **yúshì** 鱼市 and bird markets **niǎoshì (er)** 鸟市（儿）. For example, if I were in Nanjing and wanted to buy some electronics, maybe a computer, I would head to Zhujiang Road east of Nanjing University campus where the electronics district is located. All along this road for several blocks are numerous computer and camera stores, including a few large electronics malls.

Another example is Beijing's **Liúlíchǎng Xījiē** 琉璃厂西街, which is the antiques district. If you are interested in Chinese antiques, this is your market. Guangzhou's tea market **cháyè shìchǎng** 茶叶市场 is the place to go for tea connoisseurs. Many cities have such markets to explore and may have specialties that can't be found in other cities.

■ Markets geared toward foreigners and fake products
面向外国人的市场和假冒产品 **miànxiàng wàiguórén de shìchǎng hé jiǎmào chǎnpǐn**

In large cities such as Beijing, Shanghai, and Guangzhou, there are a number of markets that cater to Westerners looking for designer brands, but not willing to pay the steep price of authentic products. These kinds of markets, such as Beijing's Silk Market **xiùshuǐ jiē** 秀水街, are full of fake designer brand products. There is little attempt to convince you that the products are genuine as everyone, buyer and seller alike, knows they are fake. This is not to say they are all of poor quality. In some cases the fakes may be as well made as the genuine article. Keep in mind that selling fake products like this does violate U.S. trademark laws. Fake products are not limited to clothing and designer brands. You will also find fake pearls, gold, silver and other kinds of jewelry as well. Be careful about buying electronics such as cell phones, MP3 players and such at these kinds of markets as the electronics have an interesting way of working perfectly for about two weeks before they suddenly stop working. By this time, most tourists are long gone from China.

Be careful when shopping in these kinds of markets. Sellers are very skilled at ripping off unsuspecting, and sometimes even suspecting, foreigners. Besides getting you to pay far above the value of the product they will also use this strategy: you have decided on a pair of designer jeans and have finally settled on a price you and the seller can live with. Rather than give you the pair of jeans that you have been looking at, they will pull out the same pair from under the counter that is wrapped as if new. They will show you the size to assure you that it is the same pair of pants, but this pair is new in the package. You pay, take your new pair of jeans, and off you go only to discover that the pair of pants you were given is defective or of lower quality than the pair you were looking at. They know that the vast majority of foreign shoppers will never be back. If you do have the time and inclination to try to return it, good luck. You will have a difficult time getting any money back or making an exchange. They may not even recognize you since foreigners all look alike, and they have probably dealt with dozens if not hundreds of other customers since they last saw you.

■ Night markets 夜市 **yèshì**

Night markets are generally set up along certain streets in the city. During the day these are regular streets, but at

night the vendors come out with their portable carts to sell their goods. Sometimes these markets are on pedestrian malls where vehicular traffic is not allowed. Night markets can be great fun and bargains abound. There is often very good street food. Night markets also of-

• BEHIND THE SCENES •

Shopping Like a Native—Hit the Flea Markets

By flea markets I mean markets that sell used products. Flea markets, **tiàozao shìchǎng** 跳蚤市场, may be located on the outskirts of a city, near a park or temple, or other places. Flea markets sometimes deal with a specific product such as jade or furniture. Other large flea markets will sell just about anything you can imagine, from Cultural Revolution memorabilia to antiques and jewelry. The most famous of these kinds of markets is Beijing's **pānjiāyuán shìchǎng** 潘家园市场, also called the Dirt Market **wūgòu shìchǎng** 污垢市场, or the Sunday Market **zhōurì shìchǎng** 周日市场. Many flea markets are only open on the weekends, and it's best to get there early to get the best things. In Shanghai there is the Dongtai Road Antiques market **dōngtái lù gǔwán shìchǎng** 东台路古玩市场 which has a wide variety of knick-knacks, curios, and antiques, though most are not true antiques. Be aware that flea markets are typically very crowded, and the haggling can be fierce. (See p. 147 for more on bargaining.) At these kinds of markets, barter hard. Prices can be hugely inflated, but there are bargains galore if you are patient and have good bartering skills.

ten have carnival-type entertainment like fortune-tellers and games.

Some night markets may cater to specific kinds of goods, but there generally is a wide variety of goods sold. Bartering is the norm, so be prepared to haggle for a good deal.

You may find individual vendors or small clusters of vendors out on the streets at night. Technically these may not be night markets, and you may have to ask around to find these kinds of vendors.

A good example of night market that specializes in food is Beijing's Donghuamen Night Market **dōnghuámén yèshi** 东华门夜市. This is the place to go for adventurous eaters who want to try something different. At this market you can find things like scorpions, cicadas, silkworms, grasshoppers, and

Mongolian cheese along with more pedestrian things like kebabs of all kinds, fruit, corn on the cob, and pita bread stuffed with meat. This market is geared toward tourists, so prices are adjusted accordingly.

When you relocate to China, whether you are a student, teacher, or businessperson, you will likely need to outfit your apartment. Many apartments are furnished, so you may not have to worry about furniture or appliances.

Depending on where you are in China, your options for buying household goods include foreign chain stores, local or Chinese chain stores, and markets. The foreign stores with large presences in China include Walmart **wòěrmǎ gòuwù guǎngchǎng** 沃尔玛购物广场, or 沃尔玛 **wòěrmǎ** for short, the French counterpart to Walmart, Carrefour **jiālèfú** 家乐福, the drug store chain Watsons **qūchénshì** 屈臣氏, 7-11 Convenience Stores, Metromart **màidélóng** 麦德龙, and the relative newcomer to China, Ikea **yíjiā** 宜家. Walmart and other

Western chains in China have a distinctly Chinese feel to them, and do not stock the same goods as you would see in a Walmart in the U.S. The products, from food items to household goods, reflect Chinese tastes. In fact Walmart and Carrefour look very similar to large Chinese discount stores, carrying the same kinds of products and brands. For example, the fresh foods sections will carry things like roast duck, live fish, and a dizzying array of produce and other animal products that you would never see in the West, except at a Chinese market. The competition in China is quite fierce and look-alike stores are all over the place.

Markets are a good place to buy smaller household items like dishes, pots and pans, plastic ware, utensils, décor, and so on. You will probably get the best prices at markets where Chinese shop, but you will need to bargain to get those prices.

THE ART OF BARTERING
讨价还价 **tǎojiàhuánjià** / 讲价的艺术 **jiǎngjià de yìshù**

In many markets, especially outdoor markets, prices are often not marked and can be negotiated through bartering or haggling. This can be intimidating for some and great fun and a challenge for others. The key to successful bartering is having an idea of what something is worth. In China, this boils down to knowing what the locals pay for a given product at a market. There are a few ways to determine this. One is to hang around at a market, eavesdrop and observe what people are paying for the product in which you are interested. This is not too hard to do if you speak Chinese, because the Chinese at a market will not likely suspect that you understand what's being said. Another way to determine a fair price is to ask a Chinese friend or colleague. If they do not know off the top of their head, they may be able to accompany you to the market and even help you haggle for a good price. The sellers will likely not be very happy about this. To get the best deal, plan on using cash. It's also a good idea to have the exact amount you plan to pay in your pocket. It never looks good after a hot bartering session to pull out a thick wad of 100-yuan notes, especially when you have talked about how little money you have. It's also a good idea to come equipped with your money in small denominations. Many vendors are unwilling to break large bills, nor are they eager to give you any change back. The only kinds of markets where bartering is expected and that may take a credit card are large markets that cater to foreigners, like Beijing's Silk Market 秀水街 **xiùshuǐjiē**. And even there, only some of the stalls may accept cards.

■ The foreigner effect
外国人引起的变化 **wàiguórén yǐnqǐ de biànhuà**

As soon as any vendor sees a foreigner coming, yuan signs will light up his or her eyes. When you ask how much something costs, the vendor will probably jack up the price as much as tenfold or more, knowing that foreigners are often eager to spend money and usually are clueless about how much things should cost. The problem for the foreigner, particularly the tourist, is usually that he or she has little idea about how much something is worth, and so will tend to mentally compare with prices back home. Remember that most likely the cost of a similar product back home will be many times more than you can get it for in China. Of course, most foreigners have heard about the great deals you can get in China on fake products, like designer jeans, but still may not know what constitutes a good price.

■ Where to barter 哪里可以讲价 **nǎlǐ kěyǐ jiǎngjià**

Bartering is to be expected at most markets, outdoor shopping areas, tourist sites, some produce and meat markets, and any-

• BEHIND THE SCENES •

Cash Is King 现金为王 xiànjīn wéi wáng

In China, the vast majority of people still use cash for most purchases. This is especially true of the many markets in China: vendors generally only accept cash. Some places that cater to foreigners, like hotels, tourist sites, large restaurants, department stores, and airports, may accept plastic. (As mentioned previously though, sometimes those places will not accept foreign-issued credit cards.) For pretty much everywhere else, plan on using cash. Have small bills ready because many vendors will not give change or will not accept large denominations.

where where prices are not marked. Sometimes even when the price is marked you may try to talk them down. Bartering is not acceptable in department stores, convenience stores, large discount stores, restaurants, and other such places. While you do not barter at hotels, you can ask for a discount. This is typical in the off-season and many hotels will give you a discount just for asking. You can ask for a discount by saying,

Kěyǐ dǎzhé ma? 可以打折吗？ Can you give a discount?

Kěyǐ (gěi) piányi yīdiǎn ma? 可以（给）便宜一点吗？
Can you give it for a bit cheaper?

■ **Strategies for successful bartering**
成功的讲价策略 **chénggōng de jiǎngjià cèlüè**

The first key to getting a good price on something is to pretend that you are not that interested in the item. Look at the item skeptically, notice and verbalize negative things about the item, walk around looking at other things, then casually go back to the item you would like. Next, offer a price well below the asking price. Remember that bartering is a two-

way deal. Not only must you be satisfied with the price, but the seller must be satisfied as well. Start low, then be willing to go up in price, which the seller will expect. No vendor will sell something at a loss; they will always make sure to make a profit on all their deals.

Once you have suggested a price, the bartering begins. The vendor will likely scoff, act disgusted, give you some line about how he or she has a family to support, and so on. Don't take anything personally. This is just part of the script or game.

At this point, your next step is to simply start walking away. Remember, you have been pretending that you are not all that interested in the item anyway. The vendor will in most cases call you back, and offer a slightly higher price than what you originally offered. Now the real haggling begins. Continue to feign disinterest, that you could take it or leave it. Counter with another price lower than his. This may go on for a while. The vendor at some point will refuse to go any lower. When this happens, tell the vendor to forget it (**suàn le** 算了) and walk away again. Either the vendor will call you back again and offer a lower price, or he will let you go. At this point you need to be willing to walk on and find another vendor selling what you want. If you go back at this point, the vendor will know that he has you: that you really do want the item and probably won't leave without it! Keep in mind that in large markets there is huge overlap among the vendors and what they're selling. If you cannot find what you want at the price you're willing to pay, then move on and you will likely be able to find the exact item at another stall.

■ The flip side of bartering
思考讲价的另一面 **sīkǎo jiǎngjià de lìng yīmiàn**

There is another school of thought with regard to bartering. It's that if you are comfortable and willing to pay a specific price, then even if it is higher than what it normally sells for, it is a good deal for you. If you are content with paying a certain price, then so be it. Buy it, be glad, and move on.

Let's say that a certain pair of designer jeans sells for $140 in the U.S. At the Silk Market in Beijing you see a pair of the exact jeans you want for the equivalent of $50. You know they are fakes, but after inspecting them, you think they look pretty good. In fact, you could not tell if they were authentic or fakes. You think $50 is a pretty good deal, considering what they sell for in the U.S. With good bartering skills someone could probably get them for $10 or $15. If you are okay with spending $50 and you don't want to go through the hassle of bartering, then by all means pay the asking price and be on your way. Some people simply do not like haggling and are willing to pay the higher price. Of course, if too many tourists are doing this, it will be harder to negotiate a really good deal, because the vendor knows that someone else willing to pay the higher price will be along shortly. This is especially true of the markets frequented by tourists, and is not really applicable to markets that cater to the local population.

HOW TO GET THINGS HOME
如何搬运东西回家 **rúhé bānyùn dōngxi huíjiā**

Without having a car, it can be a challenge to get your purchases home or to your hotel if they're large or bulky. If your purchases are not too large, a taxi or car is probably the most convenient. You should be able to hail a cab in the vicinity of shopping areas.

When you're buying large items like furniture and appliances, most of the time either the store where you bought these items will deliver it, or the company that makes the product will deliver it. Sometimes there will be a small cost for delivery. Outside furniture or hardware stores, there may be trucks around that you can hire to transport your goods. You'll probably need to have pretty good Chinese skills to negotiate a price on something like this, so it would be best to have a Chinese friend or colleague with you.

If you have large items such as furniture or appliances in your apartment that you want to get rid of, you can hire a three-wheeled bike to take away your goods. You would be amazed at what these guys can fit on their bikes. I have seen mattresses, refrigerators, and furniture on them. On the back of the bike there may be a sign that says **zhuānyè huíshōu** 专业回收 which basically means "specializing in recycling" followed by a list of things that they recycle. In China, just about everything is recycled.

ONLINE SHOPPING
网上购物 **wǎngshàng gòuwù;** 网购 **wǎnggòu**

In the early 2000s, China entered the online shopping market. Though online shopping in China is probably not as common as in the West, it is gaining momentum.

It may be difficult for a foreigner to actually purchase items online because to set up an account you will be asked for your **shēnfènzhèng** 身分证, or identity card number. Since foreigners are not issued identity cards, setting up an account may not be possible as they will not accept a passport number. If you would like to buy something online you may need to get a friend or colleague to buy it for you and you can pay them back. The biggest online shopping sites are:

- Taobao **táobǎo wǎng** 淘宝网 (www.taobao.com)—Taobao is one of the biggest online shopping malls. Not only does it have business to consumer products, but also consumer to consumer shopping as well. Consumers can post new or used items to sell. Most items on Taobao are new with fixed prices, but a small percentage of their sales are done through auctions, similar to  Ebay. Aliwangwang **ālǐ wàngwàng** 阿里旺旺 is a chat service that is popular on this site so buyers can chat online with sellers to ask questions or barter for prices. This feature has become very common. The most common way to make purchases is through Alipay **zhīfù bǎo** 支付宝 (www.alipay.com).This is a third party online payment platform partnered with Visa and MasterCard and it works in much the same way as Paypal. This makes online shopping more convenient and secure.

- Dangdang **dāngdāng** 当当 (www.dangdang.com)—This is another of the big online business to consumer retailers in China that is similar to Amazon. It started out selling mostly books but has expanded to other consumer goods as well.

- Amazon China **zhuóyuè yàmǎxùn** 卓越亚马逊 (http://www.amazon.cn)—This company was originally a Beijing-based company called Joyo **zhuóyuè** 卓越 but was purchased by Amazon in 2004. It looks and functions just like Amazon in the U.S.

- Jing Dong Mall **jīngdōng shìchǎng** 京东商城 (360buy.com)—
  This company claims to be China's #1 online business to
  consumer retailer. It functions like the other online retailers
  in China and the West.

With all of these retailers, products are listed by category, such as **túshū** 图书 for books, clothing **fúzhuāng** 服装, **shípǐn** 食品 food items, **jiāyòng diànqì** 家用电器 household electronics, and so on. There are subcategories listed under these headings. Chinese online retailers do not have English versions so you will have to be able to read Chinese characters to use these sites. Since you are probably already familiar with online retailers, it should not be too difficult to navigate through these sites, even with only basic Chinese language skills. They look and function much like online retail shops in the West.

▩ Online group shopping 网上团购 **wǎngshàng tuángòu**
Group shopping is when you buy things in bulk as a group to get a better price. It is not necessary to know the other people in your group. You buy what you want and it is shipped to your home, just as if you were purchasing something individually. You can buy just about anything you want through group buying. Here's a sampling of popular group buying websites.

kāixīn tuángòu 开心团购 http://tuan.kaixin001.com/#
nuòmǐ wǎng 糯米网 (**mǎi shípǐn wéizhǔ** 买食品为主) http://www
.nuomi.com/changecity
gǎnjí wǎng 赶集网 http://www.ganji.com
wōwo tuán 窝窝团 http://beijing.55tuan.com
tuánhuá suàn 聚划算 http://ju.taobao.com
měi tuán 美团 http://www.meituan.com
lāshǒu tuán 拉手网 http://www.lashou.com
800 http://www.tuan800.com
tuángòu 58团购 http://t.58.com/bj

WHAT TO BUY IN CHINA
在中国买什么 zài zhōngguó mǎi shénme

As few as twenty years ago, consumer goods and Western food items in China were very limited, especially high quality goods. Now you can find just about anything you want, from all the latest Western and Japanese brands to high quality Chinese goods.

Shopping in China can be a wonderfully adventurous experience if you like bargaining, rummaging through countless stalls at markets, or the thrill of the pursuit of bargains and one of a kind items. Or, it can be fairly routine if you stick to established stores with set prices. The goods and places to buy things in China will appeal to all kinds of shoppers and mindsets.

For those shopaholics, keep in mind that duty rates may apply if you are returning to your own country with large quantities of purchased items. For U.S. citizens, for example, there is usually a personal exemption of up to US$1600 in goods that is duty free. Beyond that you may be responsible to pay duty charges. It is a good idea to check with U.S. Border & Customs Agency for current rules. Information can be found at http://www.cpb.gov.

One more thing to keep in mind is the proliferation of fake goods that are sold widely and openly in China. They range from designer handbags and clothing to pirated CDs, DVDs, and computer software. It is illegal to bring these items into some other countries including the United States, and they can be confiscated when you go through customs on your return to the U.S. Technically you cannot leave China with fake goods either, but the chances your goods will be confiscated in China are pretty remote, unless you had a large bag full of obviously fake handbags or something like that.

It is also illegal to bring live plants or fresh food products into the United States. I was returning to the U.S. just before Chinese New Year once, and the plane was full of Mainland Chinese going to the U.S. Most of them had packages of pressed duck. I assume this was to give to friends and relatives as gifts. What they did not know was that it couldn't be brought into the U.S. There was a garbage can literally overflowing with expensive duck and a line of many unhappy Chinese going through customs that day.

■ Souvenirs 纪念品 jìniàn pǐn

Every tourist location from the Great Wall to the Forbidden City will have dealers selling souvenirs...Chinese style paintings, knick-knacks, t-shirts, figurines, other trinkets. (When I take students to China, at the first site they get very excited about certain things and are eager to buy something thinking that they will never see anything else quite like it. I tell them to take their time, because every tourist spot sells the exact same goods. They soon learn that sure enough, exactly the same souvenirs are sold at nearly every tourist site.) These souvenir "malls" are often strategically located at the entrances to the sites. For example, at the museum of the terracotta soldiers outside Xi'an, there is a veritable gauntlet of souvenir booths located between the parking lot and the museum. You are thus forced to walk through this area, and the vendors can be aggressive and relentless. They will use all kinds of tactics to get you into their stall and buy something; they will yell out to you in broken English, and sometimes even grab you and try to physically pull you into their stall. If you express even the slightest bit of interest, they will hound you, even following you and harassing you. If you do not want to shop, simply keep your eyes straight ahead, keep walking, and ignore them. You can use the following expressions to express your disinterest.

búyào 不要 I don't need it.
búyòng 不用 I don't want it.
wǒ bùmǎi 我不买 I'm not buying it.

You may see things that look old and antique, but there is a whole industry in China that makes "antiques." Be assured that they are not authentic. You may even have someone approach you with a story that he and his friends were working out in the fields and unearthed some ancient pottery, or something like that. They will show you some things usually wrapped in newspaper and offer to take you to a nearby location and sell you these priceless treasures. To be considered a true antique in China, the item must be from the last imperial dynasty (pre-1911), and must be authenticated and stamped by the government as such. True antiques like this are not allowed out of the country. If you are caught trying to transport true antiques out of the country, the penalties are stiff, the least of which being that the item will be confiscated.

■ Arts and crafts 工艺品 gōngyì pǐn

A wide variety of arts and crafts are available in China and appeal to natives and foreigners alike. These include woodcut pictures **mùkè túpiàn** 木刻图片, paper cut pictures **jiǎnzhǐ huà** 剪纸画, kites **fēngzheng** 风筝, puppets **mù ǒu** 木偶, Beijing opera face masks **jīngjù liǎnpǔ** 京剧脸谱, chopsticks **kuàizi** 筷子, fans **shànzi** 扇子, paintings on scrolls **juǎnzhóu huà** 卷轴画, chops **yìnzhāng** 印章, calligraphy **shūfǎ** 书法 and calligraphy supplies such as brushes **máobǐ** 毛笔, ink **mò** 墨, and inkstones **yàntái** 砚台. Ceramics **táocí** 陶瓷 such as teapots **cháhú** 茶壶, tea cups **chábēi** 茶杯, bowls **wǎn** 碗, vases **huāpíng** 花瓶, figurines **nírér** 泥人儿, and such can be relatively inexpensive in China. Silk items **sīchóu** 丝绸, such as robes **shuìpáo** 睡袍, pajamas **shuìyī** 睡衣, fabric **bùliào** 布料, wall hangings **guàtǎn** 挂毯, and so on are also good finds.

Pearls **zhēnzhū** 珍珠 and jade **yùshì** 玉饰 and other jewelry **zhūbǎo** 珠宝 can be a great bargain in China.

Buddhism-related items such as statues of Buddha **fóxiàng** 佛像, incense **xiāng** 香, scriptures **jīngwén** 经文, prayer beads **niànzhū** 念珠, and other paraphernalia are popular for some. Shops that sell this kind of thing are usually clustered in and around Buddhist temples. There are usually street vendors around Buddhist temples too.

Be very careful that you are buying authentic products. It's easy to get scammed. Many vendors will sell fake and authentic products side by side, and if you don't know better you'll walk away with the fake stuff thinking it is real.

■ Antiques 古玩 **gǔwán**; 文物 **wénwù**

Most large cities have an antiques market. As mentioned above, the vast majority of "antiques" are not antiques at all but are modern reproductions made to look old. They can be very good. This is fine for most people except the serious collector. True antiques are very valuable and are also difficult to get out of the country legally. Antiques include porcelain ware, Buddhist related objects **fójiào de dōngxi** 佛教的东西, furniture **jiājù** 家具, paintings **huà** 画, chops **yìnzhāng** 印章, "ancient" coins **gǔbì** 古币, daggers **bǐshǒu** 匕首, books **shū** 书, and even Mao-era paraphernalia, such as cultural revolution socialist-realism posters **wéngé túpiàn** 文革图片, Mao buttons **máo zhǔxí xiàngzhāng** 毛主席像章, or Mao's Little Red Book **máo zhǔxí yǔlù** 毛主席语录.

■ Tea 茶 **chá**

Tea is such an integral part of Chinese culture and society that it's no wonder that tea shops abound in every city. In some cities there may be entire markets dedicated to tea leaves **cháyè** 茶叶, such as Guangzhou's **cháyè shìchǎng** 茶叶市场. At tea shops or markets a wide array of tea leaves are available

• BEHIND THE SCENES •

Avoiding Misspending

When shopping in China, it can be easy to get carried away with your spending. The foreign currency often doesn't feel like real money, and also you may not be completely familiar with the exchange rate. To keep these factors from tripping you up, remember to use the calculator on your cell phone to quickly check the amount's equivalent in your native currency. This sort of reality check can help you make sure you're paying a normal price.

(see Chapter 3 for more information on different kinds of tea). Tea shops also sell teapots, tea cups, tea diffusers, and other tea-related items like tables and chairs.

Larger tea shops offer tea tasting for the true connoisseur. You will be invited to sit at a table, often an elaborate dark burnished wood table made from tree roots. Steaming tiny cups of tea are available so that you can try a wide variety.

Tea is sold either prepackaged, or by weight then carefully wrapped for you. Of course you can buy tea, both prepackaged and bulk, at most grocery stores, but the quality of tea available at grocery stores is of much lower quality. To get really good tea and a much broader variety you need to go to a dedicated tea shop. Tea makes great gifts for tea-drinking friends back home, especially those teas that are harder to get outside China.

■ **Books 书 shū**

Bookstores abound in China. The online buying phenomenon has not affected China as much; although some Western countries' bookstores are slowly going out of business, in China book stores are still thriving. The largest bookstore chain is the state-run Xinhua Bookstore **xīnhuá shūdiàn 新华书店**, and other large and small bookstores can be found in nearly every Chinese city across the country. Chinese books tend to be very reasonably priced compared to buying books in the U.S.

The Chinese are ever anxious to learn English, and this is reflected in the quantity of English language books that are available in China. **Xīnhuá** 新华 as well as other large bookstores in major cities always have a section with English-language books. They typically carry bestsellers or other popular books as well as classics of English and world literature. These are Chinese-published books and so are quite inexpensive. If you have a hankering for some Mark Twain, Joseph Conrad, or Leo Tolstoy, you will probably be able to find it in a large Chinese bookstore. To find a bookstore in the city where you'll be, it is best to consult a travel guidebook; they usually list bookstores, especially those that carry English books. Bookstores also sell maps, CDs, VCDs, and DVDs, electronic dictionaries, and art, calligraphy, and stationery supplies. Book malls are also common in bigger cities.

■　■　■

USEFUL PHRASES

convenience store **biànlì diàn** 便利店

department stores that are typically multi-storied (an outdated term) **bǎihuò** 百货

department stores 商店 **shāngdiàn**

large department stores **shāngchǎng** 商场

discount stores or an area where there are many individual booths selling goods **gòuwù guǎngchǎng** 购物广场

flea market **tiàozao shìchǎng** 跳蚤市场

food markets; farmer's market **nóngmào shìchǎng** 农贸市场

market **shìchǎng** 市场

market that sells produce **cài shìchǎng** 菜市场

night market **yèshì** 夜市

shopping mall **gòuwù zhōngxīn** 购物中心

specialized market **zhuānxiàng shìchǎng** 专项市场

street lined with stores or a shopping district **shāngyè jiē** 商业街

store that sells only one brand of things **zhuānmài diàn** 专卖店

Sunday market **zhōurì shìchǎng** 周日市场

supermarket or other kind of store where you select items off the shelf yourself **chāoshì** 超市

bird market **niǎoshì** 鸟市
book market **shūshì** 书市
electronics market **diànnǎo chéng** 电脑城; **diànzǐ shāngchǎng** 电子商城
fish market **yúshì** 鱼市
flower market **huāhuì shìchǎng** 花卉市场; 花市儿 **huāshìr**
household goods and hardware **zhuāngshìchéng** 装饰城
knick-knacks market 小商品市场 **xiǎo shāngpǐn shìchǎng**
tea market **cháyè shìchǎng** 茶叶市场
Dirt Market **wūgòu shìchǎng** 污垢市场
Donghuamen Night Market **dōnghuámén yèshì** 东华门夜市
Dongtai Road Antiques Market in Shanghai **dōngtái lù gǔwán shìchǎng** 东台路古玩市场
Panjiayuan Market in Beijing **pānjiāyuán shìchǎng** 潘家园市场
Silk Market in Beijing **xiùshuǐjiē** 秀水街

Can you give a discount? **kěyǐ dǎzhé ma?** 可以打折吗?
Can you give it for a bit cheaper? **kěyǐ (gěi) piányi yīdiǎn ma?** 可以（给）便宜一点吗?

bartering **tǎojiàhuánjià** 讨价还价; **jiǎngjià** 讲价
cashier booths 收银 **shōuyín**
online shopping **wǎngshàng gòuwù** 网上购物; **wǎnggòu** 网购

Names of Stores
Alldays **hǎodé** 好德
CSF Market **chāoshìfā** 超市发
C-Store **xǐshìduō** 喜士多
Carrefour **jiālèfú** 家乐福
Dafang Convenience Store **dàfāng**

biànlì 大方便利
FamilyMart **quánjiā** 全家
Hualian **huálián** 华联
Ikea **yíjiā** 宜家
Jingkelong **jīngkèlóng** 京客隆
Kedi **kědì** 可的
Metromart **màidélóng** 麦德龙
QUIK **shànghǎi huálián kuàikè biànlìdiàn** 上海华联快客便利店
Suguo **súguǒ** 苏果
Wu Mart **wùměi** 物美
Walmart **wòěrmǎ gòuwù guǎngchǎng** 沃尔玛购物广场/ **wòěrmǎ** 沃尔玛
Watsons drug store chain **qūchénshì** 屈臣氏
Xinhua Bookstore **xīnhuá shūdiàn** 新华书店

USEFUL WORDS

Items to buy
"ancient" coins 古币 **gǔbì**
antiques **gǔwán** 古玩 / **wénwù** 文物
arts and crafts **gōngyì pǐn** 工艺品
Beijing opera face masks **jīngjù liǎnpǔ** 京剧脸谱
books **túshū** 图书
bowls **wǎn** 碗
Buddha statues **fóxiàng** 佛像
Buddhist related objects **fójiào de dōngxi** 佛教的东西
calligraphy **shūfǎ** 书法
calligraphy brush **máobǐ** 毛笔
ceramics **táocí** 陶瓷
chops **yìnzhāng** 印章
chopsticks **kuàizi** 筷子
clothing **fúzhuāng** 服装
cultural revolution posters **wéngé túpiàn** 文革图片
daggers **bǐshǒu** 匕首
fabric **bùliào** 布料
fans **shànzi** 扇子

figurines **nírér** 泥人儿
food **shípǐn** 食品
furniture **jiājù** 家具
household electronics **jiāyòng diànqì** 家用电器
incense **xiāng** 香
ink **mò** 墨
inkstones **yàntái** 砚台
jade **yùshì** 玉饰
jewelry **zhūbǎo** 珠宝
kites **fēngzhěng** 风筝
Mao buttons **máo zhǔxí xiàngzhāng** 毛主席像章
Mao's Little Red Book **máo zhǔxí yǔlù** 毛主席语录
paintings **huà** 画
paintings on scrolls **juǎnzhóu huà** 卷轴画
pajamas **shuìyī** 睡衣

paper cut pictures 剪纸画 **jiǎnzhǐ huà**
pearls **zhēnzhū** 珍珠
prayer beads **niànzhū** 念珠
puppets **mù ǒu** 木偶
robes **shuìpáo** 睡袍
scriptures **jīngwén** 经文
shopping **mǎi dōngxī** 买东西
silk items **sīchóu** 丝绸
souvenirs **jìniàn pǐn** 纪念品
tea **chá** 茶
tea leaves **cháyè** 茶叶
teapots **cháhú** 茶壶
tea cups **chábēi** 茶杯
vases **huāpíng** 花瓶
woodcut pictures **mùkè túpiàn** 木刻图片
wall hangings **guàtǎn** 挂毯

7

Studying

学习 xuéxí

Studying Chinese has become more and more popular over the years, even bordering on trendy. With enrollments now outnumbering other Asian languages like Japanese, and even outnumbering some European languages, the Chinese have coined the term **hànyǔrè** 汉语热, literally meaning "Chinese hot."

There are now more than half a million foreigners living in China, for reasons ranging from employment to adventure. Many of them are students. With China's increased presence and importance on the world stage, many are realizing the added value of Chinese language skills. With China's importance in the world economy, learning Chinese will become increasingly important, and those who know Chinese will be in more demand. At my university alone, enrollments in Chinese classes have almost quadrupled in the past fifteen years. Anyone with Chinese language and culture skills adds significantly to their existing business,

engineering, or other skills, and to gain professional level proficiency in Chinese it is essential to have some in-country experience.

In this chapter I discuss how the Chinese view education and how this may affect your studies, how to select a program, how to make the most of it, how to hire and use a tutor, and some tips for self-study.

WHEN TO GO TO CHINA
什么时候去中国 shénme shíhòu qù zhōngguó

Learners of Chinese often ask about the best time to go to China to study. Many students want to go as soon as possible. Some have the incorrect idea that the best way to learn a foreign language is always to study the language in the country where the language is spoken. There is no doubt that in nearly all cases this is important and a good efficient way to learn Chinese. But the question remains: when is the best time to go for a student learning Chinese?

The research on the subject shows that the best time to go abroad is after the equivalent of about four college level semesters. This equates to about two years of college level Chinese. Some programs even require this minimum proficiency.

This doesn't mean that you will not get much from your study abroad experience if you go to China as a complete beginner, or after only one year of study. The reason I recommend going after two years of formal training is that with this kind of foundation you will know enough to be able to hit the ground running (**qǐkāi déshèng** 旗开得胜). There will be much that you will be able to do, and you will be able to progress at a much faster rate than a true beginner who has little or no prior Chinese language proficiency or knowledge of the culture. Another advantage to having this base is that it means you have a solid foundation in the structure of the language—you will have a sound knowledge of pinyin **pīnyīn** 拼音 and the tones **shēngdiào** 声调 of Chinese, a good understanding of the writing system and character formation, a basic knowledge of grammar **yǔfǎ** 语法, and hopefully an understanding of basic Chinese communicative norms, including the cultural codes we discuss in this book.

Based on research in second language acquisition, for effective learning to take place there must be a great deal of comprehensible input. That is, the learner must be hearing a great deal of Chinese that is understandable, or just slightly above their level of comprehension. When true beginners go to China, there is an overload of *in*comprehensible input that can slow the process. In other words, the amount of comprehensible input available to a beginner is quite limited. For these reasons the most optimal time to study Chinese in China is after you have developed a solid foundation in the language.

I have taught many students who have first gone to China to teach English and learn Chinese "on the side." In almost all cases, even though they may have learned some Chinese during their time in China, they usually struggle more than my regular students. They have a particularly difficult time with pronunciation. I believe this is due to not having any foundation in the fundamentals of the language before going to China. This is not to say that there are not some individuals who may thrive learning Chinese in China from the very beginning. But they are the exceptions.

CHINESE ATTITUDES TOWARDS EDUCATION
中国人对教育的态度 **zhōngguórén duì jiàoyù de tàidù**

The Chinese have a different perspective on education than what we are accustomed to in the West. These attitudes or paradigms are deep seated, with roots going all the way back to traditional models of education established by Confucian **rújiā** 儒家 ideals. For most of China's history only the very elite had access to education. And education consisted of a Confucian model based on memorization of the Confucian Classics: nine books espoused by Confucian scholars as being the epitome of education. As early as the Han Dynasty (206 BCE–220 CE), this educational system was closely tied to civil service in the Chinese government. A series of civil service examinations, based on knowledge of the Confucian Classics, became the basis of all education in China and lasted until the early twentieth century. The system valued rote memorization of

> A longstanding belief in Chinese education: "once you memorize it, you will be able to use it."

those books, and the ability to regurgitate the information in lengthy, grueling exams.

China's modern education system still exhibits traces of this traditional system that has existed for so long. The Chinese are taught theory and lessons that their ancestors, previous studies, teachers, and others have acquired. They memorize with the expectation that they will be able to apply those lessons in the real world. The thinking is that once you memorize it, you will be able to use it. The Chinese typically readily accept previous learning as truth, and seldom challenge or even question established learning.

It's impossible to overestimate the importance of tests in the Chinese education system. The college entrance exams are called **gāokǎo** 高考. These very stressful tests determine if you can attend college and what college you can attend. They also may determine which major you can select. There is a whole culture surrounding these exams, and parents go to great lengths to insure their children do well on them. Consequently, there is a lot of pressure for students; the outcomes of these tests can determine one's future.

When I lead study abroad groups to China, one of the assignments I have my students do in a Chinese culture class involves interviewing a few people who are college graduates and a few who have a high school, or lower, level of education. The students ask about their jobs, living conditions, leisure time activities, and so on. They are usually surprised by what they learn. College graduates have fairly comfortable lives, typically work about forty hours a week, live in higher-priced apartments, have hobbies, have social lives. Meanwhile, it is not uncommon for the high school graduates to work six or even seven days a week, and ten or more hours a day. Their jobs are often menial with no opportunities for advancement. They have little leisure time and do not make much money. For many it is a dead-end street.

This exercise really shows people why the **gāokǎo** 高考 is so important to Chinese. If you can go to college, your chances of having a good career and a comfortable life are much greater. However, with the opening up of the Chinese economy, there are increasing numbers of entrepreneurs who are very successful, some without much education.

Just as it can be difficult for Westerners going to China to study, it can also be challenging for Chinese to come to the U.S. to study and adapt to our teaching and learning paradigms. For example, I expect students to have read the assigned material before coming to my class. Often when I ask a Chinese student about the reading, he or she has a tendency to repeat back what was in the reading, sometimes quoting verbatim from the text. When I ask what they thought of it—did they agree or disagree with it?—they typically have a very difficult time answering. Furthermore, they're sometimes uncomfortable when they are assigned to read articles with directly opposing viewpoints on an issue. And they may be uncomfortable when they learn that exams in the class may only make up 20 or 30% of their grade. In other words, it takes some time to adapt to another culture's attitudes and practices in education.

Even though Chinese may not be accustomed to expressing their opinions in a class, it does not mean that they do not have opinions. Chinese people have been trained to think that it is good to listen to others and not express your own thoughts. Younger Chinese are more willing to express their own ideas than older Chinese.

To summarize, your Chinese classes in China may have the following characteristics:

1. A heavy emphasis on reading and writing. This may include being required to memorize large numbers of characters. Even oral activities may be represented in characters.

2. A large portion of your grade based on written exams. Even oral exams may be in written form. The focus of exams may be on vocabulary and grammar, and reading and writing.

3. A traditional focus on structure rather than application. There may be more emphasis on learning about Chinese

(i.e., grammar, vocabulary), than actually learning how to use Chinese.

This is not all bad. But it is helpful for learners in China to understand what they are getting themselves into. The very act of studying Chinese in China can be a very valuable insight into Chinese attitudes, culture, and behavior. You will probably learn as much about the Chinese education system as you will Chinese language skills. This will give you valuable insight into the how the Chinese think and act.

SELECTING A STUDY PROGRAM IN CHINA 在中国选择一个 学习项目 zài zhōngguó xuǎnzé yígè xuéxí xiàngmù

There are numerous programs that offer a study abroad experience in China. In fact, there are so many programs that it is practically impossible to keep track of them all. Some are very good and some are very poor, with every variation in between. There are several programs that have excellent established track records. In this section I will only mention a few programs that we know to be well regarded in U.S.

> *When I was a young student studying in China for the first time, I took a **kǒuyǔ** 口语 or conversation class. My fellow students and I were intrigued by the fact that our textbook for this class was entirely in Chinese characters. The language was colloquial, but there was little pinyin. This meant that in order to learn the "conversational" dialogues we had to be able to read them. Furthermore, when we were tested we had to write out dialogues in Chinese characters. This is an extreme example of how the Chinese place great emphasis on the written language.*

academic circles. Keep in mind, though, that there are many other excellent programs.

Many U.S.-based universities offer formal study abroad programs. Some universities may not offer their own program, but may be part of a consortium of multiple universities that offer programs to their students. There are also numerous private organizations that offer study abroad programs in China. It's also possible to go over on your own and study at a Chinese university.

- **Study abroad through your university or a university in your area** 通过你的大学或者你所在地区的大学去留学 **tōngguò nǐ de dàxué huòzhě nǐ suǒ zài dìqū de dàxué qù liúxué**

Many universities in the U.S. offer study abroad programs in China. And many allow non-students or students from other universities to participate. These programs tend to be comprehensive and may include tuition fees for the home institution, tuition and fees at the Chinese university, housing, travel expenses, and meals. In other words, they often offer a complete package that will include all your expenses except your personal spending money.

Other universities' programs may cover only some of the costs and expect students to come up with the rest. At many

universities, any kind of financial aid, such as scholarships and loans that can be used on campus can also be applied to study abroad programs.

Going to China through a U.S. university is often one of the cheaper ways to go, especially if you are already a student at that university. Living in China is relatively inexpensive, so your American dollars go much further than if you were studying here in the U.S. Directors of study abroad programs look for motivated individuals with solid academic records and who are mature, and have good language learning potential.

American universities that have developed close working relationships with Chinese universities through years of contact and cooperation tend to have more solid academic programs.

■ **A China-based program administered by a U.S. university** 由美国大学管理的中国学习项目 **yóu měiguó dàxué guǎnlǐ de zhōngguó xuéxí xiàngmù**
These kinds of programs have an academic focus, and often a consortium of universities participate in the program. They typically have an advisory board consisting of Chinese language professors from various U.S. universities. These kinds of programs accept not only students from their consortium of universities but also students from any university.

One example is Associated Colleges in China (ACC; www.hamilton.edu/china) administered by Hamilton College in New York. The Chinese for this organization is: **měiguó gè dàxué liánhé hànyǔ zhōngxīn** 美国各大学联合汉语中心. This is an academically sound program that offers excellent Chinese language and culture programs in China. They require a language pledge, meaning you must agree to speak only Chinese while participating in the program. You must be at the intermediate or advanced level to apply.

Another example of this kind of program is the well-known and regarded Inter-University Program for Chinese Language Studies or IUP **zhōngwén zhōngxīn** 中文中心 (ieas.berkeley.edu/iup/index.html). This program is administered by UC Berkeley at Qinghua University in Beijing. Formerly it was called the Stanford Center and was located in Taibei, Taiwan.

This is a prestigious program that caters to advanced level language students. It has been a successful training program for academics for years. Teacher-to-student ratios are low, and there is an emphasis on individualized instruction. Participants are expected to use only Chinese. Offerings include a two-month summer, a four-month semester, and a year-long program.

■ **Private organizations** 私营机构 **sīyíng jīgòu**

There are numerous private organizations that offer study opportunities in China. Many of these programs are quite comprehensive and will arrange all aspects of the program for you, from visa processing to housing. Housing options range from home stays **jiātíng jìsù** 家庭寄宿, living in foreign student dorms **zhù liúxuéshēng gōngyù** 住留学生公寓 (**zhù wàiguó xuéshēng sùshè** 住外国学生宿舍), having a Chinese roommate **yǔ zhōngguó shìyǒu tóngzhù** 与中国室友同住 (**yǒu zhōngguó shìyǒu** 有中国室友), and others. There is usually a broad variety of programs and courses available and they're not limited to just language courses. Many of these kinds of programs also offer coursework in history, political science, business, cultural studies, and so on. They offer summer intensive programs, as well as programs during the regular school year, either one semester long, or an entire academic year.

An example of one of these kinds of programs is Council on International Educational Exchange (CIEE; http://www.ciee.org/study-abroad). This organization has been around for a long time and has many study abroad programs in China. There is an academic advisory board that reviews and approves their programs.

■ **Universities in China** 中国的大学 **zhōngguó de dàxué**

Many universities in China offer Chinese language and cultural studies for foreigners. Some of these universities have established programs with U.S. or other universities from around the world. Many also accept individual students. Larger, more comprehensive universities house foreign students in an academic department or school. For example, Nanjing University, a top university in China, has an Institute of International Students, **hǎiwài jiàoyù xuéyuàn** 海外教育学院. This academic unit manages all foreigners learning Chinese, as well as trains graduate students in teaching Chinese as a foreign language. Faculty in this unit are specialists in teaching Chinese as a foreign language.

These kinds of programs accept individual students whether you are a formal university student in the U.S. or not. Programs vary from intensive summer programs to one- or two-year-long comprehensive programs. There is usually a great deal of flexibility in these programs. Applying is simple and usually requires filling out an application and providing a copy of your current passport. Once you are accepted they will send you a student visa application form with a letter of admission that you will send to the Chinese embassy to apply for your China visa.

In these kinds of independent programs, your housing options are flexible as well. Large universities have foreign student dormitories. Off campus housing is also available but usually will have to be arranged yourself. (See Chapter 2 for more information on housing options in China.) With these kinds of programs you will not receive college credit for your classes unless you can convince a U.S. university to accept some transfer credit. This may require that you thoroughly document the coursework you have taken including hours per day in class, textbooks used, homework assignments, quizzes, tests, and so on.

This website provides some basic information about Chinese study programs in China: http://www.cucas.edu.cn

DIRECT ENROLLMENT IN A CHINESE UNIVERSITY
直接在中国的大学注册 zhíjiē zài zhōngguó de dàxué zhùcè

For learners with advanced level Chinese language skills, directly enrolling in a Chinese university to earn a degree is an option. This will require that you take a Chinese proficiency exam, the **hànyǔ shuǐpíng kǎoshì** 汉语水平考试. You must score a minimum of a Level 5 to study liberal arts or social sciences and a Level 4 to study the sciences. These websites show admission requirements for Chinese universities:

> http://www.cucas.edu.cn/HomePage/content/content_332 .shtml
> http://www.cucas.edu.cn/Course Search.shtml

For example, if you go to

> http://www.cucas.edu.cn/BachelorsDegree.shtml

and choose mathematics, you'll arrive at a page where you can see the HSK requirements for studying at different universities and different programs.

Studying at a Chinese university as a regular student is quite a step up from a typical, sheltered, study abroad language-only program. This will require you to attend regular classes in business, engineering, political science, or whatever your discipline is, alongside Chinese students. Lectures will be in Chinese. You will be expected to take notes in Chinese, participate in class in Chinese, take exams in Chinese, and write papers in Chinese. These regular content classes are not geared towards foreigners focusing on learning Chinese as a second language.

Once you have been accepted into a Chinese university,

detailed information will be sent to you about when to arrive and where to go on campus. There will usually be current students and faculty there to meet you and get you oriented. The university often handles tuition by giving you a bank card. You are responsible to deposit money into the account, then the university will withdraw the amounts needed for your tuition payments.

If you have not taken the HSK, you will be required to take it soon after your arrival.

■ What to expect 该期待什么 gāi qīdài shénme

U.S. university classes typically have a syllabus that clearly outlines all expectations for students including what will be covered in the class, materials and resources, how students will be evaluated including all assignments and how they are weighted, as well as other pertinent information.

The first thing you may notice about a class at a Chinese university is that there may be no syllabus, and less structure to the class than what you might expect. This may leave you wondering what will be covered in the class and how you will be evaluated.

Many classes will have course information, including required textbooks, posted online. Chinese students will understand this because they know the system well. Students also become quite close to their classmates as they attend the same classes all together for the entire four years they are students. What may seem second nature and well understood by Chinese students, may seem completely baffling to you.

It is important that as soon as possible, you find out who the class monitor or leader is, the **bānzhǎng** 班长. This person is in charge of communications between the professor and the rest of the class. To illustrate, I knew an American student who was

As soon as you can, find out who the class monitor is.

taking a class at a major university. One day he showed up for class and no one was there. The next day likewise no one was there. This went on for two weeks. He finally contacted the class monitor who told him that the professor was out of town doing some research and class was cancelled. If you are not tied into the system, and are truly an outsider, you simply do not have access to this kind of information that the Chinese students are keyed into. Get to know the class monitor early so you are in the loop with information regarding your class. Make sure that they have your contact information.

You may also be wondering what you are supposed to do to prepare for class each day. Some classes will have specific textbooks, and others will not. Some classes may have a list of suggested readings, but no required reading. When there is required reading, you may be expected to find the books wherever you can (and the Chinese students will know exactly where to find them). There may be a place on campus that only sells textbooks; some department offices may also sell textbooks for their courses; some students will buy textbooks directly from students who have taken the course previously. In other words, there may not be a central location like a university bookstore to buy all your books.

Chinese professors of content classes may treat you in

> *"Studying in China is reasonably inexpensive compared to study programs in other parts of the world. There is a huge variation in tuition costs among programs—large well-known universities in China, like Peking University, can be very expensive, and little-known colleges can be very inexpensive. Just because a school is big and famous doesn't mean it has a monopoly on good language programs: some of the smaller colleges have very good ones."*

a variety of ways. Some may not be used to having a foreigner in their class and may simply ignore you, especially if it is a large lecture class. Other professors will capitalize on the fact that there is a foreigner in the class and may call on you regularly to give the foreign perspective

on the topics that arise. Other professors will simply treat you like any other student.

■ Class participation 课堂参与 **kètáng cānyù**

In the traditional Chinese classroom, the teacher talks, and the students sit quietly and take notes. Students do not ask questions and only speak if the teacher asks them a question and expects a response. Other classes may allow more participation, small group work, student presentations, and so on. It all depends on the teacher. Pay attention at the beginning of a class and if students are not actively participating and not asking questions, then follow suit. Homework is seldom required and grades usually depend on one single heavily-weighted class presentation, term paper, or final exam, or a combination of these things.

SELF-STUDY LEARNING STRATEGIES
自学方法 **zìxué fāngfǎ**

Some people will not have the luxury of a formal university opportunity to study Chinese. Others may find themselves in China for business and without the time to enroll in a formal learning environment. Or you may find that you will need to learn a great deal of new vocabulary to function in a particular job in China. Still others may have studied some Chinese formally and want to continue their studies on their own. Actually, learning a language like Chinese really is a life-long endeavor. You will not likely come to the point where you can say, "Okay, I've learned Chinese now, what's next?" There will always be more to learn.

Successful learners of foreign languages also have mastered how to learn on their own. You can only learn so much in the classroom, then you are on your own and must know some strategies to continue learning without the benefit of a classroom and a teacher.

Below are some strategies to help you make the most of your self-study endeavors.

■ Take advantage of your environment
利用环境 **lìyòng huánjìng**

Being in China is a great advantage to your language learning efforts. You have an instant language learning lab just outside your door. You are surrounded by people speaking Chinese; there are Chinese characters everywhere you turn, and you are immersed in a living society where people act and react according to Chinese attitudes and standards. This can be intimidating, but to be a successful language learner, take every opportunity to use Chinese, even if you could use English. You will make mistakes, but you'll learn from those mistakes and improve.

■ Be positive and confident 积极自信 **jījí zìxìn**
You must believe that you can learn Chinese and use it on a regular basis. If you believe that Chinese is "just too hard," then it is a lost cause. The fact is, Chinese is challenging for the Western learner, but it is not impossible. It will take longer

to learn than European cognate languages, but you can learn it. Thousands of Westerners have. The more confident you are of your abilities and your potential, the more likely you will be a successful learner and user of Chinese.

■ Set goals 制定目标 zhìdìng mùbiāo

Making specific language goals can be a great motivator. Make daily, weekly, and monthly goals about what kinds of things you want to accomplish. It may be as simple as learning and using a few new vocabulary words each day, or as ambitious as being able to order a Chinese meal on your own by the end of the month. You may decide to read a new newspaper article each week, and talk about it with a Chinese friend or colleague.

■ Enlist your friends and colleagues
从朋友同事中得到帮助 cóng péngyǒu tóngshì zhōng dédào bāngzhù

Often we go around saying something thinking it is correct, only to discover later that we have been saying it wrong all along. This is usually because Chinese will not correct your pronunciation. This results in what we call fossilized errors, that is, errors that are difficult to change because we have been making the error repeatedly over time. So ask your Chinese friends and colleagues to correct your pronunciation. This will be hard for most Chinese to do—it's not terribly polite to correct a person, particularly in public—so be insistent. You may need to really convince them that you want them to do this.

■ Repetition is key 关键是重复 guānjiàn shì chóngfù

Learning a foreign language really involves over-learning. That is, you need to practice enough until it comes fairly naturally. Repetition is essential to mastery. The first time you do something in Chinese will probably be fairly difficult; it won't feel very natural. But the twentieth time you do it, it will feel smooth, normal, and natural. This goes for speaking as well as reading.

■ **Use what you have studied**
运用所学的知识 **yùnyòng suǒ xué de zhīshi**

Meaningful learning involves contextualization. That is, you must use the material you have studied in real-life situations, whether that be reading a sign or having a conversation with someone. When you learn a new word or grammar pattern, try to use it in your everyday interactions. Using it in context will help you remember it. Likewise, when you hear a word used by Chinese around you, try using it yourself.

■ **Use a language learning notebook**
使用语言学习笔记本 **shǐyòng yǔyán xuéxí bǐjìběn**

Get in the habit of carrying around a small notebook. Jot down things that you see and hear. Write down vocabulary items that you have studied and want to use. Write down characters on a sign that you don't recognize, or items on a Chinese menu. Later you can look these words up in a dictionary, or ask a friend what they mean. When you encounter a situation that you do not understand, jot down a few notes so you can ask someone later what was going on. This simple notebook can be a great language learning tool.

■ **Be a keen observer**
做一个细心的观察者 **zuò yígè xìxīn de guāncházhě**

Watch carefully how Chinese interact with each other. Pay attention to what they say and how they say it. Observe how people haggle over prices in a market. Watch how they greet each other, how they take leave of each other, how they pay for items at a department store, and so on. If you are ever unsure about what to do in a given communicative situation, watch and listen to what the Chinese do, then imitate their behavior. Remember that communicating in Chinese goes far beyond linguistics. It also involves behavior, mannerisms, gestures, facial expressions, use of space, and so on. You will not be successful if you think you can just do things the way you did at home, but using Chinese language to do it. You must do things the way Chinese people expect people to do things in China.

■ **There isn't always an exact English equivalent**
不是每一句话都有相同的英文表达 **búshì měi yíjù huà dōu yǒu xiāngtóng de yīngwén biǎodá**

Get used to the fact that in language learning, especially learning Chinese, there is often no one-to-one equivalent of words and expressions in English. Rather than asking "How do you say 'hi' in Chinese" the better question is "How do Chinese greet each other?" because the answer then is, it depends on the situation and your relationship with the other person. Understand and accept that the Chinese do things differently; they say things differently than we do in the West. Ordering a meal in China is done very differently than in the West. Learn to play by the Chinese rules of the game. That is, learn how the Chinese get things done and follow suit.

■ **Reading strategies** 阅读技巧 **yuèdú jìqiǎo**

Reading a Chinese text once is usually not enough. I recommend that you read a given text at least three times. The first time, read for the gist; get a feel for what the text is about. The second time, read for details. Try to understand the grammar and vocabulary. The third time, put it all together and hopefully understand the text better. Don't write pinyin or English above the written characters, because that will become a crutch: the next time you see that passage your eye will immediately go to the pinyin and not the characters. It's better to write pinyin or definitions on a separate sheet of paper, or maybe in the margin where you can cover it up when you are reading. This fosters real reading and not decoding.

■ **Flash cards are just a tool** 单词卡片仅仅是一个工具
  dāncí kǎpiàn jǐnjǐn shì yígè gōngjù
Be careful how you use flash cards. Instead of just writing the English equivalent of Chinese words, write down the word in a Chinese sentence so you better understand how it is used. Just knowing how to pronounce a character and knowing its English equivalent does not guarantee that you will actually be able to use it in an appropriate context. Remember that flash cards are simply a tool. It's important to know what words mean, but to be successful you must be able to use them in the right contexts at the right times...which goes far beyond flash cards.

■ **Consider hiring a tutor**
  考虑找一位辅导老师 **kǎolù zhǎo yíwei fúdǎo lǎoshī**
Hiring a tutor can be very beneficial. You can tailor your learning to fit your exact needs and aspirations. See below.

USING A TUTOR
个别辅导 gèbié fúdǎo

Hiring a tutor can be a very effective way to learn Chinese, maintain what language skills you have, or go beyond what you have learned in the classroom.

If you're a beginner and starting from scratch, I recommend that you find some beginning level materials to guide you in your study. I also strongly recommend that you learn pinyin, the romanization system commonly used in China. It

• BEHIND THE SCENES •

Making the Most of Your Tutor

To effectively use a tutor, it's important that you have clear objectives in mind and that those objectives are understood by your tutor. Otherwise, your "tutoring" may actually be chit-chat sessions that wander around but seldom get anywhere substantial. You will get much more mileage from your sessions with clear objectives about what you want to learn. Have clear objectives—you call the shots. In Chinese, this concept is called **quèlì míngquè de mùbiāo—yǒudìfàngshǐ** 确立明确的目标—有的放矢.

If you're using a textbook or phrase book, make a copy of the lesson you want to cover and give it to your tutor. Tell them specifically that you want to work on the material in that lesson for the appointed meeting. This way, they will come prepared, and you can work productively together on practicing the material. If you are not following any formal materials, come up with a specific plan of what you want to learn, then share it with your tutor. For example, if you are a beginner, you might want to work on basic greetings, talking about yourself and your interests, asking others about themselves, and so on. You may also want to learn how to order a meal in a restaurant. Assign each topic to a specific meeting time, so your tutor can come prepared with some vocabulary items and phrases to practice with you.

is not a good idea to make up your own pronunciation system, as this kind of approach tends to be haphazard and incomplete. Based on more than twenty-five years of teaching Chinese, I can confirm that students who know pinyin well tend to have much better pronunciation than those who do not take the time to learn it well. Pinyin is also widely used in textbooks, dictionaries, and other learning materials. Educated Chinese also will be familiar with pinyin. It is an essential tool to have for learning and maintaining your Chinese. For example, imagine if you were having a conversation with a Chinese person and they used a word you were unfamiliar with. If you knew pinyin you'd be able to write down the pronunciation of the word, then look it up in a dictionary.

■ Finding a tutor 找位辅导老师 zhǎo wèi fǔdǎo lǎoshī

The best place to find a tutor is around university campuses. Students are often looking for a chance to make a little money on the side. You may also want to arrange a language exchange—you help a Chinese person with their English in exchange for them helping you with Chinese. There are numerous Chinese students that could use help with their English. A good place to start is with the department of foreign studies, or whatever department teaches Chinese as a foreign language. Many of these kinds of departments not only teaching Chinese as a foreign language, but also have graduate programs for Chinese learning how to teach Chinese as a foreign language. You may also check the English language department, or any other department where you have interests. For example, if you are studying engineering or are an engineer working in China, an engineering student may be best suited to help you with your specialized Chinese language needs. Most campuses have an "English Corner" where people get together in the evenings to practice English. This may also be a good place to meet a potential study partner. Keep in mind that just because someone is a native Chinese person, that does not automatically qualify them as a good tutor or teacher.

Also, you may discover firsthand that some Chinese have a deep-seated belief that foreigners cannot really learn Chinese well. You may need to convince your tutor that you are serious, and that you want to go beyond basic greetings and survival language if that is your goal. Hiring a faculty member, or a retired one, may also be a good bet. Often they can use the extra money and are pleased to interact with a foreign student.

■ **Pay for services rendered** 支付报酬 **zhīfù bàochou**

If you want the best from your tutoring experience, I think it best to hire and pay for your tutoring services. You may have Chinese friends who will offer to help you out, but when they are not getting paid, they may not take it as seriously as if they were getting paid and felt the accompanying responsibility to do a good job. In terms of tutoring, you often get what you pay for.

STILL NEED HELP? SELF-STUDY LEARNING RESOURCES
自学资料 zìxué zīliào

As with study abroad programs in China, there are count-less aids from textbooks to websites to help learners master various aspects of Chinese. When you choose your resources, don't fall for the claims that Chinese is easy, or can be learned in five minutes a day, or that it can be mastered in a short time. It's a life-long process. The many resources available can be important aids in your study and can accelerate and enhance your studies, but they are no substitute for hard work and dedication. Self-study aids are also not a substitute for a formal language program with a qualified teacher.

The Internet has so many programs no one could possibly keep track of them all. Over the years I have surveyed and reviewed numerous language learning programs and aids. As with anything on the Internet, anyone can post anything. And as a result, there are quite a few really bad programs online posted by people who know nothing about teaching or learn-ing Chinese as a foreign language. However, there are some pretty good programs out there as well. Below I highlight a few that I have found helpful for my students and me.

■ **Chinese reading and reference software programs**
中文阅读参考软件 **zhōngwén yuèdú cānkǎo ruǎnjiàn**

There are a number of software programs that are powerful tools that aid in reading Chinese. These programs have built-in dictionaries that save considerable amounts of time when you're reading Chinese. They all work about the same way: when viewing a Chinese document (in characters), simply put the cursor over a Chinese character that you do not know and a pop-up appears showing the definition of the word in English. They also work with English; put the cursor over an English word and the Chinese equivalent will appear. Clicking on the character opens a dictionary of that character that will list other words using that character, as well as a great deal of other information. You can also use these programs as a regular dictionary by simply opening up a new window in the program, then typing in the pinyin for an unfamiliar word, whereupon the Chinese characters will pop up. Select the correct character and the dictionary opens up for that word. Type in an English word and easily get a Chinese equivalent.

Some of these programs work at the system level of your computer meaning that you can open a web browser, and anytime you place the cursor over a Chinese character—say on a Chinese language website—you will get an instant definition of the word. Other programs require that you first cut an article or word from the original document, then paste it into a blank page in the software. Both types of programs work well. Each uses different dictionaries, so you may prefer one program over another. These kinds of software programs include:

Wenlin (www.wenlin.com)
Keytip (http://www.cjkware.com/keytip.htm)
Clavis Sinica (http://www.clavisinica.com)

These programs are sold on their respective websites. Three additional programs are worth mentioning. One is the free online reader called Dimsum. It is available at www.man-darintools.com. This program works just like the programs listed above, but it is not as powerful, and the dictionary it uses is not as complete. I've found it to be useful in a pinch, but not as reliable as the other programs that you have to pay for. Another similar free online program is at http://www.mandarinspot.com. This site offers text annotation and dictionary features. The text annotator allows you to display pronunciation of characters in Hanyu pinyin, Taiwan zhuyin fuhao, and a few others. These two programs can be a bit quirky. Sometimes you get what you pay for. The third program is the Zhongwen Chinese-English Dictionary. This is a free app for the Google Chrome web browser. I have found this to be fairly useful, and it works at the system level so you do not have to cut and paste your documents into the program.

Two similar sites that are popular among Chinese in China are http://fanyi.youdao.com and http://www.iciba.com. The main features of these programs are translation from various languages into Chinese or vice versa, and dictionary functions. They also offer English language learning features. They do not work like annotators where you can convert a Chinese text to pinyin.

■ **Chinese dictionary apps**
汉语词典应用软件 **hànyǔ cídiǎn yīngyòng ruǎnjiàn**

There are a number of apps available for your cell phone, iPod, or other handheld device. They're very handy especially when you don't have access to a computer. Students use them in classes, and they are great for travel. One of the better apps is called Pleco (http://www.pleco.com). It allows you to input Chinese words by pinyin or English, or for an upgrade you can even write the character with your finger and the program will read your handwriting and the appropriate character will pop up. I have found this application to be very useful, especially when you don't know how to pronounce a character.

Another similar program, though not quite as good as Pleco, is Dianhua (http://dianhuadictionary.com). Like Pleco, it also is a free app for the basic program. There are numerous other apps that do basically the same thing. I highly recommend them as great tools for enhancing your Chinese studies.

A final app that is more popular among Chinese is called Kingsoft Powerword (kingsoft-powerword-2010.soft32.com). This is primarily for Chinese who are learning English, but it also has a Chinese-English dictionary and a Chinese-Chinese dictionary. This can be very helpful for advanced learners of Chinese.

■ Online resources 网上资源 wǎngshàng zīyuán

One of the more popular online programs for learning Chinese is Chinesepod, www.chinesepod.com. This program focuses mostly on listening comprehension skills by offering a vast number of short dialogues and discussions from the very basic levels to very advanced levels. It uses an informal chat-style approach that is very user-friendly and entertaining. In addition to listening comprehension, you may also see the dialogues presented in characters, along with translations.

Another Chinese language learning program that focuses on listening skills is http://cctv.cntv.cn/lm/learningchinese. This consists of video programs on a variety of topics. They cover beginning to advanced language levels.

A clearinghouse of sorts, http://www.learningchineseon line.net gives numerous links to Chinese learning resources. It is managed by a Chinese language professor and has wealth of information. It is worth looking around here as a means to find whatever specific tools you need for all aspects of your learning, including pronunciation, listening, reading, grammar, dictionaries, translation, and Chinese programs.

Another valuable resource is http://chinalinks.osu.edu. This site was also created and is maintained by a Chinese language professor. It contains more than six hundred annotated links to China and Chinese language and linguistics-related websites.

A popular online dictionary can be found at:

http://www.nciku.com and http://zhongwen.com

For intermediate level Chinese language written texts, see:

http://www.clavisinica.com/voices.html

For other Chinese language texts of various levels, see:

http://www-personal.umich.edu/ ~ dporter/sampler/sampler .html

8

Working

工作 gōngzuò

A former student who had just completed an internship in China recently told me, "If you don't do it the Chinese way, it's not going to get done." He had just returned from an internship where an American company had failed to secure a contract with a Chinese company because they insisted on playing by American business rules and were inflexible with their Chinese counterparts.

Doing business in China can be a frustrating experience for the typical American businessperson. Unless you understand, at least a little, about how the Chinese do business, it will be difficult to make inroads.

Remember the sports analogy we discussed in the Introduction? It can seem especially applicable to the cultural codes of business interactions. As a reminder, Western business practices are like the game of baseball, and Chinese business practices are like tennis. In both games, players expect their competitors to understand

and obey the rules if they want to play. If you're standing on a tennis court, but behave as though you are playing baseball, not only does the deal not go through, but there can also be other serious penalties to your business's success.

To be successful in China, one must not only understand the "rules" of conduct, but also agree to play by those rules, or at least know when to give and when to make a stand.

There are a number of excellent books on doing business in China and Chinese business etiquette. In this chapter I will only highlight some of the key things to keep in mind. For those doing business in China on a regular basis, or if you are moving to China to do business, I highly recommend that you read the books referred to at the end of the chapter. The more you know, the more likely you will be successful in your business endeavors.

HIERARCHY
等级制度 děngjí zhìdù

Hierarchy is an important and integral aspect of Chinese society and is particularly evident within all Chinese organizations, from government to education to businesses.

In Chinese organizations nearly all the power and authority is maintained with a few individuals at the top of the hierarchy. This usually means the president or owner of the organization. If it is a government organization, or a subsidiary of a government organization, this authority may not even be strictly within the organization—important decisions may be made by a high ranking official who oversees that organization. On the contrary, in U.S. companies, even lower level employees are given the power to make some decisions.

Thus, those you may be working and negotiating with may not have the authority to make any real decisions. This can be frustrating for Western businesspeople. This is also manifest in the reluctance Chinese employees have to offer their own suggestions or ideas. It is also considered inappropriate for lower ranking employees to question decisions made by those higher up. Consequently, relatively straightforward business negotiations may take a number of meetings to hash out all the details.

■ **Exchanging business cards** 交换名片 **jiāohuàn míngpiàn**
One of the first things that is done when meeting for the first time in a business setting is an exchange of business cards. This is done immediately upon meeting for two reasons: 1) so you know the rank of the individuals you are working with, and 2) so you know how to address them. This is important because addressing someone appropriately in Chinese, using their title, reflects their status and importance in the group.

To exchange business cards appropriately, offer your card while holding the card with both hands and bowing the head slightly. When receiving a business card, also take the card with two hands. After receiving the card, take a look, noting the person's name and title. Place the card on the table in front of you so you can refer to it. You may want to arrange the cards in the order that people are sitting around the table.

Most people who regularly do business with foreigners will have Chinese text on one side of their business card and English on the other side. If you will be doing business in China on a regular basis it is worthwhile to have business cards made with Chinese on one side. If you don't know Chinese, you will need someone with Chinese language skills to help you out. You can get business cards made in China very quickly and inexpensively.

■ **How to address people** 如何称呼别人 **rúhé chēnghū bié rén**
The most polite, and safest, way to address people in a business setting is by surname and title. In Chinese, surnames

always come first. Though it is common in the West to refer to someone by their given name, this is only done in China with those with whom you are very familiar. In most business and professional settings it is culturally inappropriate to call someone by their given name. For those people whom you regard as friends, or close associates, you may use their full name, that is, surname plus given name. The vast majority of all your relationships will be with these two ways of address: surname + title, or surname + given name.

In a Chinese work setting, people may abbreviate the title of a superior, such as **zhāng zǒng** 张总 for **zhāng zǒng jīnglǐ** 张总经理 (president or general manager), and **wáng bù** 王部 for **wáng bù zhǎng** 王部长 (minister or head of a section). For colleagues or coworkers who are older than you it is common to refer to them by saying the prefix **lǎo** 老 which means "old" and the surname, such as **lǎo Wáng** 老王, literally meaning "old Wang." If it is a younger colleague or coworker, people may add **xiǎo** 小 meaning "little" to their surname, such as **xiǎo Chén** 小陈, "little Chen." These terms are only used with colleagues that you know well. For all others it is most appropriate to address them by their surname and title, or by their full name.

It is only with very close friends and family that you would use a given name (first name) in Chinese. It takes quite a long time to get on familiar enough terms to use a Chinese person's given name. This is for insiders only. Likewise, the use of nicknames is reserved for the closest and most intimate relationships.

In your business associations you may deal with those who have good English language skills, and maybe have even been educated in the West. They may introduce themselves with their given name, or even an English name, knowing that this is how it is done in the West. It is usually best when in China, to follow Chinese cultural practices. In this case, stick with addressing people using their surname and title, or their full name if you already know them and are comfortable with them.

To greet a business associate appropriately, you would do the following:

Exchange business cards.

Note the person's surname and title.

If the person's surname is Wang, for example, and they are a manager, you would then say, while slightly bowing your head,

王经理，您好。 **Wáng jīnglǐ, nín hǎo.** Hello, Manager Wang.

THE IMPORTANCE OF DEVELOPING AND MAINTAINING RELATIONSHIPS 发展和维护人际关系的重要性 fāzhǎn hé wéihù rénjì guānxī de zhòngyàoxìng

I often try to convince my students that the ultimate reason they are learning Chinese is to develop and maintain relationships with people. In order to be successful in China, in any kind of business, or any other field, you must be able to present yourself in a way that puts people at ease. This means doing things the way Chinese expect people to do things. If the Chinese have to modify their behavior to accommodate you, you are less likely to be able to establish long-term relationships. If you understand how the Chinese get things done, even if you have very basic Chinese language skills, you will be able to develop and maintain important and lasting relationships.

Chinese relationships develop and progress much more slowly than in the West. This is true for personal relationships as well as business relationships. Trust is very important when dealing with the Chinese. Business negotiations with the Chinese follow a different and more gradual path than what you may expect. In the West, we are more concerned

• BEHIND THE SCENES •

Chinese Group Mentality 团队工作精神 **tuánduì gōngzuò jīngshén**

In the U.S., the individual and individualism are most valued. We teach our children to be independent from an early age. We train them to be unique, to make a name for themselves, to stand out from the crowd. This is often how we define success in our society.

The Chinese, on the other hand, find it uncomfortable to be singled out from the group. The basic unit in Chinese society is the group, and Chinese people want to fit in, assimilate, and work for the common good. This is obvious in many aspects of life in China, from dining practices to behavior in the boardroom.

In Chinese business settings group mentality is manifest in a number of ways. Decisions may be evaded or put off by individuals within an organization because if they make the wrong decision they may be criticized by their superiors or may even be punished. Efforts are made to try to get others to express your ideas, so that you yourself do not have to do it directly.

In business meetings, individuals are usually reluctant to offer their own opinions on things for fear they may not be in harmony with their boss and fellow employees. Individuals are not given a great deal of power or authority within an organization, at least at the lower levels. This is saved for those at the top. They may also be unwilling or unable to make any decisions until they have a chance to meet with their superiors thus maintaining harmony within their company's structure.

Getting along with others is of utmost importance in Chinese society and in business organizations. Even though the boss may solicit opinions and ideas, in reality everyone is expected to agree with the boss's ideas and support his decisions.

about hammering out the details of a business proposal than we are about developing relationships with our counterparts. But the Chinese feel that before you get down to the business details, it is important to get to know each other. The Chinese want to know if they can trust you and work with you. Whereas Americans tend to be more focused on contracts and the law, Chinese are more concerned with developing good relationships. In fact, in some cases, the Chinese may not necessarily see a contract as legally binding.

Formal introductions through a mutual contact go a long way in China. Connections and contacts are very important to the Chinese. Contacting a potential Chinese business partner out of the blue, when you've had no prior contact with him or her, usually will not work nearly as well as if you are introduced by a mutual colleague or associate. For example, if I wanted to start a study program at a Chinese university and I did not know anyone at that university, I would ask around among my colleagues in the field to find out if anyone has had any contact with that university. When I found someone who had, I would ask them if they would contact the people at that university in my behalf and make the initial contact. In almost all cases this is the preferred way to make contacts in China. This is not to say that you will not succeed by sending out feelers and inquiries because that sometimes works as well.

Upon arriving in China to meet with potential business partners, you will probably first attend a banquet (see Chapter 9 for more on banquets). This may be followed by other social activities including visiting tourist sites, and more meals. You may not get down to business until the second, third, or even fourth day. It is important that throughout the "relationship development" process, you portray yourself as a professional and remain formal even in what seem like informal contexts. You may be surprised that your Chinese counterparts may dress up even for visits to tourist sites or other seemingly casual activities. The bottom line is: don't let your guard down too much. Try to get to know your Chinese hosts and become familiar with their dynamic. You may be tempted to get casual, crack jokes, and lighten things up a bit. Err on the side of caution and maintain an air of professionalism at all times. For

You may be tempted to try to lighten things up a bit; don't.

example, as mentioned above, always use the correct form of address with your Chinese business partners.

Always be courteous and gracious with your hosts. It is always okay to thank your hosts for all that they have done for you. Make sure you have prepared appropriate gifts to exchange with your hosts (see Chapter 9 for more on exchanging gifts).

THE CONCEPT OF FACE
关于面子 guānyú miànzi

Face can be defined as the positive social image that you present in society. It relates to a person's reputation, dignity, and prestige. Saving face means maintaining your image or integrity in a social context. Losing face means that your reputation or image has been questioned publicly, or at least between two individuals. All societies, including the U.S., have this concept of face, but in China it has far greater social significance. The Chinese talk about face relations, and whole books have been written about face in Chinese society. Face relations are serious business in China, and losing face in public can be catastrophic.

One of the most important aspects of Chinese society is harmony, and face and harmony are intricately connected. In the group or collective mentality of the Chinese, harmony must be maintained within the group at all costs. Losing face or causing someone to lose face disrupts this harmony. This presents some interesting situations for foreigners. These beliefs may even cause you to question the ethics or morality of some situations. You need to remember that we differ from the Chinese in some very fundamental ways. These differences may even cause us to perceive the world differently and react differently to certain situations.

■ **Losing face** 丢人 **diūrén,** 丢脸 **diūliǎn,** 没面子 **méi miànzi**

It is imperative that you are very careful about avoiding causing someone to lose face, and that you avoid causing a loss of face to yourself. There are a few different ways to express this with slightly different connotations.

没面子 méi miànzi

This literally means that you "have no face." It is used when you feel that you have lost face in a social situation, or you feel that others have not respected you in front of others. This may be caused by the following situations:

- Someone criticizes you in public.

- Someone is disrespectful to you in public.

- Someone questions your beliefs or standards in public.

- Your student or employee does not perform as well as others in a competition. Even though you didn't do anything wrong, you feel this loss of face in front of the other student's or employee's teacher or boss.

- You want to date a girl, but you know another guy who also wants to date her has a nicer car than you. You would feel a loss of face picking her up in your inferior car.

丢脸 diūliǎn, 丢人 diūrén

When you do something in public, or in front of someone you feel is important, that causes you to lose face, you may feel **diūliǎn** 丢脸 or **diūrén** 丢人. **Diūliǎn** 丢脸 is the term used for less serious offenses and **diūrén** 丢人 is used for extremely serious issues. This may happen in the following situations:

- You lose your temper in public.

- You slight someone of importance, or fail to recognize them in public.

- You ask someone a question that they don't know the answer to.

- You patronize someone or give them false praise.

Another example of this happens when students from the countryside are studying at a university and their parents come to the city to visit them. People from the countryside are often not accustomed to cities and may not dress as other parents would. The students may feel **méi miànzi** 没面子 about the situation, and when the parents do something inappropriate in public, and the parents realize it, the parents would feel **diūliǎn** 丢脸 or **diūrén** 丢人. Likewise, when others think someone has done something inappropriate in public, it's felt that person has **diūrén** 丢人.

The following situations would cause a loss of face, either yours or that of another person you are dealing with.

- Criticizing someone in public, such as in a meeting.

- Being disrespectful to someone.

- Calling into question someone's beliefs or standards.

- Being caught misrepresenting yourself.

- Losing your temper.

- Embarrassing someone in public by something you say or do. This is similar to the Western situation of "putting your foot in your mouth."

■ Giving face 给面子 **gěi miànzi**

Giving face to someone is doing something for them in a public setting that increases their prestige or image. In other words, it makes them look good to others. The following situations are examples of how to give someone face.

- Praising someone in public.

- Showing support for someone, such as attending a performance or lecture.

- Agreeing with someone publicly even if you really do not agree with them.

- Helping out a friend in front of their friend, or helping out at a friend's activity; he or she will feel that you gave him/her face.

- Acting impressed by someone's job title.

- Complimenting someone on their house, car, kids, etc.

Another newer term related to **gěi miànzi** 给面子 is **gěi lì** 给力. The meaning is slightly different and has broader usage. For example, if your daughter were getting married and you had a friend who really went out of their way to help out, you would say of this person, **tā zhēn gěi lì** 他真给力. It has the general meaning of supporting you. In this context this term is interchangeable with **gěi miànzi** 给面子.

■ Having face 有面子 yǒu miànzi

This is when you do something that makes a good impression of others on you. It is also used when other people do good things for you. For example, if you invited some guests over to your house for dinner, and your spouse prepared an excellent meal, you would feel **yǒu miànzi** 有面子. Or, when other people do things for you in front of others, you would also feel **yǒu miànzi** 有面子.

■ Saving or maintaining face 留面子 liú miànzi

Maintaining harmony in the group sometimes means going to extremes to not cause anyone within the group to lose face. Saving or maintaining good face relations is the primary concern in any kind of meeting, talks, or negotiations.

The Chinese will very seldom ever tell you "no" to your face. This would cause you to lose face, which disrupts the harmony of the group and is not acceptable. Rather than say "no," they will use strategies such as saying it's not convenient **bù**

fāngbiàn 不方便, or they may say something like **kǎolǜ kǎolǜ** 考虑考虑, meaning they will consider it, or research it. Most often, both of these responses mean "no." The Chinese understand this game very well, but Americans often fail to read the signals that are given in a business meeting and become frustrated when they think their proposal is being seriously "considered" or "researched," and then nothing happens.

Another way to maintain face is to go along with the crowd. This is a difficult thing for Americans to do, because it is so ingrained in us to have opinions and to express and defend them. By agreeing and going along with others' ideas, especially those in a higher position than us, maintains harmony and good relations. Rather than directly confront someone, make suggestions in a casual or offhand way, implying that those suggestions are what others want and not necessarily what you believe. When the boss, or someone else in a higher position than you, "takes" or "borrows" your idea, make sure to give them the credit. This all sounds pretty docile and weak from an American perspective, but this kind of behavior will get the best results when communicating with the Chinese. Likewise, in China those in a position of authority over you, such as a boss or teacher, will tell you directly what you did wrong, or if something is not important they won't give you any feedback.

In order to preserve harmony and save everyone's face, the Chinese may resort to lying. To the Chinese it is better to not be forthright and even lie than to cause someone to lose face. These are generally what we call white lies. For example, if a colleague or friend invited you to a fancy meal with exotic food, and they asked you if you liked it, you would respond that it is very good, even if you had been fighting a gag reflex the whole night. By so doing you are making the host feel good. In more serious situations, Chinese are reluctant to lie about things.

When you are wrong about something, and others know it, but do not bring it up in front of others, or if you are in a weak position but others do not point it out, this is what the Chinese call **gěi nǐ liú miànzi** 给你留面子, or others helping preserve your face.

Another example: let's say you were working on a project and you made some mistakes which meant that the project could not be completed on time. Your colleagues would not say anything about your mistakes when discussing the project, and thus would preserve your face.

THE CONCEPT OF GUANXI
关于关系 guānyú guānxi

In the U.S. we often say it is not what you know but who you know. This is especially true in China. Developing relationships, **guānxi** 关系, with the Chinese is absolutely necessary to get anything done. **Guānxi** literally means "relations" or "relationship" but it has far deeper and widespread meanings as well. Chinese talk about their **guānxì wǎng** 关系网 literally meaning "connection net. This is their network of connections: those people with whom they have a relationship and who could theoretically help them get something done. The Chinese also call this **rén mài** 人脉. For example, an individual might say of a colleague that he **rén mài guǎng** 人脉广, meaning that he knows many people, and always knows important information, such as who wants to hire people.

In China, knowing people is very important in getting things done. China has a huge tradition

> *You must be careful with whom and how you offer to help someone or receive help or services. There will always be the expectation that the favor will need to be returned.*

of bureaucracy, and getting things done in a timely manner is sometimes nearly impossible. But if you have some connections, or you know someone who knows someone, you are far more likely to get what you need. This is sometimes referred to

China's huge tradition of bureaucracy makes getting things done a special challenge. The solution? Connections.

as **zǒu hòumén** 走后门 or walking in the back door. At times these connections may border on the unethical or even illegal from an American perspective, but to the Chinese it is simply viewed as how you get things done. Everyone knows it and most everyone plays the game. When you want to get something from someone, or you think they may help you, it is important to cultivate that relationship. Doing this is called **lā guānxi** 拉关系, literally meaning to "pull the relationship." This is often done with gifts, favors, invitations to meals, and so on. For example, if someone wanted to go to the U.S. to study or to work and they thought you might be able to help them out—by introducing them to someone, or helping them write a resume in English, or by pulling some strings with an admissions committee at a university, or maybe they know that you know someone that works in the embassy—they might invite you out for a nice meal. This may be followed up with a gift. Eventually, they would ask you for the favor.

Reciprocity is an important part of **guānxi** building and relations. If someone does you a favor, such as helping you get something done that you would not have been able to do on your own, then you owe them a favor in return. The favor may not be called in immediately; it might be months or even years down the road, but there is a mutual understanding that you will do them a favor in return. This kind of reciprocity is taken very seriously by the Chinese. Be careful about the favors that are granted you, because in most cases you'll be asked for a favor in return. This is not to say that careful records are kept and that the Chinese are vengeful when favors are not returned. Rather, it's simply understood that Chinese will want to help others in return.

Those within a person's in-group are expected to help each other in any way they can. Family, friends, and close associates will go to great lengths to help each other out. They will often call on those in their **guānxi** network to help get things done for each other. As such, do not expect casual acquaintances to go to great lengths to help you with a big favor, unless they see that you may be able to help them with something in the future.

> **These relationships are based on reciprocal obligations; that is, you do me a favor, and I'll return it when the right time arrives.**

This emphasis on reciprocity doesn't mean that the Chinese are selfish, greedy, and unwilling to help someone out unless there is something in it for them. The Chinese are very gracious and giving people. They're especially mindful of foreign guests in their county and will often go out of their way to make sure you are comfortable, and that your needs are met. Chinese are often very eager to help foreigners, even total strangers, from helping you buy a train ticket to giving you directions, or going so far as to show you how to get somewhere, or help you shop for a particular item.

If you are planning a career in China, it would be wise to begin as soon as possible to build your **guānxì wǎng** 关系网 or network of connections.

BUSINESS MEETINGS
会议 huìyì

Business meetings (including those in education and other fields) are usually held in a conference room specifically for meetings. Seldom will any official meeting be held in an office. Meetings typically begin on time. The seating arrangement in a conference room can vary slightly, but usually the principal host and the principal guest will sit next to each other on a sofa, or the two teams will sit across from each other at a conference table. The highest ranking individuals will sit closest to the primary host and the primary guest. You will usually be guided on where to sit in a meeting.

Small snacks, such as crackers or fresh fruit, and tea are usually provided at meetings. Sometimes bottled water may also be provided. Once the highest ranking individuals in the room have begun eating the snacks, it is okay for you to eat some.

Be prepared for some long, boring speeches. Oftentimes high ranking officials, whether from within the government or within the organization, will be present at the beginning of a meeting to welcome the guests and get things going. Flowery speeches are often offered that may discuss the organization, including its history, accomplishments, and so on. If you do not understand Chinese these speeches can be pretty painful. Even if you do understand Chinese, they can still be very dull.

Sometimes several officials will give speeches. The primary guest will often be invited to give a short speech as well. These can be formulaic, and include thanking the other party, praising them, and flowery words about the important nature and potential of the meetings. Once these formalities are over, the real discussions will begin.

Meetings can be fairly lengthy with few breaks. Be careful with your tea consumption.

WORKING IN AN OFFICE
办公室的工作 bàngōngshì de gōngzuò

As mentioned above, it is important that you always keep in mind culturally and socially appropriate ways to communicate.

One of the biggest dangers of communicating in Chinese is using the Chinese language, but not paying attention to cultural and social norms. In other words, speaking Chinese, but saying the same kinds of things you would say in English. We call this "speaking English in Chinese."

Take care: "speaking English in Chinese" won't end well.

This leads to misunderstanding, confusion, and oftentimes offense. One example is using American humor, such as sarcasm, in Chinese. Most often this results in offending the Chinese. This is particularly true if you have good Chinese language skills, because the better your Chinese is, the more Chinese will expect you to understand their culture and how to communicate like Chinese.

A Chinese company (not a joint venture or an American company's office in China) will probably be run differently than a similar kind of company in the U.S. You may find the pace of things in a Chinese office slower at times than what you would expect in an American office. Things can be very busy when the boss is around, but when he is away everything may slow down. Sometimes the amount of work will vary, from very busy times to times when there's not much to do. In an American office we are accustomed to keeping ourselves very busy and when there's not much work to do we often look for things to do to stay busy. This may not be the case in a Chinese office. One problem with large state-owned companies is that they often have more people on the payroll than they have work for them to do. The challenge for the boss then is trying to find work for everyone to do. The employees will try to find useful things to do when the boss is around to show that they're busy and useful. In private enterprises and non-state-owned companies work tends to be more along the lines of the U.S., where everyone has a specific job to do and keeps busy with their work.

It is very important that a high amount of respect is given

to your superiors in an office. It is inappropriate to ever challenge your boss on a decision or business practices, especially in front of other workers. Based on your experience in the U.S., you may feel that things are not as efficient as they could be, but it is not your place to make suggestions on how to improve things around the office, unless you are specifically asked to do so. Some Chinese business practices may even seem shady, bordering on unethical, but you must remember that things are done differently in China, and it is not your role to try to reform the Chinese business world. Even if Chinese think it is not right, there is little they can do to change the system.

For example, if another company gave your office gifts for certain aims, you may view that as a conflict of interest. But if everyone else accepts it, you have to go along with the others in your company and accept it as well. Otherwise your colleagues may be suspicious of you, feeling as if you were going to report them. This would also show that you are not a team player.

Do your best to fit in with your colleagues. Being a team player and supporting the bosses' decisions is highly valued in a Chinese workplace. Dissent is looked down upon. Even though you may not agree 100% with decisions that are made, it is important that you are supportive.

You may be accustomed to a private office in the U.S., but this is relatively rare in Chinese work settings. Space is usually

When I was in graduate school I used to eat lunch on my own. Later I discovered that all my classmates (who were native Chinese) ate together in the lunchroom. Once I began eating with them, it really helped to break down barriers. Pretty soon my classmates were inviting me to study groups and parties. It made a big difference in my academic success.

very limited—sometimes seeming crowded—and typically workspaces are shared with others. You may even be required to share a desk with coworkers.

Personal space is not a workplace priority.

In some office settings lunch may be provided in a cafeteria-type setting. You may be tempted to take off to have some quiet time alone during lunch, but if all your colleagues spend the lunch hour together, it is best that you do so as well. This too is viewed as being a team player and will help you in building good relationships in the office. Your colleagues will get to know you better and thus feel greater trust with you.

INTERNSHIPS
实习 shíxí

Internships are relatively new to China. Regardless, an internship is an excellent way to gain valuable insight into how the Chinese do business, and can greatly enhance your educational experience.

Arrangements vary with internship providers. Some may provide housing and some other benefits. Some may even provide a salary, while others will not provide anything other than the opportunity to work and gain experience.

Chinese organizations sometimes are not quite sure what to do with an American intern. They may like the idea of having a foreigner working in their company, and it can indeed boost their reputation. Unfortunately some companies will accept a foreign intern primarily for the prestige value and they may not have much for you to do. Interns may be placed in a company, and given fairly visible office space but little guidance on what to do. They usually end up doing some translation work, but often there's not enough of that to keep them very busy. Boredom can set in quite rapidly. Other internship providers may take on an intern with sincere intentions, but

• BEHIND THE SCENES •

Negotiating Like a Native

A decision making process in China, **zuòchū juédìng** 做出决定, is likely to be a slower process than one in the U.S. The primary reason for this is that decisions are usually only made after several rounds of talks or negotiations. On the Chinese side, various levels of hierarchy need to meet to discuss the issues at hand. Often those directly negotiating with a U.S. team do not have the authority to make a final decision on a matter. After an initial meeting with their U.S. counterparts, they may convene other meetings with other officials in their organization. The frustration that many in the U.S. have with this process is that it's difficult to know who is actually making the decisions and when a decision will be made.

As explained in this chapter, you need to be able to read the signals that are communicated in a business meeting. Remember that the Chinese are not likely say "no" or directly turn down a proposal. It will instead be done in a vague, roundabout way. If you understand the signals, you can be prepared to alter your approach or make changes to your proposal.

may not really know how to utilize that foreigner, especially when they're unsure of your mastery of Chinese, and your set of skills.

It's a common situation I have encountered when students are placed in an internship with a Chinese company: At first there is not much for them to do, beside the occasional translation work. If the student maintains a good attitude, works hard, and displays a willingness to do whatever is asked, things usually turn out well. If you have strong Chinese language skills and some expertise in the business, be patient. Let your boss know what you can and are willing to do. Sometimes it just takes some time for the boss to get to know you and understand your skills. Once a relationship of trust has been developed, and the boss more fully understands your strengths, you will usually be given more and more responsibility.

Some of my former students have started out with hardly anything to do, and ended up attending business meetings, going on business trips with the CEO, doing presentations in business meetings, and working directly with clients. In order for these kinds of developments to happen, it's important that you have a positive attitude, be open-minded to Chinese ways of doing things, work hard, and fit in as well as you can.

■　■　■

FURTHER READING

The following books are highly recommended for those planning to do business in China.

- Bucknall, Kevin. 2002. *Chinese Business Etiquette and Culture*. Raleigh, NC: Boson Books. Offers quite a bit of detail about doing business in China in a straightforward, conversational style.
- Clissold, Timothy. 2006. *Mr. China: A Memoir*. New York: HarperCollins. A memoir detailing the ups and downs of a British businessman trying to buy shares of Chinese businesses in an attempt to make them more profitable. His personal stories are very enlightening.
- Gao, Ge, and Stella Ting-Toomey. 1998. *Communicating Effectively with the Chinese*. Thousand Oaks, CA: Sage Publications. Treats the specifics of Chinese communication from both insiders' and outsiders' perspectives. All key terms are introduced in Chinese characters and pinyin. This book may be more useful for those who speak Chinese, but will be valuable to all.
- Hu, et al. 2010. *Encountering the Chinese*. 3rd Edition. Boston: Intercultural Press. Covers topics for those visiting or going to live in China. Several chapters specifically discuss Chinese business culture.

• BEHIND THE SCENES •

The Importance of Cultural Knowledge 文化背景知识 wénhuà bèijǐng zhīshi

Having Chinese language skills is certainly valuable when doing business in China. Even basic Chinese skills and trying to use Chinese whenever possible will be appreciated by your Chinese business associates. But perhaps even more important is understanding how the Chinese get things done. Understanding what will happen next in a typical situation is valuable knowledge, letting you focus your energies on the task at hand, and not on wondering what's going on and what will happen next.

The future will provide innumerable opportunities to do business in China. Important contacts, contracts, and deals are fumbled all the time due to insensitive and unknowing (but sincere) American businesspeople. Those who know how to play the game have an inside track, and will ultimately be the most successful.

• Seligman, Scott D. 1999. *Chinese Business Etiquette: A Guide to Protocol, Manners, and Culture in the People's Republic of China.* New York: Warner Books. An excellent book that covers all aspects of doing business in China, from how to get in touch with potential partners to dealing with Chinese bureaucracy.

USEFUL PHRASES

exchanging business cards **jiāohuàn míngpiàn** 交换名片
old **lǎo** 老 as in **lǎo wáng** 老王 old Wang; used to address someone older than you and familiar
little **xiǎo** 小 as in **xiǎo chén** 小陈 little Chen; used to address someone younger than you and familiar
Hello, Manager Wang. **Wáng jīnglǐ, nín hǎo** 王经理，您好

face **miànzi** 面子

lose face **diūrén** 丢人, **diūliǎn** 丢脸, **méi miànzi** 没面子
give face **gěi miànzi** 给面子
give support **gěi lì** 给力
he really gave support **tāi zhēn gěi lì** 他真给力
to have face **yǒu miànzi** 有面子
save or maintain face **liú miànzi** 留面子

big connections network that people have **rén mài guǎng** 人脉广
connections network **guānxì wǎng** 关系网

develop relationships or connections with others 拉关系 **lā guānxi**

relationships; connections **guānxi** 关系

relationships that people have with others **rénmài** 人脉

not convenient **bù fāngbiàn** 不方便

to consider it **kǎolǜ kǎolǜ** 考虑考虑

to help preserve your face **gěi nǐ liú miànzi** 给你留面子

walking in the back door; using your connections **zǒu hòumén** 走后门

working in an office; office work **bàngōngshì de gōngzuò** 办公室的工作

USEFUL WORDS

business meetings **huìyì** 会议

hierarchy **děngjí zhìdù** 等级制度

internships **shíxí** 实习

working **gōngzuò** 工作

9

Visiting & Hosting

做客与待客 zuòkè yǔ dàikè

Visiting and hosting are important aspects of Chinese culture. The Chinese are eager to be good hosts, and to be a good host, certain behavior is expected among their guests. To be a good guest you need to know how to show respect and appreciation for your host.

If you spend any amount of time in China, sooner or later, someone will invite you to their home, they'll invite you out for a meal, you'll be a guest at a banquet, or you'll want to invite some friend out for a meal or drink.

In this chapter I'll cover the basics of relationship building in Chinese culture, and some of the rules of social etiquette that are important to understand for a range of social situations you're likely to encounter. Developing lasting relationships with Chinese and cultivating your networks will provide you with much more social mobility.

BUILDING AND MAINTAINING RELATIONSHIPS
建立和维护人际关系 **jiànlì hé wéihù rénjì guānxi**

There are some significant differences between China and the U.S. in the ways we develop and maintain relationships. From an early age, Chinese children are socialized with their classmates in school. And each group of high school students within a specific track takes all their classes together, thus maintaining close contact and relationships throughout their school-age years. Chinese society is also much less mobile than American society. It is unusual for families to move frequently to different cities and parts of the country. The Chinese have more opportunities to maintain the relationships they've developed from an early age.

Those students who go on to college may develop new relationships with their classmates. In Chinese universities, students of the same major all take the same classes at the same time throughout their four-year college careers. This system also helps foster long-term relationships with their classmates. These relationships often last a lifetime. One day I was talking with some elderly men at a park. I asked if they were friends with each other, and one of them replied, "No, we are elementary school classmates!"

The Chinese tend to have fewer close friends but maintain those relationships over longer periods of time than Americans. Americans will often have numerous friends from different periods of their lives, and may not maintain all these friendships throughout their lives. We also have friends with whom we do only specific activities, for example, friends you play basketball with. Though the Chinese may also have these kinds of relationships, it's relatively less common.

Friends are expected to watch out for and help each other out. These obligations seem to run deeper than with friendships in the West. If you have the time and money to help out a friend in need, in China, it is expected that you will. Even without much time or money, a Chinese person would still do all that they could to help out a friend in need. Friendships are developed based on mutual interest, just like anywhere else in the world. But once the relationship is well established, then reciprocal obligations are the expectation. Chinese place great importance on their **guānxì wǎng** 关系网, meaning their "connection net": the people they've built relationships with, who could in theory help them if needed. In the example I give at the right, the aunt was happy to write the letter and it was a very small thing for her to do to help out her nephew's friend. Insiders, such as family members and close friends, will go to great lengths to help each other out. This extends to the other networks that members of the in-group have. The relationships you have with people can greatly enhance your social mobility in China.

> *A friend of mine was living in China and was having a hard time getting an extension on his visa that was about to expire. He learned that the aunt of one of his friends living in New York was a low level government official in Guilin, where he happened to be traveling. She wrote a letter for him, which he took to the local Public Security Bureau (PSB) office and within a few minutes he had his visa extension.*

(For more on the implications **guānxi** has in the world of business, see Chapter 8.)

■ **Male-female relationships and dating**
异性朋友及约会 **yìxìng péngyǒu jí yuēhuì**
Just as with any relationship, in China, male-female relations tend to develop and progress rather slowly and cautiously. Potential partners are often introduced by a third party, such

as a mutual friend or parents or other relatives. Dating as we know it in the West—that is, casual relationships and flirting—is not common in China. Chinese individuals typically do not become exclusive partners unless the relationship is very serious. The Chinese may go out together, but they do not call it dating. Americans need to be cautious when developing relationships with members of the opposite sex. What may appear to you to be casual flirting or dating, may be interpreted as much more serious intentions by the Chinese.

Casual dating? It's just not Chinese.

After a period of time associating with classmates, friends, and colleagues, people may of course begin to have romantic feelings toward someone. Usually a person won't ask out another until they already know the person quite well. (In the U.S. we often will ask someone out to *get* to know them, but in China you typically would not ask someone out on a date unless you already knew them and had strong feelings for them.) The notion of dating, **yuēhuì** 约会, is reserved for serious relationships that often lead to marriage. If a young man and woman are introduced by a third party, they both know the aim, and they will already know about each other pretty well. After the first or second time going out together, they will decide if they want to further develop the relationship. In this kind of situation, the first time the couple gets together is called **jiànmiàn** 见面, meaning "to see face" or to simply see each other. Subsequent outings are called **yuēhuì** 约会, or what we would call dating. If they continue to see each other and have mutual affection, they will often introduce each other to family and friends, and they become boyfriend and girlfriend. However, in general, most people do not continue a dating relationship after the first meetings.

■ **Expressions of affection** 感情的表达 **gǎnqíng de biǎodá**

New students of Chinese often ask how to say "I love you" in Chinese. I'm not sure why they want to know this, but the answer I give them is, "You don't say that in Chinese." This is usually met with some confusion.

The Chinese are not verbally expressive with their emotions. It is rare for Chinese to openly say that they love each other. Several years ago I was curious about this and surveyed a few native Chinese female colleagues. My questioning went something like this:

"Do you ever say 'I love you' to anyone?"
"No, we don't say that." (nervous giggling)
"What about with your husband?"
"No way." (more nervous giggling)
"Why not?"
"Because if you have to say it, then there is something wrong, and it will sound contrived."
"What about to your kids, or your parents?"
"No."

The Chinese are more likely to express affection for each other through their actions and not through what they would consider empty words. In other words, you show your affection for someone not by saying it, but with kind acts that show them you love and care about them. Even the seemingly innocent expression **wǒ xǐhuān nǐ** 我喜欢你 "I like you" is considered quite serious. That is, you wouldn't say it to someone of the opposite sex unless the relationship was very serious.

The Chinese are also less likely to open up and talk about their feelings, particularly with regard to a relationship. There are seldom the deep conversations about the relationship between a boyfriend and girlfriend, such as the DTR (Define the Relationship) talk, common in the U.S.

In the past decade, relationships have become more

casual, no doubt due to globalization, but in general they are still much more conservative than in the West. Those who overtly flirt with the opposite sex are still considered to have loose morals. However, with Westerners, sometimes Chinese are more straightforward, because that is how they expect us to be.

GIVING AND RECEIVING COMPLIMENTS
给予和接受赞扬 jǐyǔ hé jiēshòu zànyáng

In the West we have been conditioned to accept compliments with graciousness. When we are complimented on something it is appropriate to say "thank you" or "that is very kind of you," or something along those lines. In other words, we acknowledge the compliment and thank the person for giving it.

In Chinese culture, the appropriate way to accept a compliment is to downplay, deflect, or deny it. In China the Chinese will compliment you in a variety of ways and for a variety of purposes. If you speak any Chinese at all, they will probably say something like **nǐ shuō zhōngwén shuō de hěn hǎo** 你说中文说得很好, "You speak Chinese very well." You may have been studying it for years; you might want to say "thank you **xièxie** 谢谢," but the appropriate response is to downplay, deflect, or deny the compliment, by saying something like **búshì, wǒ zhǐ huì shuō yìdiǎn(er)** 不是，我只会说一点（儿）, "No, I only can speak a little." Or you can be even

more emphatic and say something like, **búhuì, wǒ zhēnde hěn bèn** 不会，我真的很笨！, "No I don't, I'm really an idiot." Or you can use the generic response for denying a compliment and say **nǎlǐ nǎlǐ** 哪里哪里 "No, no." Remember that by downplaying, deflecting, or declining a compliment, you are acknowledging and accepting the compliment in a culturally appropriate way.

A compliment? Be sure to downplay, deflect, or deny.

I remember the first time I encountered the practice of denying compliments. I was living in Hong Kong and had met a young mother with two adorable little kids. I told her that her kids were really cute. Her response astonished me. She said the equivalent of "What? These little brats; they're useless; all they do is sit around and watch TV." My immediate reaction was "verbal child abuse!" In my naivete, I was thinking that the poor kids were sure to grow up with some serious self-esteem issues.

When someone has complimented you, it is appropriate to give a compliment back. If someone has complimented you on your Chinese you might compliment them on their English. Or you could respond to the compliment about your Chinese with something like **méiyǒu nǐ de yīngwén nàme hǎo** 没有你的英文那么好, "It's not as good as your English."

You need to be careful about how you compliment someone. For example, if you really like a painting hanging on the wall of a friend's home, rather than say **wǒ hěn xǐhuān nàzhāng huà(er)** 我很喜欢那张画（儿）"I really like that painting," say **nàzhāng huà(er) hěn piàoliàng** 那张画（儿）很漂亮 "That painting is pretty." With the former compliment, the Chinese may feel inclined to offer the painting to you as a gift, whereas the second compliment will be received without any pressure.

Knowing when to compliment someone is pretty straightforward and not too different than what you're used to. Here are some times you might give someone a compliment:

For a skill (like speaking English, or doing well at their job)
For an attractive object or article of clothing
For a job a well done
For their apartment

For their car
For their children

I recommend that you practice paying compliments with people you won't see again, before trying it out on work associates or other long-term relationships. For example, if you jump in a taxi to go someplace, practice complimenting the driver on his car or on his driving. Notice how he responds and do likewise when someone compliments you. That way you can become comfortable giving and receiving compliments before you are in a "high stakes" situation.

A WORD ABOUT "THANK YOU" AND "PLEASE"
关于谢谢和请 **guānyú xièxie hé qǐng**

In American culture we say "thank you" and "please" almost constantly. We use these polite phrases in nearly all situations, formal and informal alike. For example, at the store, we might thank a clerk for ringing up our purchase. And we'll say "please" to practically anyone.

When interacting with people the Chinese are very aware of in-group and out-group relations. In-group people are those you are very familiar with, such as family members, close friends, maybe certain colleagues. Out-group individuals include everyone else.

With in-group individuals, polite language is not necessary because you are so close to these people. (If you were to insist on using polite language with your in-group people, they would see this as your intentionally wanting to distance yourself from them. In other words, it would be rude.) And the Chinese are not as likely to use polite language with strangers they will probably never see again. This may seem rude to an American, but it is common in Chinese interactions. Polite language is used in formal occasions such as in business or educational settings, when meeting someone for the first time, and when dealing with people with higher social status than you, such as a boss, teacher, someone higher up in a company than you, and so on.

You may notice that Chinese may use more polite language with foreigners than they do with each other. This is a reflection of the idea that foreigners are considered guests and should be treated with preference.

It can be hard for Americans to drop these phrases as their use is so ingrained in our thinking. Students in China for the first time tend to overuse "thank you" **xièxie** 谢谢, saying it to everyone, seemingly all the time. The Chinese find it odd, even downright strange, that you would say thank you to a total stranger, or to someone of an obviously lower social status than you, like a person selling fruit on the street. The appropriate way to interact in these situations is to simply not use "please" or "thank you." When at a store, instead of saying "May I please see such-and-such item" just say "I want to see such-and-such." When you have made a purchase, gather your things and leave; no thank you is needed. Sometimes a clerk will say thank you to *you* as you're leaving.

GIFT GIVING
赠送礼物 zèngsòng lǐwù

Gift giving is an integral part of Chinese social interactions. It's another way of creating and building **guānxi** or relationships with people. There are a variety of occasions when gift giving is appropriate, even expected, in China. If you're going to China to study or work, they might include:

- Visiting a friend or colleague at their home, such as for a dinner appointment.
- To show appreciation to an individual for a special service or kindness.

- To show appreciation to an institution for hospitality or services.
- Visiting a sick person.
- When you're an invited guest, for instance visiting a company or school.
- When a friend opens a new company or shop.
- When you have asked for help from someone, or someone has helped you out.

So, obviously, it's important that when planning any trip to China, you prepare a variety of gifts. Some gifts may be designated for specific individuals or occasions, but there will likely also be unanticipated times when you'll need a gift. When packing your bags, have a good supply of gifts on hand, from more expensive planned gifts to several inexpensive just-in-case gifts.

Gifts that are most appreciated are often associated with the country, or even better, the specific location you are from. These kinds of gifts may include coffee table picture books of your city or national parks, or mugs, t-shirts, paperweights, and so on that display your company or school logo.

■ Whom to give gifts 送给谁礼物 sònggěi shéi lǐwù

It is not necessary to give gifts to everyone you encounter, but it is important to give gifts to those with whom you have regular contact. This may include teachers, school administrators, tutors, government officials, company officials, colleagues in business, education, or government, and close friends. You may also give small gifts to people like tour bus drivers, tour guides, children of colleagues, and any other person who has done you a favor.

■ Accepting gifts 接受礼物 jiēshòu lǐwù

It is common among the Chinese to gently refuse a gift when it is given. The giver will then insist. After a couple of gentle

• BEHIND THE SCENES •

What Kinds of Gifts Should You Give?

A thoughtful list of appropriate gift ideas is offered in the pages of **Encountering the Chinese** by Hu, et al. (Intercultural Press). These ideas include books, CDs, maps, posters, and art prints, calendars (at the appropriate time of year), food items unique to your home region, stamps, clothing like t-shirts, hats, and scarves with logos on them, toys and games for children, souvenir items such as pins, pens, and so on, and local handicrafts.

Remember that the more important the person is to whom you are presenting a gift, the nicer the gift should be. For example, you would not want to present a New York Yankees pin to the CEO of a company you are doing business with, but that might be appropriate to give to the child of a colleague. The type of gift to give also depends on the relationship you have with the person. For close friends, relatives, and people who are important to you, you will want gifts that are more deluxe. For all others, smaller, more inexpensive gifts are appropriate. When visiting people in a professional context, I have given pens, paperweights, deluxe coffee table books, and so on.

refusals, the receiver should graciously accept the gift. This gentle refusal is the Chinese way to express humility and gratitude. When accepting a gift, you may say things like:

nín tài kèqi le 您太客气了。 You're too polite.

nín kàn nín hái pòfei 您看您还破费。 You're spending too much.

ràng nín pòfei le 让您破费了。 You're squandering your money.

The person giving the gift might respond with phrases like:

Yīdiǎn (er) xiǎo yìsi 一点（儿）小意思。 It's a small thing.

yīdiǎn (er) xiǎo lǐwù 一点（儿）小礼物。 It's just a small gift.

yīdiǎn (er) xīnyì 一点（儿）心意。 It's just a small token (of my regard).

Be careful that you do not give or accept gifts that are too expensive, especially in a business context. You would not want

> *A caution about gift giving: Remember that it's a reciprocal activity. That is, when you give a gift to someone, there's an unwritten obligation that they also must give you a gift. So be careful to whom you present gifts. And because you may unexpectedly receive a gift from someone, it's a good idea to have several generic "just in case" gifts at the ready.*

to present a very nice expensive gift, only to have your host lose face by presenting something of obvious lesser quality. It is also very important that you do not *accept* a large, expensive gift. By accepting these kinds of gifts you are opening the door for a favor being required from you in the future. The person giving an expensive gift will most likely expect some favor in return. One way to decline expensive gifts is to say that your company or institution does not allow its employees to accept expensive gifts.

■ **What not to give 不合适的礼物 bù héshì de lǐwù**

In general people do not like to receive clocks as gifts, especially older people, as this signifies death. Young people do not give cups, because in Internet language the word for "tragedy" sounds the same as the word for "cup." Do not give friends scissors or knives as this is symbolic of a break up, and for older people do not give shoes, which in Chinese has the same pronunciation as "evil."

ACCEPTING AND DECLINING INVITATIONS
接受和拒绝邀请 jiēshòu hé jùjué yāoqǐng

Undoubtedly there will be numerous occasions when you will be invited to do something for one reason or another. This may be for a meal, to visit someone at their home, to go on an excursion together, or to simply go out shopping, drinking, or clubbing. When accepting an invitation it is important to act tentative, like they are going to a lot of trouble by inviting you. It is common to use expressions like:

Nín tài kèqi le. 您太客气了。 You're too polite.

Tài máfan nǐ le. 太麻烦你了。 This is troublesome to you.

Nǐ búyòng nàme kèqi. 你不用那么客气。
You don't need to be so polite (gracious).

In other words, it's polite to reluctantly accept an invitation.

You may have a number of reasons to decline an invitation, but don't go into any details about why you cannot accept. The most common expression used to decline an invitation is simply, **wǒ yǒu shì (er)** 我有事（儿）, meaning literally "I have things." You may also be more apologetic by saying, **duìbùqǐ wǒ yǒu shì (er)** 对不起，我有事（儿）, "Sorry, I have something." This is a very handy phrase to know and use. When using this expression, the Chinese understand that you are not available. The reason is not important. In fact, it is not polite to explain why you cannot accept the invitation. The reason for this is that if the person inviting feels as though your excuse is weak, or that the other business you have to attend to is not deemed as important as their offer, face is lost. When it is left vague using the above expression, both parties retain face and social harmony is maintained. If you are close to the person it is appropriate to negotiate another time to get together. Another common expression used to decline an invitation is to say **bútài fāngbian** 不太方便, meaning "It's not too convenient," or **bùhǎo yìsi, bútài fāngbiàn** 不好意思，不太方便 meaning "I'm really sorry, it's not too convenient." This is a common code for expressing that you cannot accept the invitation for some reason. Another common expression is **wǒ yǐjīng yǒu ānpái le** 我已经有安排了 meaning "I already have something arranged or planned." You may also make up an excuse such as:

Wǒ yǒu diǎn(er) bù shūfu. 我有点（儿）不舒服。
I'm not feeling too well.

Jiālǐ yǒu diǎn(er) shì (er). 家里有点（儿）事（儿）。
I have something at home.

VISITING SOMEONE AT THEIR HOME
去别人家里做客 qù biérén jiā zuòkè

It is not uncommon for a Chinese friend, classmate, or colleague to invite you to their home. It may be for a meal, or it may be just for a visit although that is rare. Sometimes more affluent Chinese like to show off their house to guests.

It is important when visiting someone at their home to be gracious and appreciative. When preparing for your visit, bring a small gift. It may be a bottle of wine, flowers, or something from home, or something with your institutional logo if you're in China from a university or company. Appropriate gifts may also include a coffee table book of photographs from the region where you come from, or other books. If your host has small children, consider offering small toys.

It is important to show up on time, or even a little early. The Chinese often show up early (as much as 10 minutes), with the reasoning that they do not want to use up your valuable time. If you're going to be late, perhaps because of traffic problems, it's best to call and let your host know. Remember to be apologetic.

Your host may insist on picking you up and escorting you to their house, or meeting you somewhere close by, then walking you to their house. When you arrive at the door, you will be expected to take off your shoes. Your hosts will usually provide a pair of slippers or house shoes for you to wear. Once you are in the house, present your gift to the host. If you have been invited for a meal, you will probably spend some time visiting before the meal is served. Always be gracious and appreciative of their hospitality. If you don't have a meal at their home, it will often be at a restaurant near their home. Your host will, in most cases, offer you a drink, usually tea, soda, juice, or maybe beer or another drink. It is important that you accept a drink from your host, even if you are not thirsty. If they offer you something

Accept a drink, even if you are not thirsty.

that you do not drink, such as alcohol, respectfully ask for something else that's likely to be on hand. The important thing is to accept something. It is not as important that you actually drink, but that you accept their hospitality. When Chinese visit you, you should also offer them something to drink. Tea is the most common thing to offer.

When the Chinese invite you to a meal they will often prepare or order far more than can be consumed. This is a polite way of showing their regard for you. In the past, leftover food at a restaurant was not taken home. But in recent years more and more Chinese are taking the leftovers home with them.

You may use the following expressions to express your gratitude:

Nǐ zhēn de tài kèqi le. 你真的太客气了。You're really too polite.
Nǐ búyòng nàme kèqi 你不用那么客气。Don't be so polite.
Máfan nǐmen le. 麻烦你们了。This is really troublesome for you.

When visiting someone's home it's also appropriate to compliment them on their home. The following phrases are commonly used.

Nǐmen jiā zhēn piàoliàng. 你们家真漂亮。
Your home is really beautiful.

Zhè fángzi zhēn búcuò. 这房子真不错。Your home is really great.
Nǐmen jiā zhēn shūfu. 你们家真舒服。Your home is so comfortable.

These kinds of expressions convey your appreciation for their hospitality. It's also appropriate to praise the meal, with expressions like these:

After a colleague had spent time showing me and some family members around his city for a few days, we visited his apartment the last evening. We gave him and his family some small sauce dishes made from recycled glass that are unique to the town where my brother lives. They were simple, yet beautifully handcrafted, and they were very well received.

Nǐ zuò de cài zhēn hǎochī. 你做的菜真好吃。
This meal is really delicious.

Nǐ hěn huì zuòcài. 你很会做菜。
You really know how to cook.

Sometimes it can be difficult to know when it is time to leave. Look for small cues by your host. After a meal try to help clear and clean the table, although they probably won't let you do that. Generally, the wife will clean up while the husband sits and talks to you. After the wife cleans up, she may bring some fruit to the living room, or add water to your tea. At this time she may sit down and visit. After talking for a little while, you can say something like:

Máfan nǐmen bàntiān le, wǒmen yě gāi zǒu le.
麻烦你们半天了，我们也该走了。
I've troubled you for so long. We should leave.

Nǐ zhème máng, bú zài dǎrǎo/ máfan nǐ le. 你这么忙，不再打扰/要麻烦 你了。
You're so busy, I don't want to trouble you.

Hěn wǎn le, wǒ yīnggāi zǒu le. 很晚了，我应该走了。
It's late, I should leave.

Your hosts may respond with something like:

Méi shìr. 没事儿。 It's nothing.

Búlèi, búlèi. 不累不累。 We're not tired.

Hái zǎo ne. 还早呢。 It's still early.

Zài zuò huǐr ba. 再坐会儿吧。 Sit for a while longer.

At this point you should insist on leaving by saying something like:

Tài máfan nǐmen le. 太麻烦你们了。 We've really troubled you.

Huíqù hái yào... 回去还要...
We need to go to … (Indicate that you need to prepare for tomorrow, or something similar.)

They will then agree. In general, when the host adds more water to your tea, or refills your cup, or gives you some more fruit, it's a cue for you to express your intent to leave. If you feel like the host is searching for something to say, or for a new topic, it is time to leave. Do not look at your watch during a conversation as this may be considered rude. If your host glances at his or her watch, this is another indication that it's time for you to leave. Pay attention to these cues, and be sure you don't overstay your welcome.

Unless there is a large group of visitors, your host will in most cases escort you out. The Chinese term for this is **sòng**

When my family and I were living in a Chinese city a colleague invited us to visit a nearby city for the day. I knew she was very busy and that it would take some time and effort to arrange the transportation, meals, and details. I told her that she didn't need to go to all that trouble, that she was being too polite, and so on. She insisted; I gently declined; but eventually I reluctantly agreed and made sure to express my thanks many times in the days to come. Later when she was visiting the U.S., we treated her to an outing in our home state.

送 which means to see someone off, accompany, or escort. This may be a fairly drawn out process; its length will depend on how highly the host regards your relationship. The more important the relationship the longer the **sòng** 送 will be. A female guest will be escorted farther than a male guest. If you live a distance from your host, you may find that they will walk with you to the bus stop, or subway station, or they will help you hail a cab and wait until you are literally out of sight. They may even try to pay for the taxi fare in advance. Though this may feel a little awkward for an American, you should view this gesture of hospitality as it's meant. To the Chinese, not walking someone to the door, and farther, seems rather abrupt and even rude.

THE CONCEPT OF PRIVACY IN CHINA
中国的隐私概念 zhōngguó de yǐnsī gàiniàn

As the United States is a very individualistic society we highly value personal privacy, "alone time," and personal space, whether that be our apartment, bedroom, office, or other space. To understand the Chinese notion of privacy, or lack thereof, it is important to understand the population density that exists in China. China is a very crowded place and personal space is practically non-existent. The geographical size of China (9,706,961 sq km) is similar to that of the United States (9,629,091 sq km). However, the big difference lies in the amount of arable land, and areas suitable for comfortable living. Much of western China is high plateau, mountains, or desert, and not very conducive to human habitation. The U.S. has a population of about 311 million and China's population is 1.3 billion, or a billion more people than in the U.S. With China's west being mostly non-arable, most of those 1.3 billion live in eastern China. To get a sense of how crowded China is, imagine putting about 900 million people, or three times the population of the U.S., east of the Mississippi River. That is very crowded.

Many in the West are accustomed to large homes with multiple rooms. It is not uncommon for children to have their own bedrooms. Through most of Chinese history, on the other hand, this was not the case. Most living spaces were shared, and belongings were shared as well.

The notion of privacy is a relatively new concept in China. Even the term is problematic. The term for privacy is **yǐnsī** 隐私 and can be interpreted as hidden things or personal secrets. Needless to say, it has a negative connotation in China. The term **zìsī** 自私, meaning "selfish," shares the same character.

The Chinese may find it strange that Westerners want to spend time alone, or do not want to be bothered at times.

To you it's just privacy. To the Chinese, it's suspicious.

It's common in work settings to share office space, sometimes with several other individuals. Unless you are the boss, you will probably be sharing space with other coworkers.

In dorm or apartment type settings it is not uncommon for friends to show up unannounced, at just about any hour, and walk right into your dorm or apartment. This is especially true in more rural areas. The Chinese may have a difficult time understanding why someone would want to be alone. In fact, they may even be suspicious that something odd is going on. It may make you feel better to remember that unannounced visits are reserved only for close friends and associates (if you're not very close to a person, the practice is to call in advance).

If you feel close enough to a person to drop in without prior arrangement make sure you do not show up near the dinner hour. If you do, you will most certainly be invited to eat, even if it is inconvenient for your friends. They will feel obligated to feed you.

THE CHINESE BANQUET
中国式的宴会 zhōngguó shì de yànhuì

The banquet is an important part of Chinese culture. In fact, banquets can seem to be omnipresent. The Chinese have banquets for numerous reasons: welcoming or saying farewell to a foreign delegation or group of students, celebrating a birthday or wedding, or a festival or holiday, sending off a friend who is going away, and so on. Banquets vary in formality depending on the occasion and guests involved.

Banquet tables are round, and seat from 8 to 20 guests.

The primary purpose of a banquet is to create and maintain social harmony. As such, banquets are not always held for the benefit of the guest. They are a time when groups can get together and have a nice meal and drinks, often at the expense of someone else. Banquets and hosting are so important that some organizations will have a specific budget just for this purpose.

I was once in China at a university that was celebrating its one-hundredth anniversary. In a week's time, I was invited to four banquets. One banquet was hosted by the college I was associated with, two were hosted by different departments, and one by a group of teachers. Those visiting China on any kind of official business may become weary of banquets. The rich food and the huge quantities will leave you feeling overfed and tired. You may be welcomed with a banquet at every city you visit. Likewise there may be a banquet hosted by each individual institution or group you meet with. The Chinese call this **yìngchou** 应酬, which means "to treat with courtesy." It carries the notion that you have to communicate with people in an appropriate way, especially in these kinds of social engagements. These people may not be your friends, and you may not want to spend a lot of time with them, but you are obligated because of your business. The Chinese also get tired of banquets.

The food at banquets is usually not the typical fare that you find on the streets or in small, casual restaurants. At more formal banquets the food is rich, expensive, and exotic. In fact, there may be some dishes that will be difficult for you to identify. At various banquets I have eaten everything from duck blood soup to snake meat to duck web. It is best to at least try each dish that is presented.

When you arrive at a banquet, if you are not sure where to sit, do not just sit anywhere. Wait for someone to tell you where to sit. The primary host and the primary guest will sit at the head table, and important other guests and officials will also be seated there. The more important the people, the closer they will sit to the host.

On your arrival the table will usually already be set with four to six cold dishes intended as appetizers. Once the host has begun eating, you may follow. After the cold dishes are mostly consumed the hot dishes will begin to arrive. They will arrive as they are prepared. It is very important at a banquet that you pace yourself. Even if you really like a particular dish, restrain yourself and keep in mind that many more dishes will be arriving. It is very bad form to fill up early in the meal and then not eat any of the later dishes. Sometimes the better dishes are served late in the meal. At large elaborate banquets, a soup dish may be served after about every fourth or fifth dish. Do not ask for rice at the beginning of the meal! Many foreigners are accustomed to eating rice with their meal and may feel the need to ask for it. But the emphasis at a banquet is on the var-

Do not ask for rice at the beginning of the meal!

ied, delicious dishes, so rice is not usually eaten as part of the main meal. Near the end of the meal, fried rice, noodles, dumplings or other starchy, filling courses will be brought.

The purpose of this is to "top you off" if you're not totally full already. Nearly all banquets end with platters of fresh fruit, often melon. This is your sign that the banquet has come to an end.

Keep banquet table conversation light. Avoid discussing politics, religion, or other potentially sensitive subjects. Avoid also serious business discussions or negotiations. A banquet is a time to build and maintain relationships, relax, and have a good time.

■ The lazy Susan 转盘 zhuànpán

As with most dining situations in China, banquet tables are round and seat anywhere from eight to twenty people. In the center of the table will be a lazy Susan. All dishes are placed on the lazy Susan and shared. When new dishes are brought they are placed in front of the person who is deemed the host or perhaps the guest. It is okay to rotate the lazy Susan yourself, but make sure no one is taking food when you do so, and that you move the lazy Susan very slowly.

■ Dealing with food you don't like
处理不喜欢吃的食物 chǔlǐ bùxǐhuān chī de shíwù

There will likely be some dishes served that will not agree with you. It is polite to try everything that is offered. If you do not like something, leave it in your bowl or on the small plates that are provided for bones, shells, and such. If there is an item served that you are prohibited from eating, such as pork for Muslims, it is okay to not eat those dishes.

■ Drinking and giving a toast 喝酒和祝酒 hē jiǔ hé zhùjiǔ

Drinking alcohol and toasting are integral parts of any banquet. There may be up to three different glasses: a medium sized glass for beer, soda, or juice, a smaller wine glass, and an additional glass, like stemware or a shot glass for hard liquor. The host will often begin the banquet with a short speech and a toast, **zhùjiǔ** 祝酒. All present will likewise toast with the host. Do not drink any liquor until the host offers this toast, or at least takes a drink himself. If you do not drink alcohol, you may request soda or juice in place of alcohol. The host or oth-

> *In more informal situations, such as going out to eat with friends, you may indicate a toast by simply saying* **gān le** 干了 *which also means "bottoms up." You may also say or hear the expression* **suíyì** 随意 *which means "drink as you please," or "drink however much you would like."*

ers at the banquet may press you to drink. Alcohol has become a pervasive part of business meals and banquets. It is said that some businesspeople will not trust you unless you drink with them. However, there are also plenty of Chinese who prefer not to drink alcohol. If that is your preference, make it known to the host or your colleagues or friends. You may be razzed a bit for not drinking alcohol but the important thing is that you do drink something else and participate in the toasts.

You may be pressed to drink a fair amount of alcohol. The usual sign that you have had enough is to place your glass upside down on the table. You may also participate in a toast without actually drinking. Just raise your glass, toast, then put your full glass back down on the table.

The term for a toast is **gān bēi** 干杯 which literally means "dry cup" and is the equivalent of the English expression "bottoms up." If you are a guest at a banquet, you will also be expected to give a toast. After a toast, it is common to gently bump glasses with those at your table. When toasting and bumping glasses with those in a higher position than you, particularly your host, it is important that when bumping

---

When toasting, take care to bump your glass low enough.

---

glasses, your glass should be held lower than the other person's glass. When you are toasting peers, there may be a friendly competition of who can get their glass lower than the other.

At banquets you do not need to worry about paying the bill, or even pretending that you want to pay the bill.

If you are the one who is organizing the banquet, you will need to make preparations in advance. The restaurant you select and the dishes you order will depend on the occasion and your guests. In general, your friends or other Chinese associates can help you by giving you some suggestions. The staff at the restaurant can also help with selecting dishes. Make sure that you order enough food. Like the Chinese, err on the side of ordering too much.

■　■　■

USEFUL PHRASES

"bottoms up"; literally means "dry cup" **gān bēi** 干杯; **gān le** 干了

Chinese banquet **zhōngguó shì de yànhuì** 中国式的宴会

connections network **guānxi wǎng** 关系网

develop a connection **lā guānxi** 拉关系

"drink as you please," drink however much you would like **suíyì** 随意

see someone off, accompany, or escort **sòng** 送

"to see face" or to simply see each other **jiànmiàn** 见面

walking in the back door (using your connections) **zǒu hòumén** 走后门

You speak Chinese very well. **nǐ shuō zhōngwén shuō de hěn hǎo** 你说中文说得很好

No, I only can speak a little. **búshì, wǒ zhǐ huì shuō yìdiǎn(er)** 不是, 我只会说一点（儿）

No I don't, I'm really an idiot. **búhuì, wǒ zhēnde hěn bèn** 不会, 我真的很笨

No, no. 哪里哪里 **nǎlǐ nǎlǐ**

It's a small thing. **yìdiǎn (er) xiǎo yìsi** 一点（儿）小意思

It's just a small gift. **yìdiǎn (er) xiǎo lǐwù** 一点（儿）小礼物

It's just a small token (of my regard). **yìdiǎn (er) xīnyì** 一点（儿）心意

You're too polite. **nín tài kèqi le** 您太客气了

This is a bother for you. **tài máfan nǐ le** 太麻烦你了

You don't need to be so polite (gracious). **nǐ búyòng nàme kèqi** 你不用那么客气

I have something. **wǒ yǒu shì(er)** 我有事（儿）

Sorry, I have something. **duìbùqǐ wǒ yǒu shì(er)** 对不起，我有事（儿）

It's not too convenient. **bútài fāngbian** 不太方便

I'm really sorry, it's not too convenient. **bùhǎo yìsi, bútài fāngbiàn** 不好意思，不太方便

I already have something arranged/planned. **wǒ yǐjīng yǒu ānpái le.** 我已经有安排了

I'm not feeling too well. **wǒ yǒu diǎn(er) bù shūfu** 我有点（儿）不舒服

I have something at home. **jiālǐ yǒu diǎn(er) shì** 家里有点（儿）事（儿）

This is really troublesome for you. **máfan nǐmen le** 麻烦你们了

Your home is really beautiful. **nǐmen jiā zhēn piàoliàng** 你们家真漂亮

Your home is really tidy. **nǐmen jiā shōushi de zhēn hǎo** 你们家收拾得真好

Your home is really big. **nǐmen jiā zhēn dà** 你们家真大

Your home is really great. **zhè fángzi zhēn búcuò** 这房子真不错

Your home is so comfortable. **nǐmen jiā zhēn shūfu** 你们家真舒服

This meal is really delicious. **nǐ zuò de cài zhēn hǎochī** 你做的菜真好吃

You really know how to cook. **nǐ hěn huì zuòcài** 你很会做菜

You should rest now; we'll leave now. **nǐmen yě gāi xiūxi le, wǒmen huí qù le** 你们也该休息了，我们回去了

It's late, I should leave. **hěn wǎn le, wǒ yīnggāi zǒu le** 很晚了，我应该走了

It's nothing. **méi shìr** 没事儿

We've really troubled you. **tài máfan nǐmen le** 太麻烦你们了

USEFUL WORDS

dating **yuēhuì** 约会
lazy Susan **zhuànpán** 转盘
relationships, connections **guānxi** 关系
selfish **zìsī** 自私
thank you **xièxie** 谢谢
toast **zhùjiǔ** 祝酒

10

Surviving

生存 shēngcún

The large metropolitan areas of China are certainly not third-world, but they are not as fully developed as large cities in the West either. Staying healthy in China is not too difficult if you take a few precautions. Living, working, or traveling in rural areas, especially remote areas of China, can be more challenging to your health. Of course, nothing will make you totally immune from illness or injury, but taking a few preventive measures will increase your odds of a safe and healthy time in China. Knowing what to expect can help you stay healthy.

CULTURE SHOCK
文化冲击 wénhuà chōngjī

Culture shock is the difficulty one experiences in adjusting to a new culture. It's often precipitated by encountering things that go against one's expectations. In a place like China you'll be dealing with many things that you're not used to, such as the food, the climate, even the behavior of people. Missing loved ones, being overly tired (jet lag), and being faced with the unknown, that is, not knowing what to do in a given situation, also contribute to culture shock. The language barrier can significantly increase the chances of experiencing culture shock, especially if you are traveling independently.

Culture shock can be quite severe and can result in physical illness. Most everyone, even experienced China visitors, experiences culture shock to some degree. Often it is experienced almost immediately, but its onset can be delayed until quite some time after your arrival.

Culture shock is usually categorized into stages.

■ Honeymoon stage 蜜月期 mìyuè qī

This stage lasts from when you first arrive to a few weeks to a few months out. This is when you are dazzled by the new culture and find everything interesting and exotic. You may love the food, the bustling of life on the streets, the new language and so on. During this stage you may be enthusiastic, eager, and energetic. Like all honeymoons, this stage will come to an end.

■ Negotiation stage 障碍期 zhàng'ài qī

This is the stage where reality sets in; it usually occurs after about three months. During this stage, you fully realize that things are really different. You may be having a hard time adjusting to your new life. This may include adapting to the local cuisine, hygiene practices, and the language. This is the stage where many people feel homesick and overwhelmed at the prospect of doing everything in a foreign language. The overall strain of living in a completely new environment without the usual support networks, like family and friends, is taking its toll. This can be a time of high anxiety and stress.

■ Adjustment stage 适应期 shìyìng qī

This stage typically comes along somewhere between three and six months after your arrival, but can be longer or shorter for some individuals. This is when you come to terms with your new life, make some adjustments, and begin to settle into normal routines. You are now seeing things with new eyes and are able to adapt your behavior to fit in with native expectations. What used to seem exotic early on, and later annoying, seems pretty normal now. Things are making sense now and you are able to go through your days without a great deal of stress.

■ Mastery stage 熟悉期 shúxì qī

This is when you are able to participate fully and actively in the foreign culture with a considerable degree of comfort. You know what to expect and how to get things done. This stage can come much sooner the more Chinese language and culture skills you have.

We naturally have a tendency to use our own culture and practices to measure and evaluate all differences. It's important to realize that there are many different ways of doing things, and one way is not necessarily better or worse than another way. For example, the Chinese typically bathe at night. Their thinking is that it is repulsive to get into bed dirty from the day's activities. You may think this strange coming from a culture where many of us bathe in the morning. Our reasoning is that we want a shower in the morning so we'll look fresh for the day. Neither of these options is right or wrong, just different.

VACCINATIONS
疫苗 yìmiáo

Check your country's government guidelines (for example, the Centers for Disease Control website is http://wwwnc.cdc .gov/travel/destinations/china.htm) to see what vaccinations they recommend for China. They also offer a great deal of health related information for travelers.

Generally, when traveling to China it's a good idea to be current with your basic vaccinations like MMR (measles/mumps/rubella) and DPT (diphtheria/pertussis/tetanus). It may not seem urgent to be vaccinated with these mostly childhood vaccines, but remember that getting ill in a foreign country can be much more serious than at home. The other vaccinations that are recommended for urban areas of China include hepatitis A and B, and typhoid. Other vaccines may be recommended if you're going to be traveling in rural areas. Most doctors and health departments will recommend a malaria shot for just about any destination in Asia; it may not be necessary for China unless you are visiting the tropical regions of southwest China. But it is safest to follow your health department's recommendations.

JET LAG
时差反应 shíchā fǎnyìng

The time difference between the U.S. and China varies from 12 to 15 hours ahead (or 13 to 16 hours ahead during the summer). This can cause considerable jet lag when you first arrive. For most people, it seems more difficult to adjust to the time change when returning to the U.S. than when going to China.

When you arrive in China you will likely be very tired from

all the travel. It is best to try to follow China time as soon as possible. If you arrive in the evening, try to sleep. If you wake up in the middle of the night, rather than get up, try to lay in bed and at least rest. During the day, do your best to not nap for the first few days, or at least keep your naps short. By forcing yourself to stay awake during the day, you'll help your body to adjust faster. It usually takes about a week for your body to adjust completely to the time difference.

Some people like to take a sleeping pill on the plane and, for the first few days, again when going to bed. It's a good idea to have a hotel or other place to sleep arranged in advance of your arrival. That way, once you get off the plane you can go straight to bed. This works best if your plane arrives late in the afternoon or evening. It is nice to know where you are going to sleep, and how to get there when you step off the plane. China can be overwhelming when one's exhausted, but after a night's sleep things usually look a lot better.

One other piece of advice is to try and nap about every four hours on the airplane. That way when you arrive you are not too tired and your body does not have a clue what time it is. This will make it easier to adjust to the new time zone.

DEALING WITH FOOD AND DRINK
注意饮食 zhùyì yǐnshí

Any time you radically change your diet, you often will feel it in your stomach. This usually manifests in a mild case of diarrhea **fùxiè** 腹泻 / **lādùzi** 拉肚子. It usually takes a couple to a few days for your body to acclimate to the new diet and climate. Once your body adapts, you should feel better and your digestive system should get back to normal. It's probably best to not be too adventurous with your meals for the first few days in China. Don't order that big plate of spicy Mapo Tofu **mápó dòufu** 麻婆豆腐 on the day you arrive.

■ Don't drink the water

不要直接饮用自来水 **búyào zhíjiē yǐnyòng zìláishuǐ**

China's tap water is not potable, so don't drink it under any circumstances. Even the locals do not drink tap water. Since the Chinese drink tea on a regular basis, they're in the habit of regularly boiling water. No matter whether you're living in a hotel, an apartment, a dorm, or another dwelling it is important that you boil all drinking water; many hotels provide an electric kettle for this purpose. If you are spending a longer period in China, buy a large electric kettle. Some dorm rooms will have a container of drinking water delivered daily, oftentimes left sitting outside your door every morning.

Another option is to buy bottled water. Bottled water in China is either from a spring **kuàngquánshuǐ** 矿泉水, or is purified **chúnjìngshuǐ** 纯净水. Nearly all stores, from small convenience stores to large discount stores, sell bottled water in a variety of sizes. When buying bottled water from small shops or restaurants, check to make sure the seal is intact. This is very important, especially in rural areas. If you're staying in a larger hotel, they may provide a few bottles of water free of charge each day.

Using a filter **guòlǜqì** 过滤器 is another possibility. Backpacking stores in the U.S. sell these for treating suspect water. Reliable brands include MSR, Katadyn, Sawyer, and Aquamira. A

A student related a story about eating in a large university cafeteria in Beijing as a study abroad student. One day the price of the food went up. When asked about this, the staff replied that they were now using soap to wash the dishes, and the increased prices were to pay for the soap. I also once had to pay extra at a small rural restaurant in Guangxi so that they would use soap to wash the dishes.

> *Some travelers swear by yogurt to keep their systems healthy. The idea is that the good bacteria in yogurt will strengthen the gut so you're less likely to get sick. And there has been quite a lot written about the various "off label" uses of Coca-Cola, like cleaning your drains and the engine block on your car. So some travelers' thinking is that if Coke can clean your drains, it ought to work well on your gut, keeping things healthy down there. I firmly believe that a can of Coke once or twice a week has kept me from ever getting seriously ill from the food in China.*

filter will filter out bacteria and protozoa, but not viruses. A water purifier will also treat viruses, which is recommended for China. An excellent choice for complete water treatment is Aquamira (www.aquamira.com) tablets and liquid drops. They use chlorine dioxide to successfully treat viruses as well as everything else.

If it is hot and humid out it's a good idea to carry water in your purse or bag. You can quickly get dehydrated in hot summer weather. It's also best to avoid ice in your drinks as the ice may have been made with untreated water. Also be careful with fresh fruit juices because they're sometimes watered down with unpurified water.

■ Wash fruits and vegetables
清洗水果和蔬菜 **qīngxǐ shuǐguǒ hé shūcài**

If you plan to eat raw fruits and vegetables it is important to wash them thoroughly in purified water with detergent before consuming. To be even safer, you can wash them in one teaspoon of bleach per quart of water. This applies to fruits like apples and pears if you plan to eat the skin. You don't

• BEHIND THE SCENES •

Easing Culture Shock 缓解文化冲击的小窍门 **huǎnjiě wénhuà chōngjī de xiǎo qiàomén**
Here are a few tips to help you adapt to living in China and avoid serious culture shock.

- Go with an open mind. Remember that things will be different. Try to adapt to the changes, keeping in mind that things are not inferior, just different. Trying new things won't kill you.

- Get proper rest. Try to acclimate to the new time zone as quickly as possible.

- Avoid isolating yourself and sleeping too much. Get out there and get into a normal routine as soon as possible.

- Stay healthy by eating well. Chinese menus can be intimidating and you may find that you are ordering the same things all the time, because that is what you know how to say. Learn how to say, and read if possible, many different kinds of foods.

- Make friends as soon as possible. Having a support group early on will help with unforeseen problems. This may include fellow classmates, colleagues in your office, and so on.

- Study the language. The more Chinese you know and can use, the more integrated into society you will be.

need to worry about fruit that you peel, like oranges, lychee, and so on.

Leafy vegetables like lettuce are good carriers of bacteria. Fortunately, the Chinese seldom eat raw vegetables. Most everything is cooked. One exception is cucumbers. They are usually peeled, but not always. If you don't want to wash these kinds of vegetables simply peel them first.

■ Is the food safe to eat? 食品安全吗？ **shípǐn ānquán ma**

The Chinese have a saying, **bùgānbújìng chī le méi bìng** 不干不净吃了没病; its meaning something like "If it is not clean and you eat it, you won't get sick." As odd as this may sound, there is some truth to this. Every region of the world has bacteria specific to that area. The local population will be acclimated to those bacteria and are not bothered by it. When Chinese students come to the U.S. to study, they often have diarrhea for a few days when they are adjusting to the new diet. Your body will adapt to the local bacteria as well. Eat the local food and enjoy it.

I jokingly, but with a serious undertone, warn my students to just enjoy the food, but never look back in the kitchen. The conditions in many food prep areas in China are not very sanitary. Nor are there government agencies going around checking on restaurants. I have seen pigs being butchered on the sidewalk, meat hanging on hooks outside in the sun for hours on end, vegetables being washed in basins of water on the curb of the street, and so on. The good news is that most Chinese food is either cooked in a very hot wok in hot oil, or is stewed or

> *A friend was once traveling in Yunnan Province. He really wanted to try a local pork stew that was reputedly very good and was a local delicacy. He found a restaurant serving the dish, but there was a long line winding out the door. Because he was very hungry after a long bus ride, he chose another restaurant next door serving the same thing, with no line. In fact, there were hardly any customers at all. He ate two large bowls of pork stew. Hours later he was violently ill. He had a bad case of food poisoning. After two days of severe illness he slowly regained his strength and had learned an important lesson about eating in China.*

boiled well. This kind of cooking likely kills most really bad bacteria. However, keep in mind too that in many small restaurants, even though the food may be safe to eat, dishes and chopsticks may not be very sanitary. I like to carry my own set of travel chopsticks. They are more sanitary and more environmentally friendly (disposable chopsticks contribute to the downing of countless trees).

It helps to eat at restaurants that are popular and have a high turnover rate. That way the food is not sitting around waiting for customers. Ask for recommendations from friends and colleagues or simply go to restaurants that are fairly busy.

■ **Street food** 马路餐桌 **mǎlù cānzhuō,** 路边摊（儿）
lùbiāntān(er); 路摊（儿）**lùtān(er)**

Some foreigners are reluctant to eat street food. However, street food is usually very fresh and freshly prepared. And food stalls on the street are usually crowded, ensuring that there won't be any food sitting around for too long. Actually you are probably just as likely to get sick eating at a big fancy Western-style hotel buffet because the food has been sitting around and is more susceptible to spoilage. But use good judgment when selecting street stalls, and avoid those that are visibly dirty or otherwise seem unsanitary.

One other tip that really helps some people is to take some chewable antacid tablets, like Maalox or a similar type. If your stomach feels queasy after a meal, sometimes chewing one or two tablets will do the trick.

DEALING WITH INJURY OR ILLNESS
治病 **zhìbìng**

If you're living in China for more than a few weeks, it is a good idea to find out where medical facilities are located in the city in which you live. You have a few options for dealing with illness or injury in China—Western medical clinics, hospitals (traditional or Western), and traditional Chinese medicine clinics. Most Chinese go to a hospital when they get sick or injured. There are three levels of hospitals in China, First, Second, and Third Level, with Third Level being the biggest and most comprehensive. People living in the countryside will usually go to a clinic instead, as hospitals may not be accessible. There are more and more smaller clinics also showing up in China's large cities.

■ **Western medical clinics** 西医诊所 **xīyī zhěnsuǒ**
Large Chinese cities such as Beijing, Shanghai, Guangzhou, Nanjing, Tianjin, and Chongqing will usually have a Western medical clinic. At these clinics the medical staff will be trained in Western medicine, often in the U.S. or Europe. Some of these clinics may even have a Western doctor. Regardless, Western medical clinics usually have English speaking staff. This can be quite reassuring when you are sick or injured. These facilities are clean, sanitary, and are usually not crowded. They are run like medical offices in the U.S. The downside to Western medical clinics is that they can be very expensive.

Before going to China it's a good idea to check with your health insurance provider to find out what is covered overseas. Some insurers require that you pay the full bill up

> *Back in 2005 my wife needed a simple blood test for a preexisting condition. We decided to go to a Western medical clinic in the city where we lived. It was the clinic recommended by our international health insurance provider. We were very happy with the German doctor and the treatment we received. However, I was shocked to learn that the office visit cost US$200 and had to be paid in full on the spot.*

front, then will reimburse you later. Some offer you very limited services while you are abroad, while others will require that you get treatment only at certain clinics. Still other insurers don't offer coverage while you're out of the country. An option to consider is international coverage from a provider that specializes in insurance for travelers, like International SOS (http://www.internationalsos.com/en/asia-pacific_china.htm). SOS has its own clinics in four major cities in China, and has a hospital with an emergency room in Beijing.

■ Pharmacies in China
中国的药房 **zhōngguó de yàofáng** / 药店 **yàodiàn**

Pharmacies are not too difficult to find in China. They can be Western style with modern drugs, traditional Chinese style that dispense herbal remedies, or a combination of the two. They can be identified with the character **yào** 药 meaning medicine. Many drugs that are only available by prescription in the U.S. may be available over the counter in China. Examples of this are antibiotics such as penicillin and its derivatives, antidepressants like Prozac, and asthma inhalers.

Traditional Chinese pharmacies may not be totally obvious from the outside, but once you're inside, they can be identified by the large apothecary cabinets against one of the walls. These cabinets have numerous small drawers where a dizzying variety of herbs, animal parts, and other ingredients is stored. The pharmacist will measure out the ingredients, usually by weight, and pour them onto a paper, adding each ingredient needed for a particular formula. Many of these traditional herbs are steeped like tea and drunk.

Many Chinese feel that Western drugs only treat the symptoms and don't get to the cause of the problem.

Some traditional Chinese medicine looks like Western medicine, but is made of traditional Chinese medicinal herbs. It is called **zhōng chéng yào** 中成药 or just **zhōng yào** 中药. Medical doctors trained in Western medicine may also prescribe this kind of traditional Chinese medicine.

■ Traditional Chinese medicine 中医 **zhōngyī**

Many hospitals in China have Western medicine as well as traditional Chinese medical options. Sometimes these are separated by different wings in a larger building or they may be in different buildings. Still, some clinics and hospitals deal only with traditional healing techniques. Traditional Chinese medicine includes acupuncture **zhēnjiǔ** 针灸, cupping therapy **bá huǒguàn er** 拔火罐儿, massage **ànmó** 按摩, exercise and breathing techniques **qìgōng** 气功, and herbal remedies **zhōng cǎo yào** 中草药.

■ **Acupuncture** 针灸 **zhēnjiǔ**

Acupuncture is a means of treating illness and disorder by inserting very fine needles into the body to stimulate energy channels that promote healing. The Chinese believe that all living things have a vital force or energy called **qì** 气 that circulates through your body through channels called meridians **jīngluò** 经络. When there is a blockage of this energy, pain or illness is the result.

■ **Cupping therapy** 拔火罐（儿） **bá huǒguàn (er)**

Cupping therapy is another way to stimulate points along the acupuncture meridians. It is done by suctioning small glass, metal, or wood jars on the affected area. The suction is created by placing a small flame in the jar, then quickly attaching the jar to the body. This simulates the area by causing coagulation of the blood. Once the jars have been placed on your body, you will feel a pulling sensation on the skin inside the cup, that gradually eases in a few minutes.

> For some, cupping therapy is even more relaxing than a good massage.

Cupping therapy is commonly used for backaches, soft tissue injuries, sprains, acne, colds, asthma, and more. I have found cupping therapy very effective in relieving a tense back and neck. After cupping therapy I feel very loose and relaxed, even more so than after a good massage. Cupping therapy does leave large, round red marks on your body that gradually go away in about four to five days. Sometimes cupping therapy is done in public parks.

■ **Traditional Chinese massage** 中医按摩 **zhōngyī ànmó**

Traditionally, massage therapists in Chinese are blind. This is still the case at many clinics, but you will find many massage therapists that are sighted as well. A Chinese massage is usually done while you're clothed. The massage therapist will put a sheet or light towel over your clothes while massaging, so they are not actually touching you directly. You can select a full body massage or just your shoulders and neck, or wherever else you are having trouble. A full body massage will last about an hour and is very reasonably priced, especially compared to what you would pay in the U.S. Traditional Chinese massages can be pretty intense and you may be sore for a couple of days afterward.

It is common in many hair-cutting salons to give customers a scalp, neck, and shoulder massage with a haircut. It usually comes with the price of the haircut, and is quite relaxing. At some salons you can get your hair washed and get a massage without getting your hair cut.

■ Chinese herbs 中草药 zhōng cǎoyào

The Chinese use herbs in their daily lives to nourish and maintain good health. For example, Chinese wolfberries or goji berries 枸杞 gǒuqǐ are often steeped in tea or added to soups to give general nourishment or when nursing yourself back to health after an illness.

Chinese herbs are generally classified into food herbs and medicinal herbs. Food herbs are eaten with food, or added to dishes as a means to strengthen, nourish, and maintain health. Sometimes food herbs and medicinal herbs are the same; the only difference is in how they are taken. Herbs taken medicinally are usually stronger than when added to foods. Medicinal herbs are taken like medicine, often in the form of a tea. There are more than a thousand common herbs used for medicinal purposes. Most formulas consist of ten to fifteen different herbs selected to work together to treat the illness. Herbal formulas are commonly used for colds, flu, bronchitis, and a variety of other ailments.

When Chinese get sick, they often will take traditional Chinese medicine as prescribed by a traditional Chinese doctor.

Even if you have good Chinese skills you may not know how to say everything that you may need. I had a colleague who was living in China and suspected that his wife was pregnant. They wanted to buy a pregnancy test to find out, so he headed to the nearest pharmacy. Because he did not know how to say "pregnancy test" he simply described it the best he could. He said something like, "I think my wife is pregnant. Do you have one of those kits that has a little stick that you pee on?" The pharmacist did not know what he was talking about, so called another colleague. Pretty soon they were calling people in off the street and before long there was a crowd of Chinese people in the pharmacy trying to figure out what the foreigner wanted. He was finally relieved, and a bit embarrassed, to find just what he was looking for practically right in front of him on the counter.

In general, one bag of the prescribed herbs is boiled twice per day. In the morning it is boiled and then drunk as a tea. In the evening new water is added to the same herbs and it is drunk again. After the second time, it is thrown away. The next day, you will use a new bag of herbs. Doctors will tell you specifically how to prepare it, when to drink it (before or after meals), and what things you can and cannot eat with the medicine. Doctors may explain to you a little about the formula, such as which herbs are used for what purposes, but in general terms. Sometimes these formulas are a secret and the doctor will not tell you exactly what is in it.

HEALTH INSURANCE
医疗保险 yīliáo bǎoxiǎn

Hospitals and health care is generally covered by the state in China. However, most hospitals and clinics do require payment, usually before services are provided.

If you're going to China for work, your employer will often provide health insurance benefits. Chinese health insurance is rather complicated. If you work for the government or a state owned company or school, you are covered by a government insurance policy. If you work for a private company, you may get insurance directly from an insurance company or the company will provide health insurance for its own staff. When you're sick, how much you pay and how much may be reimbursed depends on your plan. For government policies, what medicines can be paid by insurance are specified. A special insurance card (with an amount of money programmed in it) is used when going to the hospital. If the medicine you need cannot be paid by your insurance policy, you need to pay for it by yourself. If the medicine is more than the money on the card, you pay first, then according to your plan, you will get a certain percentage of money back.

VISITING A HOSPITAL
去医院 qù yīyuàn

If you are injured or sick and require medical help, you may desire to go to a Western clinic. However, these kinds of modern, clean, and sanitary clinics are usually only available in large cities. If one of these clinics is not available, you'll most likely need to go to the nearest hospital. Chinese go to a hospital when they are sick and not to a doctor's office. This is the standard practice as there are few doctors' offices around;

• BEHIND THE SCENES •

Chinese Attitudes towards Healthcare
中国人的健康观念 zhōngguórén de jiànkāng guānniàn

The traditional Chinese approach to treating illness is much more holistic than the approach in the West. A traditional Chinese doctor will not only look at the symptoms, but also seek to understand the cause of the illness and how it relates to other functions of the body. There is an emphasis on balance in the body as manifest through the principles of yin **yīn** 阴 and yang **yáng** 阳. When there is too much of one thing, such as heat, in the body, then it causes an imbalance that may cause a variety of illnesses. The five elements (air **qì** 气, earth **tǔ** 土, fire **huǒ** 火, metal **jīn** 金, wood **mù** 木) are also an integral part of traditional Chinese medicine.

For example, if you have a headache, the problem may not be in your head. Traditional Chinese medicine tries to solve the underlying problem instead of treating your headache directly. After taking traditional medicine, you may not feel the effectiveness of the medicine immediately, and you may still have a headache, but within a certain time of taking the medicine, the source problem will be treated and the headache will thus go away. While Western medicine may make your headache go away more immediately, it is only a temporary fix.

Many Chinese in China will first go to a Western medical hospital, and will be treated mostly with Western medicine. If Western medical methods cannot solve the real problem, the Chinese will go to a traditional Chinese medical hospital or use traditional Chinese medical methods.

In general, for acute disease, the Chinese use Western medicine, but for chronic disease, they usually think traditional Chinese medical methods are more effective. Sometimes there are situations where you may not be sick, but you are still not very healthy. For these kinds of situations, Chinese take traditional medicine to **tiáolǐ shēntǐ** 调理身体 or **tiáoyǎng shēntǐ** 调养身体, which means to nurse your body back to full health.

Chinese go to a hospital— not a doctor's office— when they are sick.

the vast majority of doctors work out of hospitals.

When you arrive at the hospital, you will generally follow the procedure described below. Hospitals can be confusing places as things are not always clearly marked. What seems routine for native Chinese can be very non-intuitive to the foreigner. I strongly recommend that you take a native Chinese friend or colleague with you. They will understand better what to do and how to get things done in a hospital.

■ Register 挂号 guàhào

When you arrive at the hospital, if your situation is not life threatening, you will first need to register. This entails showing identification, telling the nature of your ailment, etc. If you have health insurance, they will want to see your card. You will be given a slip of paper telling you which exam room to go to.

■ Payment 付款 fù kuǎn

You will not be able to see a doctor until you have paid. You will be directed to a cashier where you'll pay for the services that are anticipated. Payment may range from 1 yuan to up to 20 yuan.

■ Waiting 候诊 hòuzhěn

You will then be directed where to go to find a doctor. As is the case with many socialized medical systems, you typically will not have a regular doctor, but will see whomever is available. You will most likely have to wait, sometimes for quite a long time. You may be waiting in the doctor's exam area while other patients are being examined. Things can seem chaotic as there may be many people jockeying for position to see the

• BEHIND THE SCENES •

Tips for Staying Healthy in China 在中国保持健康的小窍门
zài zhōngguó bǎochí jiànkāng de xiǎo qiàomén

- Stay hydrated. It is easy to get dehydrated in hot, humid climates. And summer weather in much of China is hot and humid, from Beijing in the North, to Guangzhou in the South. Keep a water bottle with you and drink regularly.

- Carry a first aid kit when traveling. Even a basic kit is better than nothing. Because medical facilities are not always as sanitary as you might like them to be, carrying some basic supplies like bandages, antibacterial ointment, and anti-diarrhea medicine is a good idea. If you are in the countryside, insect repellent is also important.

- Some travelers will even carry their own needles just in case they need sutures for an injury. (Chinese hospitals have been known to reuse needles.) Some hospitals or clinics may require you to buy your own needles. Needles can also be bought at most pharmacies.

- During the hot and humid summers some kind of antifungal cream is a must. Warm moist areas, like the armpits and crotch area, can get prickly heat rashes.

- Bring a familiar cold medicine with you to China. Many people pick up a cold when they move to China, and having a familiar remedy can be comforting.

- Get plenty of rest and take time to relax. People often get stressed by the pressures of daily life in China, and it literally makes them sick. Take things one day at a time with plenty of rest and the transition will be smoother.

doctor. It is not uncommon for people to try to cut in front of you. Sometimes a nurse will be there to maintain order. This is where having a native friend or colleague comes in. They will know what to do in order to be seen.

Be aware that many doctors will take a long, two-hour lunch break, during which they will not see patients. This usually occurs between noon and two o'clock PM. That means if you have been waiting to see the doctor since 11:00 AM, and have still not seen him or her at 12:00, you'll need to wait until 2:00 PM to resume your waiting. When you register, they will tell you the doctor's hours.

■ Seeing the doctor 看病 kànbìng; 看大夫 kàn dàifu; 看医生 kàn yīshēng

There is not much privacy in Chinese hospitals. You may also be alarmed at the lack of sanitary conditions. A few years ago I brought a student, who had twisted his ankle playing basketball, to the hospital. We watched as the doctor ran some water over his hands, then wiped them on a very dirty towel. He then proceeded to examine a young patient. Bigger, more modern hospitals and clinics are more sanitary.

While you are being examined by a doctor, other patients may approach the doctor with questions or the results of lab tests. This is considered normal. There are many lines to wait in at a hospital, so everyone is trying to get taken care of as soon as possible. A Chinese hospital is a good way of really understanding the pressures on a society with more than a billion people. It may also give you some insight into the one-child policy and why many Chinese think it is a good idea.

Once you have been treated by the doctor, you may receive a prescription. Hospitals will have an in-house pharmacy where you can pick up your medications. Compared to prices in the U.S., medications, visits to a doctor, and medical procedures are very inexpensive.

WOMEN'S HEALTH
妇女保健 fùnǚ bǎojiàn

Birth control pills **bìyùn yào** 避孕药 are available in China. Two popular brands of birth control pills in China are Marvelon **māfùlóng** 妈富隆 and Levonorgestrel **zuǒquēnuò yùn tóng piàn** 左炔诺孕酮片. Birth control pills can be purchased at most pharmacies with a doctor's prescription. There is a type of birth control pill that is used in temporary situations, such as when Chinese couples only see each other a few times during the year at holidays. They are called **tànqīn bìyùn yào** 探亲避孕药. There is another type of birth control pill that is taken one time, directly after intercourse. They are called **jǐnjí bìyùn yào** 紧急避孕药. Two popular brands are Yuting **yùtíng** 毓婷 and Anting **āntíng jǐnjí bìyùn yào** 安婷紧急避孕药. They can be purchased at most pharmacies without a prescription.

Feminine products, such as pads, are also widely available in just about any convenience store or supermarket. Though pads are easy to find, tampons are very difficult if not impossible to find in China. You might be able to find them in big cities, at Western drug stores like Watsons.

Condoms are sold in convenience stores all over China. For the Chinese, birth control items, such as condoms, are usually provided free if you work for the government or a state-owned company. Birth control items may also be provided free by the government office that has jurisdiction for the area in which you live. This office is called the **jiēdào** 街道 or **jūwěihuì** 居委会. Outside these offices there is often a box, like a mailbox, where people can freely take what they need.

■ ■ ■

USEFUL PHRASES

breathing techniques; qigong
  qìgōng 气功
not sick, but still not very healthy
  yà jiàn kāng 亚健康
to nurse your body back to full
  health **tiáolǐ shēntǐ** 调理身体;
  tiáoyǎng shēntǐ 调养身体
to see a doctor **kànbìng** 看病/**kàn
  dàifu** 看大夫/**kàn yīshēng** 看医生
to stay at a hospital (as a patient)
  zhù yuàn 住院
to visit a hospital **qù yīyuàn** 去医院

USEFUL WORDS

acupuncture **zhēnjiǔ** 针灸
acupuncture points **xuéwèi** 穴位
bottled spring water **kuàngquánshuǐ**
  矿泉水
bottled purified water **chúnjìngshuǐ**
  纯净水
Chinese herbs **zhōng cǎo yào** 中草
  药
culture shock **wénhuà chōngjī** 文化
  冲击
cupping therapy **bá huǒguàn er** 拔
  火罐儿

diarrhea **fùxiè** 腹泻; **lā dúzi** 拉肚子
filter **guòlùqì** 过滤器
goji berries **gǒuqǐ** 枸杞
health insurance **yīliáo bǎoxiǎn** 医
  疗保险
jet lag **shíchā fǎnyìng** 时差反应
meridians **jīngluò** 经络
payment **fùkuǎn** 付款
pharmacy **yàofáng** 药房; **yàodiàn**
  药店
qi (vital energy) **qì** 气
register **guàhào** 挂号
street food **mǎlù cānzhuō** 马路餐
  桌; **lùbiāntān(er)** 路边摊（儿）;
  lùtān(er) 路摊（儿）
traditional Chinese massage **zhōngyī
  ànmó** 中医按摩
traditional Chinese medicine
  zhōngyī 中医
vaccinations **yìmiáo** 疫苗
Western medicine **xīyī** 西医
waiting room in a hospital or clinic
  hòuzhěnshì 候诊室
Western medical clinics **xīyī
  zhěnsuǒ** 西医诊所

Conclusion

SAFELY AVOIDING THE UGLY AMERICAN SYNDROME

You can usually see, and hear, a group of American tourists from a mile away. There is something about Americans—they want to be heard, seen, liked, accommodated. The term "ugly American" refers to the perceptions many foreigners have of Americans as being loud, arrogant, demeaning, and ethnocentric. When foreigners come to the United States, we expect them to adapt to our way of life, speaking English and doing things as we expect things to be done. Why is it, then, that when Americans travel abroad, we sometimes expect everyone to adapt to us and our ideals?

It is probably not possible to fully blend in when in China. For many Westerners, physical characteristics almost always rule out the possibility that they would be taken for a native. But even if we could speak Chinese like a native, dress like the locals, and look like them, we would still probably have a hard time completely blending in. The anthropologist Mayfair Mei-Hui Yang tells of when she was in Beijing early in her career doing fieldwork. As an ethnic Chinese, who spoke Chinese growing up in America, she did all that she could to blend in. She wore Chinese clothing, spoke only Chinese, ate Chinese food, associated with Chinese friends, and so on. Even so, her American posture and gait always gave her away. It was only after about six months of diligent effort that she was able to pass for a local.*

Avoiding being mistaken for an "ugly American" does not

---

* Yang, Mayfair Mei-Hui. *Gifts, Favors, and Banquets: The Art of Social Relationships in China* (Ithaca and London: Cornell Univ. Press, 1994), 20.

mean that you should mimic every aspect of Chinese behavior and society. But it is important to understand what those behaviors and norms are. You will need to decide what aspects of American culture you are not willing to give up, and what aspects of Chinese culture you *are* willing to adopt. For example, even though most Chinese bathe in the evening, you may still wish to shower in the morning as is common in America.

BLENDING IN

There are several other things one can do to blend in better with Chinese society. In the group consciousness that the Chinese value, people attempt to fit in and conform to those around them. In fact, most Chinese go to great lengths to fit in with their associates, in dress, actions, thoughts, and so on. Your objective is not to be noticed, not to draw attention to yourself, but to mesh well with your surroundings.

Being a keen observer of what is going on around you will enable you to understand expectations and norms in whatever environment you are living, working, or studying. Here are some general guidelines that will help you make the transition.

Basic strategies for blending in

- Avoid loud, flashy clothing.

  Wear clothing that is similar to the clothes of those with whom you work or study. Err on the side of conservative dress. Avoid overly revealing clothing. Extreme clothing styles will only draw attention to you. This is especially true in professional settings. Shorts, sandals, a bright flowery shirt, and a baseball cap do not go over very well in China and will make you stand out like a sore thumb.

- Dress appropriately for the occasion.

  If everyone at the office is wearing shirts and ties, or skirts and blouses, then you should also. Be aware that Chinese may dress up when you would not expect it, for example, for outdoor outings.

- Don't insist on American-style goods and services.
  This is especially applicable if you're in rural areas or smaller cities. Sometimes Western goods are not available or are at the least hard to acquire. For instance, potatoes are not common fare in most areas of China.

- Eat what is placed before you.
  At least pretend that you appreciate the food and nibble on it. Shunning food given to you, especially at a banquet, can be very offensive to your hosts.

- Learn at least a few phrases in Chinese.
  Learning a few phrases in Chinese and using them when you can will go a long way in China. The Chinese understand how hard their language is and appreciate when foreigners try to speak Chinese.

- Smile.
  Even if you are confused, frustrated, and don't know what is going on, smile. It will ease the tension for both you and others.

- Take it easy.
  Avoid public displays of anger or frustration. Keep your cool and be patient. Logic and reason do not always work. Trying to force your way seldom works. Try to understand the situation, be open to alternatives, and generally try to be pleasant no matter how ugly things get.

- Don't flirt.
  American style flirting is often misunderstood in China. While you may think it is innocent and not serious, Chinese usually interpret this sort of behavior as serious affection.

- Pay attention to mannerisms.

This is especially true with non-Chinese minority groups who may have different behaviors and mannerisms for you to blend with. If you are traveling to the Western provinces, such as Gansu, Xinjiang, Tibet, Yunan, and Western Sichuan, you'll want to pay close attention to how people interact with each other.

- Be humble.
  Look people in the eye when you talk to them to acknowledge their humanity. Treat people with respect and dignity.

- Go slower, but go deeper.
  Become a regular by frequenting the same places repeatedly. Get to know local people, like your neighbors, the lady who sells breakfast items from a cart on the street, the bicycle repairman on the street corner, and so on.

- Have patience with yourself and those around you.
  China can be a difficult place. Allow yourself some time to adjust and adapt to the differences.

- Don't expect things to be the same all over China.
  Each area of China has different food, cultural icons, and ways of doing things.

In the ten preceding chapters you've learned the main cultural codes that form the "norms" in China: that network of understandings that people have accepted as the ways to handle the most basic interactions of everyday life.

You may not find these different approaches the most comfortable ones from your own perspective; after all, each one of us views "normal" from the safety of our own culture's understandings. But knowing them allows you to "decode" them and reach deeper understanding—whether you use that to help you get things done effectively in China, or whether you simply enjoy the broadening of your awareness.

You now have many coping strategies for getting things done in the way Chinese expect, which in China is always the most effective way. Following these will go a long way in helping you to integrate smoothly into Chinese society if you'll be living, studying, or working there for a period of time, or in helping you to interact smoothly if you're visiting China for a shorter time. Either way, best wishes in your travels and your adventures as you experience China.

Appendix 1

USEFUL WEBSITES FOR BEFORE YOU GO

GENERAL INFORMATION

U.S. Department of State

http://www.state.gov/p/eap/ci/ch
Information about China, Hong Kong and Macau. Includes background notes as well as the Library of Congress country study of China.

http://www.state.gov/p/eap/ci/taiwan
Background notes about Taiwan.

TRAVEL

General Information

http://www.chinatour360.com
Provides private and package tours to all areas of China, as well as airline and train ticketing services.

http://www.travelchinaguide.com
Offers private, small group, and package tours to China. Descriptions of top attractions, city guides, and other travel related resources.

http://www.synotrip.com
A Chinese travel agency that helps tourists connect with tour guides, and also arranges other travel related services.

http://wikitravel.org/en/China
This wiki provides a wealth of information on everything related to traveling in China. Content is organized according to topic and subtopic making it easy to navigate and use.

Ticket Booking

http://www.ctrip.com
A well known and trusted online travel agency similar to Travelocity.

http://www.elong.net
Another well-known online travel agency, providing the same services as Ctrip above.

http://www.flychina.com
Has a long history of providing discount international airline tickets to China. They now also offer domestic tickets and hotel, tour, and visa bookings.

Discussion Forums

http://www.lonelyplanet.com/thorntree/forum.jspa?forumID = 19&keywordid = 84
The Thorn Tree Discussion Forum for China is a forum for travelers to ask questions and

swap information on traveling in China. Discussions are searchable with separate threads for different areas of Northeast Asia. There are also forums for Taiwan, Tibet, etc.; use the index at **http://www.lonelyplanet.com/thorntree/index.jspa**

Train Travel

http://www.seat61.com/China.htm
General train travel information including ticketing, schedules, fares, and recommended trains for popular routes.

WEATHER

http://weather.com.cn
Detailed weather forecasts for all major cities and an amazing number of small towns in China. Cities are arranged alphabetically by pinyin. An English mirror site is provided.

LIVING

General Online Classified Advertisements

http://58.com
In Chinese, but very easy to navigate and use. Simply choose the city, district and category you are looking for.

http://www.chinese-forums.com/index.php?/forum/29-classifieds
Targets English-speaking expats. Jobs and housing seem to be the most popular postings.

http://www.zhantai.com
Craigslist in Chinese. Choose any major city on the right-hand side.

http://geo.craigslist.org/iso/cn
Craigslist for China! The format and functionality is exactly the same as for U.S. cities. A great place to find an apartment or room for rent.

http://www.justlanded.com/english/China
For expats new to China. Find a place to live. Find a job. Find a friend.

Housing-Specific Online Classifieds

http://www.5i5j.com
Makes finding a place to buy or rent seem easy. New or used apartments in a variety of cities.

http://www.at0086.com/two/provider.aspx?cid = 523
Apartments for rent in Shanghai, Beijing, Wuhan, or Shenzhen. In English.

http://www.wanhai.com.cn
Specializes in selling and renting properties in Beijing. In English, and very user-friendly.

Yellow Pages

http://www.wo116114.com
Get 411-type info here. Pretty good for the Beijing area, but not so great for other cities.

CITY-SPECIFIC RESOURCES

Beijing

http://www.agendabeijing.com
An online English language
magazine catering to the Beijing
expat community.

http://beijing.asiaxpat.com
Articles, classifieds and personals
for the expats in the capital.

groups.yahoo.com/group/
Beijingcafe
A Yahoo! Groups listserv,
essentially for expats living in
Beijing.

http://www.beijingchina.net
.cn/transportation
In English. Lists train schedules
for Beijing as well as taxi, bus,
and metro information.

http://www.beijinghikers.com
An eco-friendly company that
leads group and private hikes.

http://www.cityweekend.com
.cn/beijing
A variety of resources for the
Beijing expat. (Also available for
Shanghai and Guangzhou.)

www.innbeijing.org
At International Newcomers'
Network, find out about group
gatherings for those fresh off the
plane and the "old China hand"
alike.

http://www.thebeijinger.com
Classifieds, a blog, and forums for
the Beijing expat community.

http://www.timeout.com/cn/
en/beijing
The latest and hippest happenings
in the capital. (Also serves
Shanghai.)

Nanjing

http://www.3dnanjing.com
A 3-D map of Nanjing with
bus and metro routes is useful
for finding your way around.
However, the site may not work
on all computers.

http://www.hellonanjing.net
Resources, classified ads, and
discussion boards for the growing
Nanjing expat community.

http://www.nanjingexpat.com
A variety of resources for the
Nanjing expat.

Shanghai

http://www.cityweekend.com
.cn/shanghai
Good resource for finding an
apartment and a job in Shanghai.

http://shanghai.asiaxpat.com
Resources for the foreigner in
Shanghai.

http://www.shanghaiexpat.com
A clearinghouse of all things
expat in Shanghai. This
community is very active.

NEWS AND INFORMATION

Newspapers Published in China

http://libguides.mit.edu/content
.php?pid = 146063&sid = 1247887

http://en.wikipedia.org/wiki/
List_of_newspapers_in_the_
People's_Republic_of_China

http://www.world-newspapers
.com/china.html

Chinese News Sources

CCTV http://www.cntv.cn/
index.shtml
China Daily http://www
.chinadaily.com.cn
Chinese News Digest http://
www.cnd.org

Chinese News Net http://www
.chinesenewsnet.com
Peoples Daily http://www
.people.com.cn

Xinhua News Agency http://
www.xinhuanet.com/english/
index.htm

English News Sources

CCTV http://english.cntv.cn/01/
index.shtml
China Daily http://www
.chinadaily.com.cn/index.html
Global Times http://www
.globaltimes.cn
International Business Times
China/Hong Kong http://
cn.ibtimes.com
Peoples Daily http://english
.peopledaily.com.cn

Straits Times http://www
.straitstimes.com:80/Home.html
The South China Morning Post
http://www.scmp.com
Xinhua News Agency http://
www.xinhuanet.com/english

Other Asian Pacific News Sites

BBC News http://www.bbc.co
.uk/news/world/asia_pacific
China Digital Times http://
chinadigitaltimes.net
New York Times http://www
.nytimes.com/pages/world/asia/
index.html
Guardian http://www.guardian
.co.uk/world/china
The Epoch Times China Page
http://www.theepochtimes.com

COMMUNICATING

Search Engines

http://www.baidu.com
Often referred to as the Chinese
Google.

http://www.163.com
http://www.sina.com.cn
http://www.sohu.com
These three sites are very similar
and feel like a Chinese Yahoo, but
much more overwhelming.

http://google.hk
The real Chinese Google, based in
Hong Kong.

Social Networking

http://www.kaixin001.com
http://www.renren.com
Two very popular social

networking sites similar to Facebook.

http://www.qq.com
Free instant messaging program used by most young people in China.

Online Video

http://www.56.com
http://www.joy.cn
http://www.ku6.com
http://www.qiyi.com
http://www.tudou.com
http://www.youku.com
These six video-sharing websites are all very similar to YouTube, allowing users to upload, view, and share videos. They also contain many TV programs and movies; Ku6.com is very similar to the U.S. site hulu.com.

Radio

http://www.cri.cn/index1.htm
China Radio International, a comprehensive news outlet. Listen live over the Internet.

http://radiotime.com/region/c_100322/China.aspx
Lists radio stations by province and provides direct links to listen live.

Television

www.wcetv.com
A sort of clearinghouse of TV station broadcasts in China such as the CCTV stations. Links allow you to watch each station live.

http://www.chinaontv.com/
A collection of television videos from around China, together in one location.

Online Magazines

http://chinasite.com/Media/Magazine.html
A comprehensive list of magazines related to China.

http://www.chinatoday.com.cn/ctenglish/index.htm
http://www.thechinaperspective.com
Two of many magazines that cover contemporary Chinese news and culture.

SHOPPING

Online Shopping

http://www.360buy.com
A popular online shopping website with a wide variety of products.

https://www.alipay.com
A third party online payment platform that works like Paypal; partnered with Visa and MasterCard.

http://www.amazon.cn
The Chinese language version of the popular shopping website.

http://dangdang.com
Another of the big online business-to-consumer retailers in China that is similar to Amazon.

http://taobao.com
Like a combination of Amazon and Ebay. You can even bargain a little on it. It is used by many expats.

Group Shopping

http://tuan.kaixin001.com#
http://www.nuomi.com/
changecity
http://www.ganji.com
http://beijing.55tuan.com
http://ju.taobao.com
http://www.meituan.com
http://www.lashou.com
http://www.tuan800.com
http://t.58.com/bj
Group shopping offers just about anything you want, and the prices are hard to beat.

STUDYING

Study Abroad

http://www.ciee.org/study/
index.aspx
The Council on International Educational Exchange has been around for a long time and has many study abroad programs in China. There is an academic advisory board that reviews and approves their programs.

http://www.cucas.edu.cn
Some basic information about Chinese study programs in China including available programs, admission and program requirements and required HSK levels.

http://www.hamilton.edu/china
The Associated Colleges in China is administered by Hamilton College. An academically sound program that offers excellent Chinese language and culture programs in China.

http://ieas.berkeley.edu/iup/
index.html
The well-known and regarded Inter-University Program for Chinese Language Studies or IUP is a prestigious program that caters to advanced level language students.

Chinese Reading and Reference Software Programs

http://www.cjkware.com
http://www.clavisinica.com
http://www.wenlin.com
These three websites sell text-annotating software that allow the reader to move their cursor over a Chinese character to get an instant definition of the word.

http://www.mandarinspot.com
Offers text annotation and dictionary features. The text annotator lets you display pronunciation of characters in Hanyu pinyin, Taiwan zhuyin fuhao, and a few others.

Apps

http://www.pleco.com
This excellent dictionary app allows you to input Chinese words by pinyin, English, or for

an upgrade you can even write the character with your finger.

http://dianhuadictionary.com
A free dictionary app similar to Pleco.

Online Resources

http://chinalinks.osu.edu
This site, managed by a Chinese language professor, contains more than 600 annotated links to China and Chinese language- and linguistics-related websites.

http://chinesepod.com
This program focuses mostly on listening comprehension skills by offering a vast number of short dialogues and discussions from basic to very advanced levels.

http://www.learningchinese online.net
A clearinghouse with numerous links to online Chinese language learning. Managed by a Chinese language professor and offers a wealth of information.

http://www.mandarintools.com
A variety of resources useful to the Chinese learner including a free downloadable text annotating tool called DimSum Chinese Tools.

Online Dictionaries

http://www.nciku.com
Has a useful English, pinyin and character dictionary. You can look up characters by writing them with your mouse.

http://zhongwen.com
A popular dictionary based on character etymology.

Texts for Learners

http://www.clavisinica.com/ voices.html
Short essays written for the intermediate and low advanced learner of Chinese.

http://www-personal.umich .edu/ ~ dporter/sampler/ sampler.html
A variety of learner texts organized by genre.

Modern Chinese Literature and Culture Resource Center

http://mclc.osu.edu/default.htm
The MCLC resource center contains modern and contemporary Chinese literature, film, art, music, and culture. Highly recommended.

http://mclc.osu.edu/rc/LIST.htm
MCLC email listserv subscription information.

http://www.facebook.com/ pages/MCLC/185091461514265
The MCLC Facebook page.

http://twitter.com/#!/mclclist
The MCLC Twitter page.

HEALTH

http://wwwnc.cdc.gov/travel/ destinations/china.htm
The Center for Disease Control and Prevention website provides

current health information for travelers to China.

**http://www.internationalsos
.com/en/asia-pacific_china.htm**
An international health insurance and health care provider with clinics in several major cities in China.

OTHER

www.cyclechina.com
A tour agency specializing in bicycle tours of China.

Appendix 2

TRAIN TICKETS

Train tickets are pretty standard all around the country, though they may come in different colors. The pink ticket below is a typical train ticket. The blue ticket (on the next page) is for the bullet trains.

Train tickets usually contain the following information.

date

place of origin and destination with an arrow pointing from one to the other

train car number; berth number and bunk (if a sleeper car).

the type and number of the train (T42 below)

price of the ticket

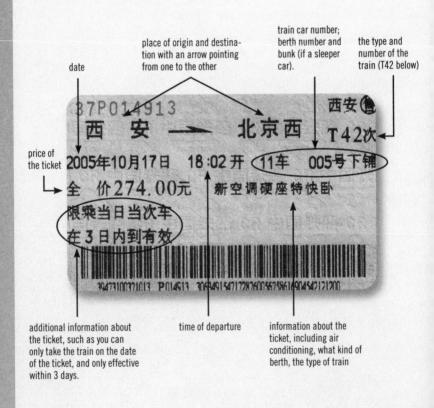

additional information about the ticket, such as you can only take the train on the date of the ticket, and only effective within 3 days.

time of departure

information about the ticket, including air conditioning, what kind of berth, the type of train

The bullet-train ticket contains the following information.

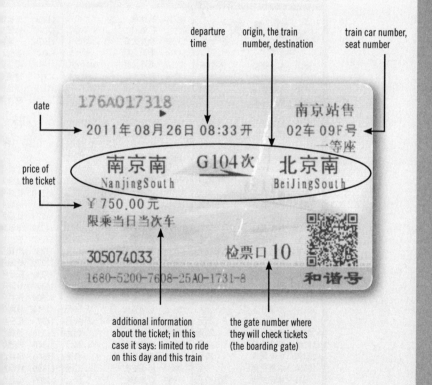

date

departure time

origin, the train number, destination

train car number, seat number

price of the ticket

additional information about the ticket; in this case it says: limited to ride on this day and this train

the gate number where they will check tickets (the boarding gate)

A TYPICAL CHINESE RESTAURANT MENU

As mentioned in Chapter 3, menus are usually arranged by categories of food served. The menu shown here is typical of a smaller to medium sized restaurant. In bigger and more expensive restaurants, it is becoming increasingly popular to have large elaborate menus that include photographs of each dish.

清真 宴宾楼饭庄　清真 宴

凉菜类

10010	凉拌鸭掌	大/70元
10011	凉拌鸭掌	小/35元
10020	老醋蜇皮	30元
10030	鸡丝大皮	18元
10040	水果沙拉	18元
10050	椒麻鸡	20元
10060	凉拌枝子粉	14元
10070	糟香鸭舌果仁	20元
10080	凉拌木耳	14元
10090	老干妈鸭胗	20元
10100	泰国小黄鱼	20元
10110	卤水鸭心肝	18元
10120	特色鸭头	只/4元
10140	酱牛肉	25元
10150	青芥菜心	18元
10160	杲珍糯米藕	18元
10170	老醋果仁	12元
10180	冰梅苦瓜	15元
10190	炝黄瓜条	15元
10200	炒红果	12元
10220	红酒雪梨	14元
10250	沙律苦苣菜	18元
10260	宴宾山药泥	25元
10270	美味牛肚卷	22元
10280	特色小拌鱼	14元
10290	美味凤爪	20元
10210	水果拼盘	小/25元
10211	水果拼盘	大/40元

海鲜类

10710	扒鲍鱼	大/300元
10720	扒鲍鱼	小/150元
10730	煎烹大虾	只/50元
10740	惹油大虾	只/50元
10750	两吃大虾	只/50元
10760	盘龙大虾	只/50元
10770	两吃虾钱	半份/200元
10771	两吃虾钱	份/400元
10780	煎烹虾钱	半份/100元
10781	煎烹虾钱	份/200元
10790	炒虾球	半份/100元
10791	炒虾球	份/200元
10800	红烧干贝	110元
10810	白汁鱼肚	88元
10820	鲍汁鱼肚	88元
10830	温拌全贝	48元
10840	炝全贝	48元
10870	蕃茄虾球	半份/100元
10871	蕃茄虾球	份/200元
10880	醋椒扇贝	小/38元
10881	醋椒扇贝	大/76元
10910	全家福	70元
10920	红烧鲢鱼	斤/70元
10921	干烧鲢鱼	斤/70元
10922	清蒸鲢鱼	斤/70元
10940	红烧黄鱼	斤/60元
10941	干烧黄鱼	斤/60元
10950	香辣虾	46元
10960	清炒虾仁	86元
10970	蕃茄虾仁	86元
10980	腰果虾仁	82元
11000	软炸虾仁	60元
11010	葱烧海参	56元
11020	红烧海参	56元
11030	葱烧海参蹄筋	56元
11040	全爆	48元

11050	鱼香...	
11060	炝鱿鱼...	
11070	干煸鱿...	
11080	溜鱼片...	
11090	蕃茄鱼...	
11100	银鳕鱼...	
11110	炒鱼片...	
11120	鲍汁哪...	

特

11200	红烧牛...
11201	红烧牛...
11210	红烧牛...
11211	红烧牛...
11220	红烧舌...
11230	炒羊肉...
11240	杏仁豆...
11250	海鲜豆...
11270	蚝油牛...
11280	蒜子牛...
11290	香辣羊...
11300	孜然牛...
11310	爆两样...
11320	烧三丝...
11330	芫爆肚...
11340	炒肚丝...
11350	辣烧肚...
11360	红烧肚...
11390	烩肚仁...
11391	烩肚丝...
11400	西柿牛...
11410	黄焖牛...
11420	辣烧牛...

On this menu, the following categories are listed, in order:

Cold Dishes	**liángcài lei** 凉菜类
Seafood Dishes	**hǎixiān lei** 海鲜类
Special Dishes	**tèsè lei** 特色类
Chicken and Duck Dishes	**jīyā lei** 鸡鸭类
Sweet Dishes	**tiáncài lei** 甜菜类
Vegetable Dishes	**shūcài lei** 蔬菜类
Staples, Sweets, and Soup	**zhǔshí tiándiǎn tāng** 主食甜点汤

庄 清真 宴宾楼饭庄

	11430	醋溜肉片加木须	30元
40元	11440	炖蹄筋	34元
40元	11450	辣烧蹄筋	34元
38元	11460	锅塌三样	36元
35元	11470	鱼香肉丝	32元
38元	11480	水煮牛肉	34元
88元	11500	虾仁独面筋	28元
38元	11510	新疆爆牛肉	32元
78元	11530	香酥羊腿	82元
	11540	老炖三	50元
	11550	特色牛窝骨	62元
	11560	杏鲍菇牛柳	38元
68元	11570	特色牛腩	38元
36元	11580	茶树菇牛柳	38元

蔬菜类

10300	腰果西芹	28元
10320	腰果尚素	28元
10330	虾仁菊花茄子	30元
10340	素烧四宝	28元
10350	鲍汁菌菇	32元
10360	合炒茶树菇	38元
10380	松仁玉米	28元
10390	金沙玉米粒	28元
10420	蒜茸生菜	18元
10430	蚝油生菜	18元
10440	素炒苦瓜	20元
10450	辣炒娃娃菜	22元
10460	白灼娃娃菜	22元

鸡鸭类

42元	10510	虾酱鸡翅	40元
84元	10520	飘香仔鸡	28元
10元	10540	京酱鸭片	28元
70元	10560	甘肃鸡翅	40元
28元	10570	酱爆腰果鸡丁	30元
48元	10580	宫保鸡丁	28元
32元	10590	鱼香鸡丝	28元
32元	10600	香酥鸡腿	30元
56元			
40元			
45元			
38元			

主食甜点汤

39元	11710	果木烤鸭	套/130元
39元	11711	果木烤鸭	半套/65元
39元	11712	果木烤鸭小料	个/4元
39元	11713	果木烤鸭小料	半份/2元
34元	11720	春饼	张/0.5元
68元	11730	米饭	碗/2元
	11740	银丝卷	个/2元

甜菜类

	11750	炸银丝卷	个/2元
	11760	香麻饼	个/15元
	11770	三鲜炒饭	半份/25元
46元	11600	蜜汁金瓜饼	30元	11771	三鲜炒饭	份/50元
38元	11610	脆皮鲜奶	26元	11780	蛋炒饭	半份/18元
38元	11620	脆皮豆沙饼	26元	11781	蛋炒饭	份/36元
				11790	三鲜烧麦 ★	屉/30元

LONG DISTANCE IP PHONE CARD

This is a typical IP phone card that can easily be used for long distance calls. This particular card advertises on the front that calls can be made to the U.S. **měiguó** 美国, Canada **jiānádà** 加拿大, Singapore **xīnjiāpō** 新加坡, Hong Kong **xiānggǎng** 香港, and via internal long distance **guónèi chángtú** 国内长途.

To use these you first dial the card company number, in this case 17900. You will then be prompted to use Chinese or English. You then punch in the scratch off card account number, shown on the bottom left, then the scratch off password shown on the bottom right. Finally you dial the telephone number you are trying to reach.

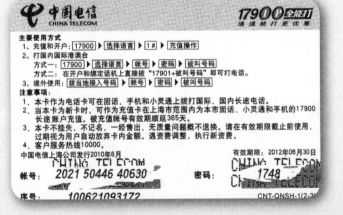

SIGNS

Here are some photographs of signs you will likely encounter.

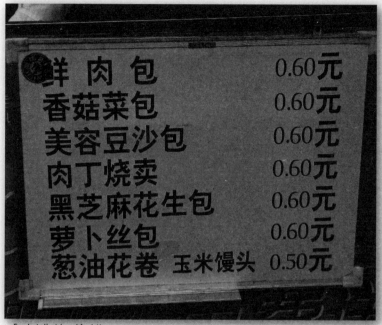

a. Food stall at breakfast time

This sign is at a stall selling steamed bread dumplings or **bāozi** 包子. This stall has a variety of dumplings, from the very common **xiānròubāo** 鲜肉包 "fresh meat dumpling" to the less common **hēi zhīma huāshēng bāo** 黑芝麻花生包 "black sesame and peanut dumpling."

b. A board advertising apartments for rent

The advertising board says **chūzū xìnxī** 出租信息 meaning "rental news or messages." The first column is the name of the place. The third column indicates the size of the apartment: **dān** 单 means it is for one person, **xiǎotào** 小套 is a small apartment with bathroom and sitting room, **zhōngtào** 中套 is a medium sized apartment, and **dàtào** 大套 is a large apartment. The last column is additional information about the apartment. **Zhuāngxiū** 装修 means the apartment has been remodeled; **jīngxiū** 精修 is a complete remodel, and **jiǎnxiū** 简修 is a basic remodel. **Shèquán** 设全 indicates that all utilities are included.

c. Cashier sign in a department store

This sign says **shōu yín** 收银 which literally means "receive money." The cashier's booth may also be called the **shōu yín tái** 收银台.

This sign says **shōu fèi biāozhǔn** 收费标准, or "the standard for collecting fees," meaning the fee rates. The first row lists bicycles, **zìxíngchē** 自行车; the second row has assisted bikes **zhùlìchē** 助力车, three-wheeled bikes **sān lún chē** 三轮车, electric bikes **diàndòng zìxíngchē** 电动自行车, and mopeds **qīngqí** 轻骑, and the third row is two-wheeled motorcycles **liǎnglún mótuōchē** 两轮摩托车.

d. Sign for parking rates for bikes, scooters, motor-cycles, etc.

e. Public phones sign

Gōngyòng 公用 means "public."

f. Domestic long distance phone sign

Guónèi 国内 is domestic, or within the country, and **chángtú** 长途 is "long distance."

Appendix 2 | 283

g. Mailbox on the street

The term for *mailbox* is either **xìn tǒng** 信筒 as here, or **xìn xiāng** 信箱 as in Photo h. This term is more common for an individual mailbox or those at apartment buildings. There are two slots. The one on the left is labeled **wài bù** 外埠 meaning towns or cities outside where you are. The slot on the right is labeled **běn bù** 本埠 meaning "this city," the city where you are.

h. Mailbox in a post office

TRAIN STATION SIGNS

1. *Train Board*

This is a typical electronic board in a train station, found above the ticket counter, that shows when trains depart, destination, and status information. The information, from left to right, includes:

Date **yuè/rì** 月／日; train number **chēcì** 车次; Destination **dàozhàn** 到站; departure time **kāidiǎn** 开点. The next five columns indicate the type of seat

and include: hard seat **yìngzuò** 硬座; soft seat **ruǎnzuò** 软座; hard sleeper **yìngwò** 硬卧; soft sleeper **ruǎnwò** 软卧; no seat **wúzuò** 无座. Below these shows how many seats are available. Under the "no seats" column it indicates whether they are available or not with **yǒu** 有 "available" and **wú** 无 "not available."

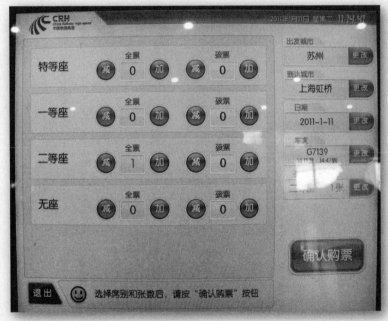

2. *Train Arrival Board*

This sign contains the following information, from left to right:
Train number **chēcì** 车次, place of origin station **shǐfā zhàn** 始发站, final destination station **zhōngdào zhàn** 终到站, arrival time **dàodiǎn** 到点, platform **zhàntái** 站台, status **zhuāngtài** 状态.

3. *Self-service Ticket Machine* 自助售票处

Self-service machines are becoming more popular, especially with the bullet trains. This machine shows the following information, from top to bottom.

First line: special class seats **tèděng zuò** 特等座, first class seats **yīděng zuò**

一等座, second class seats **èrděng zuò** 二等座, no seats **wúzuò** 无座.

Next to each category you can subtract (**jiǎn** 减) or add (**jiā** 加) the number of tickets you want to buy. 全票 indicates an adult ticket, and 孩票 indicates a child ticket. On the far right is shown the city of origin **chūfā chéngshì** 出发城市, and the destination city **dàodá chéngshì** 到达城市.

4. *Sign outside train station*

This sign says **Kāi chē qián 5 fēn zhōng tíngzhǐ jiǎn piào** meaning "No tickets will be checked five minutes before departure." This means that you have to check in at least five minutes before the train departs.